I0793418

IMAGES
of America

SOTTERLEY PLANTATION

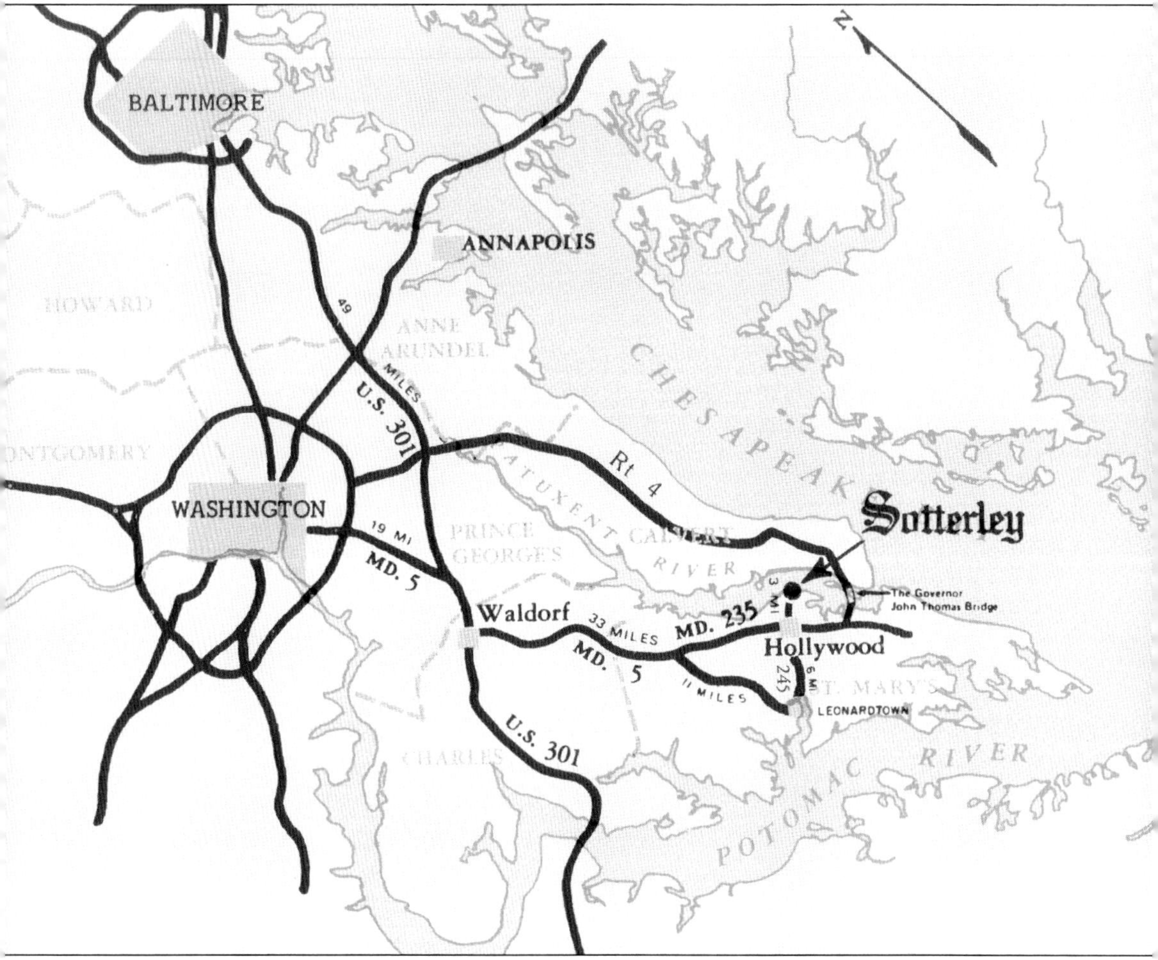

This road map from Sotterley Plantation's early museum literature invites guests to visit the historic site. Sotterley became a nonprofit foundation and was opened to the public by its last family owner, Mabel Satterlee Ingalls, in 1961. Following her death in 1993, Sotterley was turned over to the foundation. Without a financial endowment, Sotterley was in danger of closing in the 1990s, but it was saved by the tireless work and fundraising efforts of descendants, trustees, staff, and volunteers. As its prominence grew, grants awarded by the Save America's Treasures initiative helped rescue Sotterley. An easy day trip from Baltimore, Washington, DC, and Richmond, Sotterley Plantation continues to serve visitors from Maryland and beyond. (Courtesy of Sotterley Plantation.)

On the Cover: Herbert Livingston Satterlee stands at the gate of Sotterley Plantation in his later years. He purchased Sotterley in 1910 and restored it during the American Colonial Revival period. In this 1930 photograph, the farm is seen in the background with the south gatehouse, built by Satterlee, in the foreground. Satterlee transformed the plantation into his masterpiece of Colonial romance and helped to create a thriving farming community. Today, Sotterley Plantation is visited and studied by thousands of people each year as a microcosm of American history. (Courtesy of Sotterley Plantation.)

IMAGES
of America

SOTTERLEY PLANTATION

Jeanne K. Pirtle

ARCADIA
PUBLISHING

ISBN 978-1-4671-1999-3

Published by Arcadia Publishing
Charleston, South Carolina

Printed in the United States of America

Library of Congress Control Number: 2013930706

For all general information, please contact Arcadia Publishing:
Telephone 843-853-2070
Fax 843-853-0044
E-mail sales@arcadiapublishing.com
For customer service and orders:
Toll-Free 1-888-313-2665

Visit us on the Internet at www.arcadiapublishing.com

To my husband, children, and grandchildren and to all the people who have lived, worked, and served at Sotterley Plantation

Contents

Acknowledgments		6
Introduction		7
1.	Prosperity and Bondage: 1699–1822	9
2.	Family and Freedom: 1823–1909	37
3.	Vision and Revival: 1910–1947	61
4.	Past and Promise: 1948–2012	101
Bibliography		126
About Sotterley Plantation		127

Acknowledgments

I would like to thank all of the sponsors, members, and volunteers that support Sotterley Plantation's important mission. Thanks to my coworkers, past and present, especially Nancy Easterling for her support and encouragement. Thanks to Eileen Miller, Piper Carlson, and Chuck Pirtle for their photography. Special gratitude goes to Sheila Gibbons Hiebert and Merideth Taylor for their editing help and suggestions and also to Merideth for her leadership during the reinterpretation process that ignited new research.

Thanks to professor Kenneth Cohen of St. Mary's College of Maryland for his work and guidance to help Sotterley move forward as a museum. Thanks to the Sotterley trustees and descendants for their confidence; to the members of the interpretation, collections, and education committees; and to our wonderful group of docents and instructors that know and love Sotterley so well.

I was fortunate to have Sotterley's restoration manager, John O'Rourke, working on site these past few months. I thank him for his work, dedication, and sharing his knowledge. Thanks to Dave Brown for keeping the archives in good condition and being a Sotterley supporter. I found myself looking up details in Dave's book *Sotterley: Her People and Their Worlds* many times. Thanks to Richard Knott and Agnes Kane Callum for sharing their memories, research, and history and to Peter Himmelheber for his maps and research. Thanks to Betty Hill, the granddaughter of Julius Clifton Callis, for coming forward and supplying her family history and photographs.

Thanks to all of those supporters, staff, and volunteers from years past that I visit in the memories, documents, and photographs that are left behind. Thanks to Lissie Cain, Rebekah Collinswoth, and Ryan Easterling, editors at Arcadia Publishing, for keeping me encouraged and on track throughout this process. Love and thanks goes to my family for their support.

Unless otherwise noted, all images are courtesy of Sotterley Plantation.

INTRODUCTION

Sotterley Plantation is located in Hollywood, Maryland, on the Patuxent River in St. Mary's County. Part of the Tidewater region on the western shore of the Chesapeake Bay, the river is named for the small band of native people whose presence was recorded by Capt. John Smith in 1612. The Patuxent people spoke an Algonquin dialect. Like the Piscataway on the Potomac River and other native peoples in the area, they were pressured by European encroachment of their lands, political unrest, and disease. They eventually died out or joined other local native groups.

The Patuxent River had provided almost unlimited resources to native peoples for thousands of years. Early European settlers found these natural resources, rich farmland, and access to travel and trade on the Patuxent as an opportunity for wealth and prosperity. Originally governed by English Catholics seeking religious toleration, Maryland and its government's definition of toleration changed with the seats of power in England.

By the time James Bowles, a Protestant, came to Maryland in 1699 and then purchased 2,000 acres of what later became Sotterley Plantation, the first capital of Colonial Maryland, St. Mary's City, 14 miles to the southeast, had been relocated. The capital was moved to Annapolis four years prior as a result of the political and religious unrest that continued to plague England and the colony. Bowles's land, renamed Bowles Preservation, was purchased from a land grant known as Resurrection Manor.

Set up in business by his merchant father to trade slaves and act as an agent for the Royal African Company on the Patuxent, Bowles began clearing his land, constructing support buildings, and planting a tobacco crop. He prospered by selling and using slaves imported from the Gold Coast of Africa, and by exporting lumber, tobacco, and other goods produced on the farm. By 1703, he had built the first two-room house on his land overlooking the river, which is still part of Sotterley's plantation house today. As a successful merchant and planter, and with powerful family connections through birth and marriage, Bowles and his family became part of the Maryland elite.

James Bowles died in 1727, leaving his land and property, which included 41 slaves, to his three daughters and his widow, Rebecca. In 1729, Rebecca Bowles married politically connected Annapolis lawyer George Plater II. This union made them one of the wealthiest and most powerful families in Colonial Maryland. Their eldest son, George Plater III, inherited the plantation by 1755. It was under his ownership that the estate became known as Sotterley, named for the Platers' ancestral home, Sotterley, in Suffolk, England. The Platers continued to rely on enslaved laborers from the domestic slave trade to work the plantation. At almost 7,000 acres, it was one of Maryland's largest. In 1790, Plater III owned 93 slaves. There were many examples of flight and resistance in the enslaved population at Sotterley under Plater ownership.

George Plater III also prospered under British rule and received important political appointments. His second wife, Elizabeth Rousby, came from a prominent family in Calvert County. He remained loyal to the British leading up to the American Revolution, but decided to join the Patriot cause before the Declaration of Independence was signed. Plater served in the Second Continental

Congress, was president of the Maryland Senate, and later became the sixth governor of Maryland, helping to develop Maryland's first state constitution. Vulnerable to attack along the Patuxent River, Sotterley was raided by the British in 1781 and 1783. Plater's overseer was hanged during the second raid, and, on both occasions, Sotterley slaves escaped to the British.

George Plater IV inherited Sotterley after his father's death, but growing debts, economic downturns, and the challenges and changes brought on by the new form of government brought about the beginning of the plantation's decline. Plater IV died in 1802, leaving his estate to his minor son. His brother John Rousby Plater was named guardian and master of Sotterley until George Plater V came of age.

During the War of 1812, the British harassed and burned farms along the Patuxent River. Sotterley's plantation house was spared, but crops and food stores were plundered. In 1814, a total of 49 enslaved men, women, and children from Sotterley escaped to the British. Some, including Lewis and Grace Munroe and their children, went to Halifax, Nova Scotia. Others, like James Bowie, escaped to serve in the Colonial Marines alongside the British and were given land in Trinidad.

By the time George Plater V became the master of Sotterley, he was laden with inherited debt and had lost his labor force. In 1822, he sold Sotterley to William Clarke Somerville, his step-uncle and executor. Thomas Barber purchased it soon after. He died in 1826, leaving his property, including his slaves, to his daughter Lydia and his stepdaughter Emeline Dallam, with Emeline inheriting 400 acres and the plantation house.

Emeline married Walter Hanson Stone Briscoe of Charles County. They were married for nearly 60 years and had 13 children. Briscoe supplemented his income from the farm by practicing medicine and running a girls' boarding school on the property. An enslaved labor force of about 50 worked the farm, growing wheat, corn, cotton, and tobacco. One of the several slave cabins built between 1830 and 1850 still survives today.

With the outbreak of the Civil War, Maryland, a border, slaveholding state, remained in the Union. The Briscoes were Confederate sympathizers, as were many landed slave owners. Three of their sons joined the Army of Virginia, while at least one of Dr. Briscoe's slaves, George W. Barnes, joined the United States Union Colored Troops. Barnes's name was changed to Briscoe upon his enlistment. After the end of the Civil War, with the plantation economy broken, St. Mary's County remained rural and economically depressed until the outbreak of World War II.

In 1910, the last Briscoe owner sold Sotterley to Herbert Livingston Satterlee, a wealthy business lawyer from New York. He had married Louisa Pierpont Morgan, the oldest daughter of the financial giant John Pierpont Morgan, in 1900. Their two daughters, Mabel and Eleanor, were nine and five years old, respectively, when they first visited Sotterley, their new family retreat from their busy lives in New York. Herbert Satterlee proceeded to remove 19th-century aspects of the house and grounds and restore them to his vision of an idyllic 18th-century gentleman's estate. Generations of the Barber, Knott, and Scriber families worked as part of this farming community for over half a century.

Upon Herbert Satterlee's death in 1947, Mabel Satterlee Ingalls purchased Sotterley from her father's estate. She visited Sotterley about four weeks a year, indulging her love of hunting, fishing, and entertaining friends. In 1961, she opened Sotterley as a nonprofit historical foundation to help maintain the property and share Sotterley's environmental, historical, and cultural assets with the public. After Mabel Ingalls's death in 1993, a financially strapped foundation was kept alive by the hard work of various Sotterley family descendants, including Sandra Ingalls Van Heerden, John Hanson Briscoe, Donald Barber, and Sotterley slave descendant Agnes Kane Callum. Today, Historic Sotterley offers educational programs and events for all ages and remains an important community, state, and national treasure.

One

Prosperity and Bondage 1699–1822

James Bowles was the only son of Tobias Bowles, who was from the city of Deal in the county of Kent, England. His father was a successful merchant of sugar, tobacco, and slaves, and James came to Maryland by 1699 to expand the family business on the Patuxent River and to grow tobacco on land he had purchased there. By this time, indentured servitude by white Europeans was already on the decline, and African slave labor had become more affordable and lucrative.

Many records from the Royal African Company in the early 1700s did not survive, but there is a record of the slave ship *Generous Jenny*, which left London for Cape Coast Castle on the Gold Coast of Africa to acquire 260 slaves for James Bowles on the Patuxent River. Bowles recorded the ship's arrival on September 21, 1720. At least 29 slaves had died of smallpox during the 11-week middle passage. Most of the human cargo that remained was shipped on to Virginia to be sold. Chattel slavery would be a way of life at Sotterley Plantation for 165 years.

James Bowles was related by blood and marriage to powerful Maryland families and held high offices in Colonial government. By his mid-30s, he was a widower. He remarried, to Rebecca Tasker Addison, in 1719. In 1727, Bowles left his family and traveled to England to prove his father's will. He died there that August.

Rebecca Bowles and their three daughters inherited the property and possessions. Rebecca then married George Plater II in 1729 and became the matriarch to the four generations of the Plater family who owned and lived at Sotterley Plantation for almost a century. George Plater II served in the highest seats of Colonial power, including on the governor's council and in the upper house.

Their son George Plater III was a participant in the end of the Colonial government and the formation of a new nation. He corresponded with and served with the nation's founders, including George Washington and Thomas Jefferson. He helped Maryland ratify the Constitution and the Bill of Rights, and he represented Maryland as the state's sixth governor.

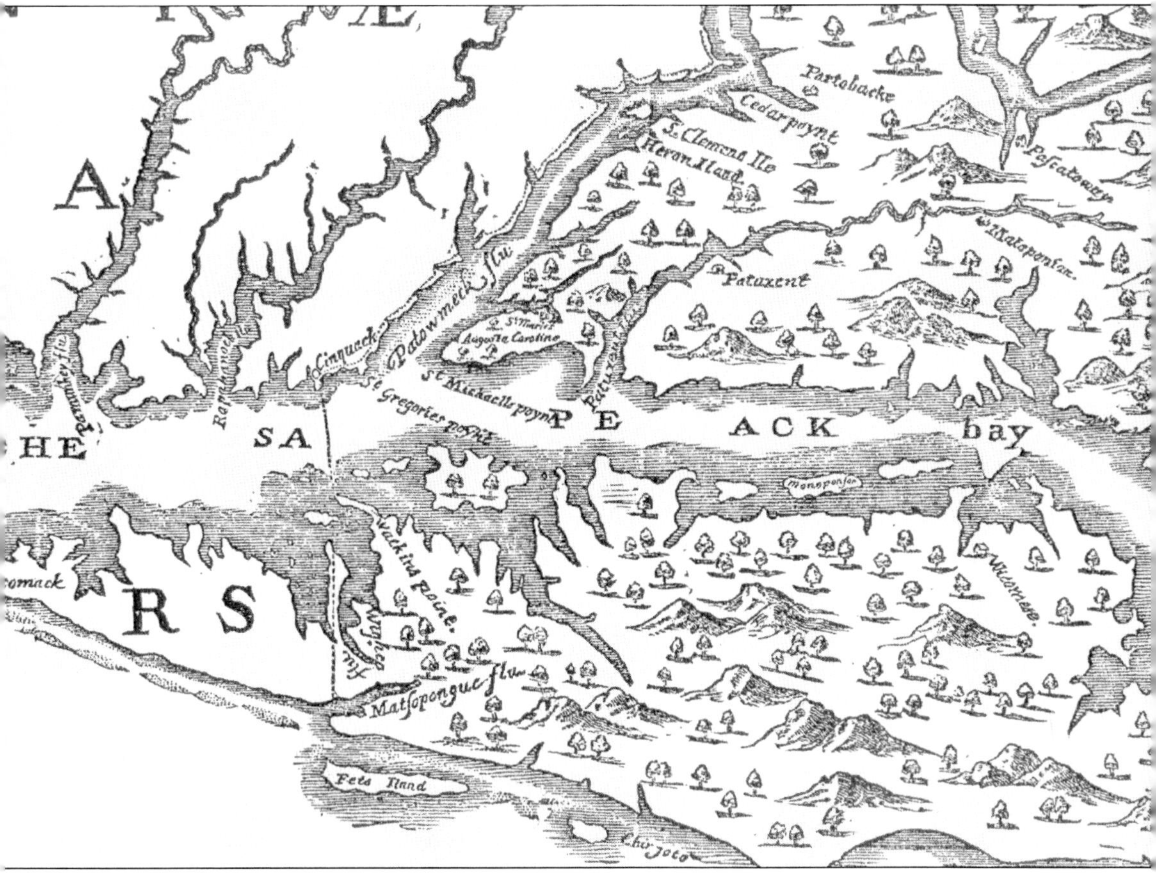

This portion of a 1635 map of Virginia and Maryland clearly places the Native American peoples along the Patuxent and Potomac Rivers. Archaeological evidence of a small band of native people was found within what is now Jefferson Patterson Park and Museum in Calvert County, which is within sight of Sotterley Plantation across the Patuxent River. The Piscataway people are also noted on the map, along the northern Potomac. St. Mary's City, founded by the Catholic, noble Calvert family, was already established by 1634 and remained the Colonial capital of Maryland until 1695. In the early 1900s, the same enthusiasm for the early founders that transformed Sotterley Plantation also transformed St. Mary's City into a National Historic Landmark and a Colonial museum. (Courtesy of FCIT.)

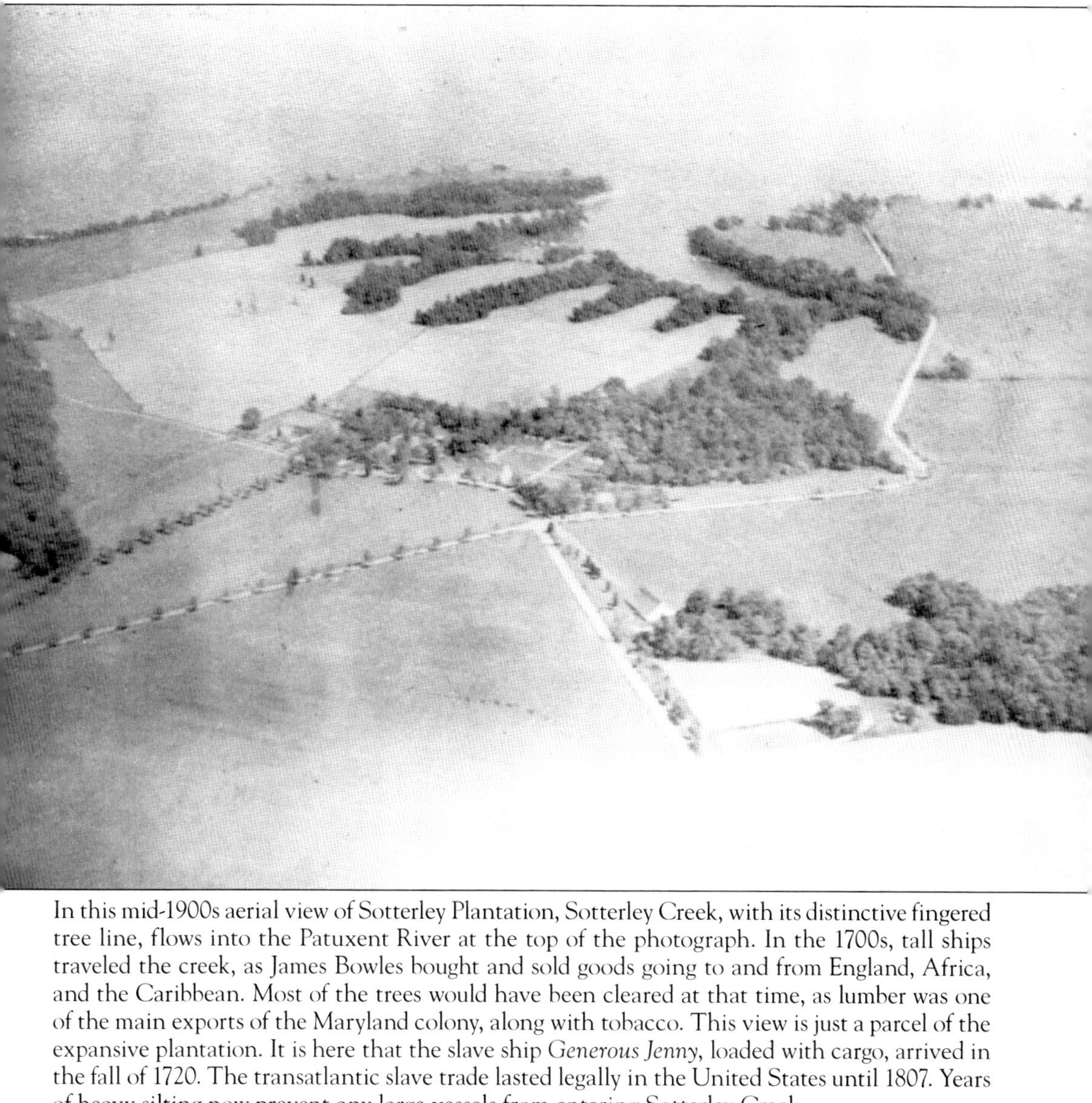

In this mid-1900s aerial view of Sotterley Plantation, Sotterley Creek, with its distinctive fingered tree line, flows into the Patuxent River at the top of the photograph. In the 1700s, tall ships traveled the creek, as James Bowles bought and sold goods going to and from England, Africa, and the Caribbean. Most of the trees would have been cleared at that time, as lumber was one of the main exports of the Maryland colony, along with tobacco. This view is just a parcel of the expansive plantation. It is here that the slave ship *Generous Jenny*, loaded with cargo, arrived in the fall of 1720. The transatlantic slave trade lasted legally in the United States until 1807. Years of heavy silting now prevent any large vessels from entering Sotterley Creek.

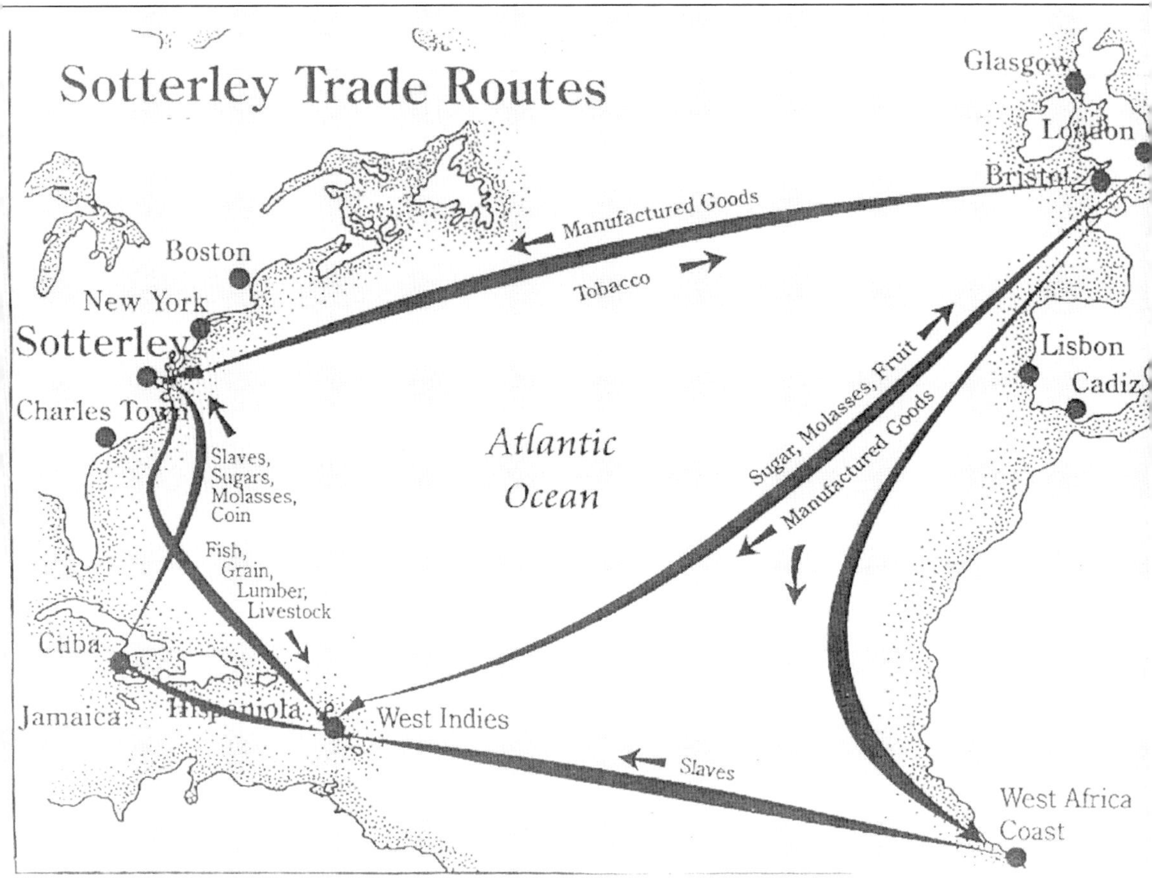

This map of the triangular trade route shows the movement of goods and people between England, Africa, and North America. Coastal West African kings sold enslaved people who had been captured or kidnapped from the interior to Europeans for rum, guns, and other status goods. Starved, sick, and frightened, shackled together, and marched miles without clothes, food, or shelter, captives were taken to holding areas like Cape Coast Castle, as were those on the *Generous Jenny*. They could languish there in crowded squalor and disease for weeks before being rowed out to waiting ships to endure even more suffering on the middle passage across the Atlantic. James Bowles had a lucrative business in slaves, resupplying incoming ships as well as selling tobacco and lumber. Bowles bought many imported luxury goods of the day, such as china, books, expensive fabrics, and wines.

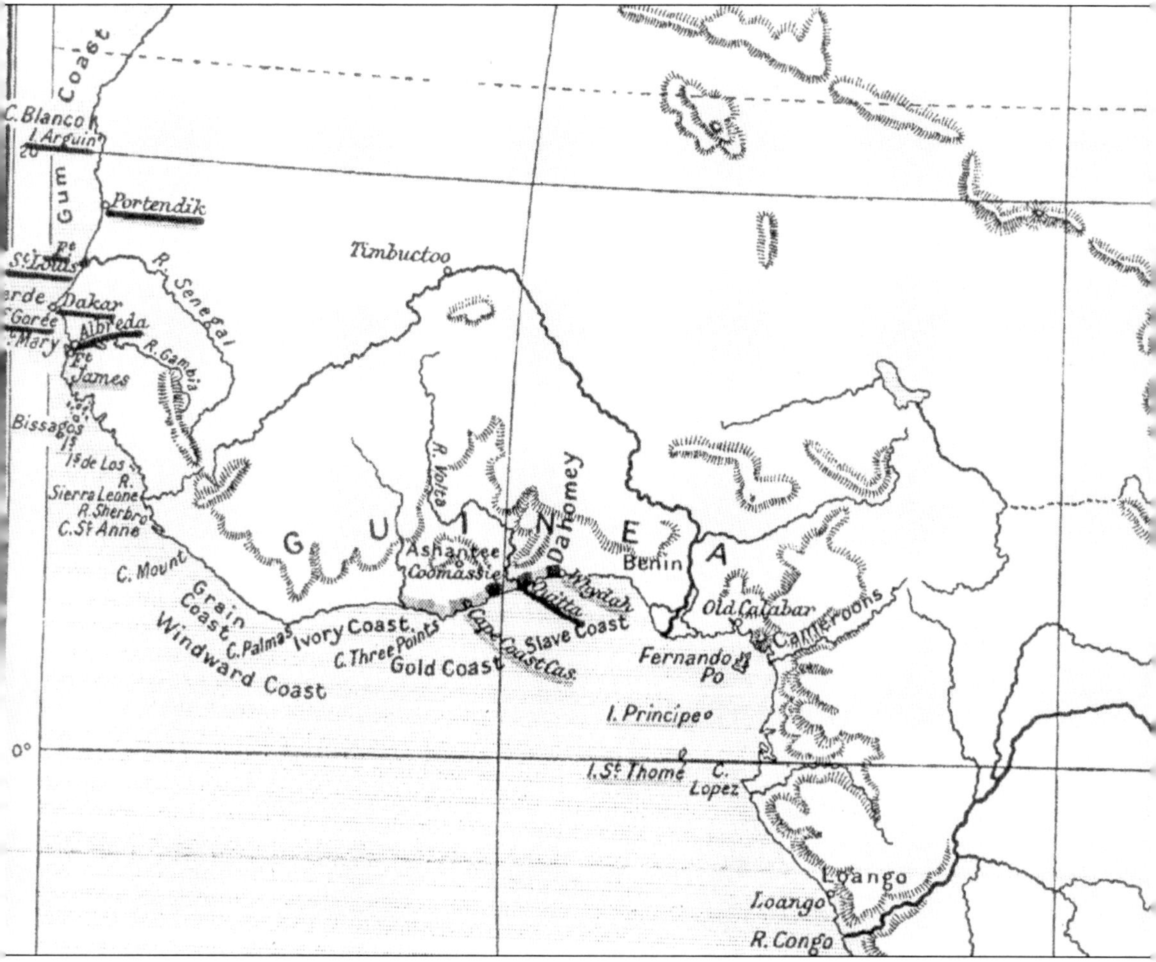

This 1783 map of West Africa highlights the trading centers for the transatlantic slave trade. In November 1719, Capt. Richard Lamberth sailed from London on the 230-ton, 10-gun *Generous Jenny* bound for Cape Coast Castle. By March 1720, he had arrived but had not found enough slaves to fill the large order for James Bowles. For the next four months, Lamberth lingered along the Gold and Windward Coasts, trading for more and better cargo. By July, he sailed for the Patuxent River with 270 slaves. When he arrived in September, Lamberth reported that 29 slaves had died from disease, their bodies thrown overboard. James Bowles received about 230 slaves but complained to the company that the slaves arrived in poor condition and after the planting season. The Royal African Company blamed Captain Lamberth for disobeying orders and engaging in unsanctioned private trading. A few slaves remained with Bowles, some were sold in a private sale, and the remaining 211 were shipped on to Virginia to be sold to waiting planters for a profit. (Courtesy of FCIT.)

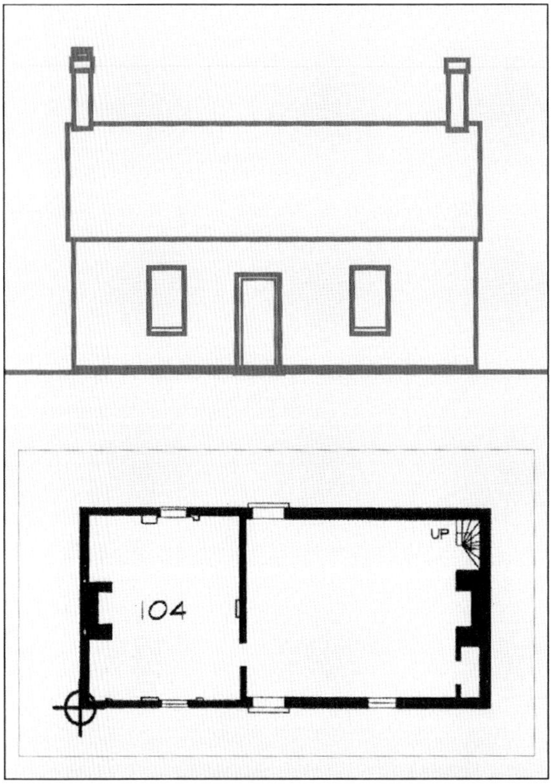

Dendrochronology dates the first build of James Bowles's two-room house to about 1703. Like Resurrection Manor, it was a hall and parlor plan, but it was built using cypress post-in-ground construction. The smaller room was the bedchamber, later called Madame Bowles' Room. The plantation had many support buildings, including a kitchen and a dairy, some of which surely predated the house.

Resurrection Manor was a 5,000-acre land patent first granted in 1650. By the 1670s, the manor house pictured below was constructed. It is an example of a hall and chamber plan. This house, once designated a National Historic Landmark, was demolished in 2002 by its owners. It was located about five miles to the southwest of present day Sotterley. The land on which James Bowles built his plantation was part of this original patent. (Courtesy of National Park Service.)

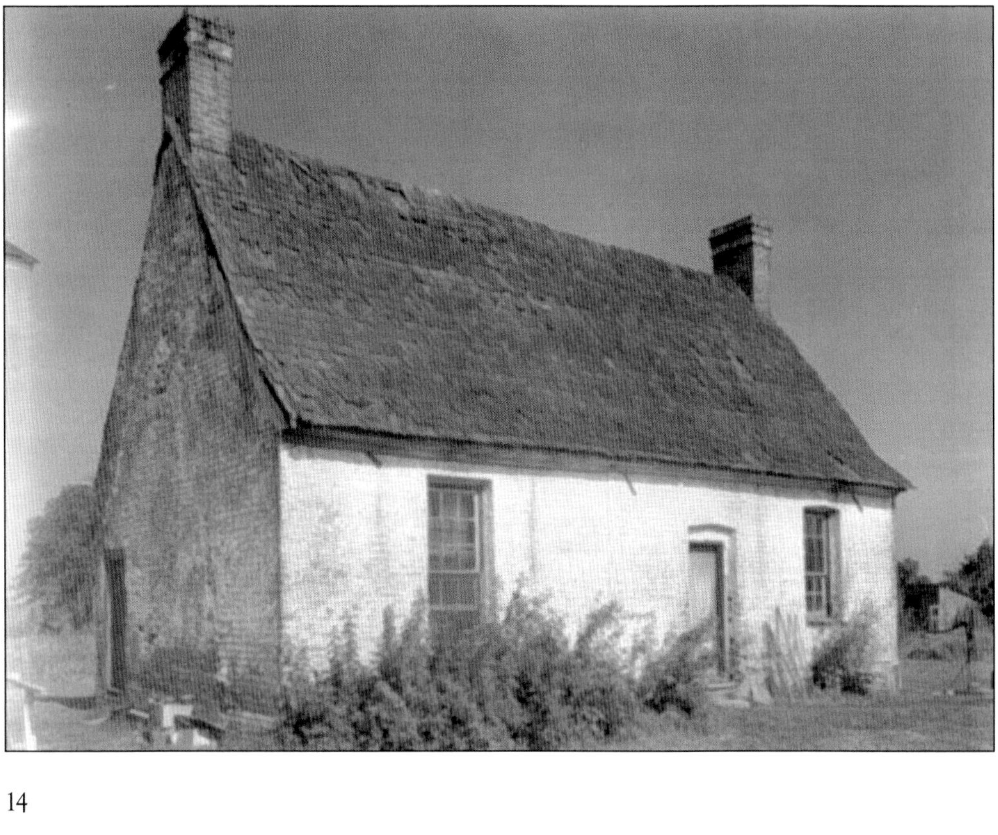

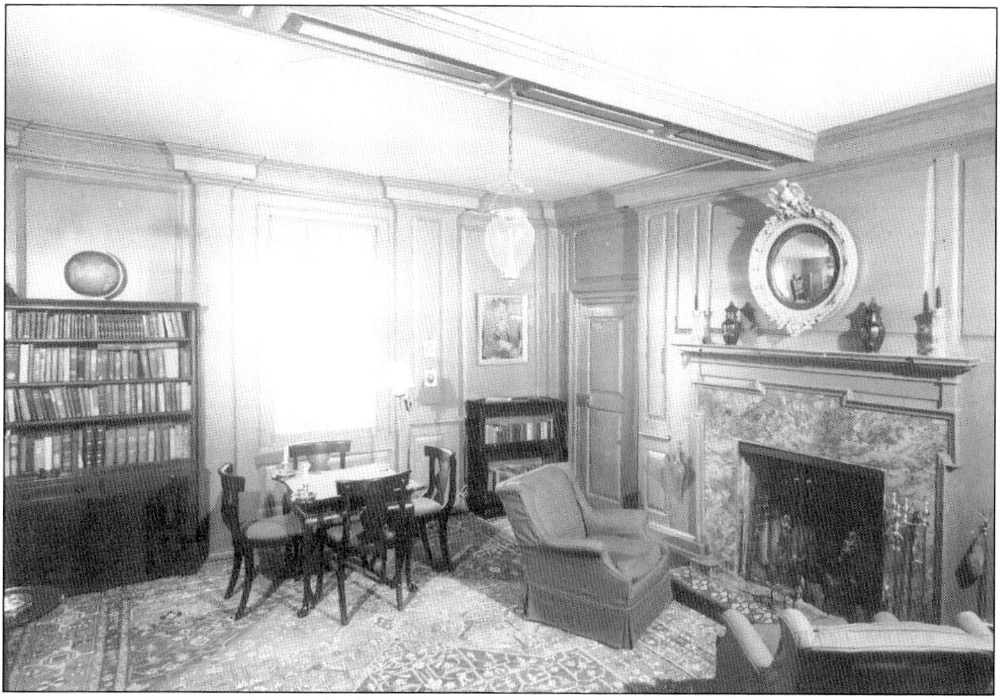

This interior photograph from the late 1960s shows one of the original rooms of the Bowles house. Although the walls and posts were covered by paneling in the mid-1700s, visitors are still able to see the post-in-ground construction. This room is the least structurally altered of the two rooms. The paneled house interiors were originally painted with red ochre, sometimes called Spanish brown, a pleasant and inexpensive brownish red. The door on the left leads to a closet. At one time, it was an entrance to the 1750s dining room passage.

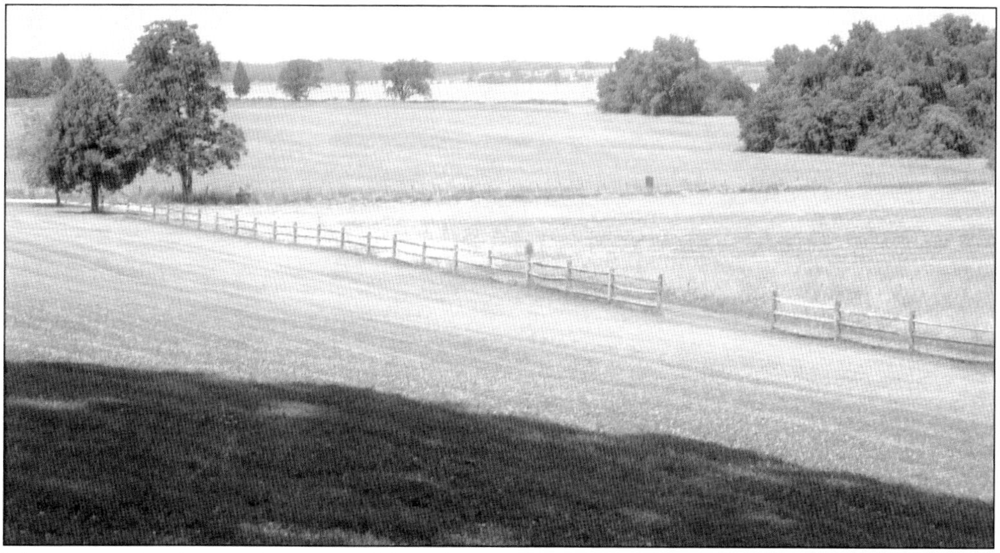

This view to the Patuxent River would have been enjoyed by Rebecca Bowles from her bedchamber. Instead of manicured lawns, however, she would have seen herds and flocks of grazing animals, fields of tobacco, and perhaps a tall ship sailing down the river. Her personal house slave, who helped her bathe, dress, and care for her children and the household, would have been nearby.

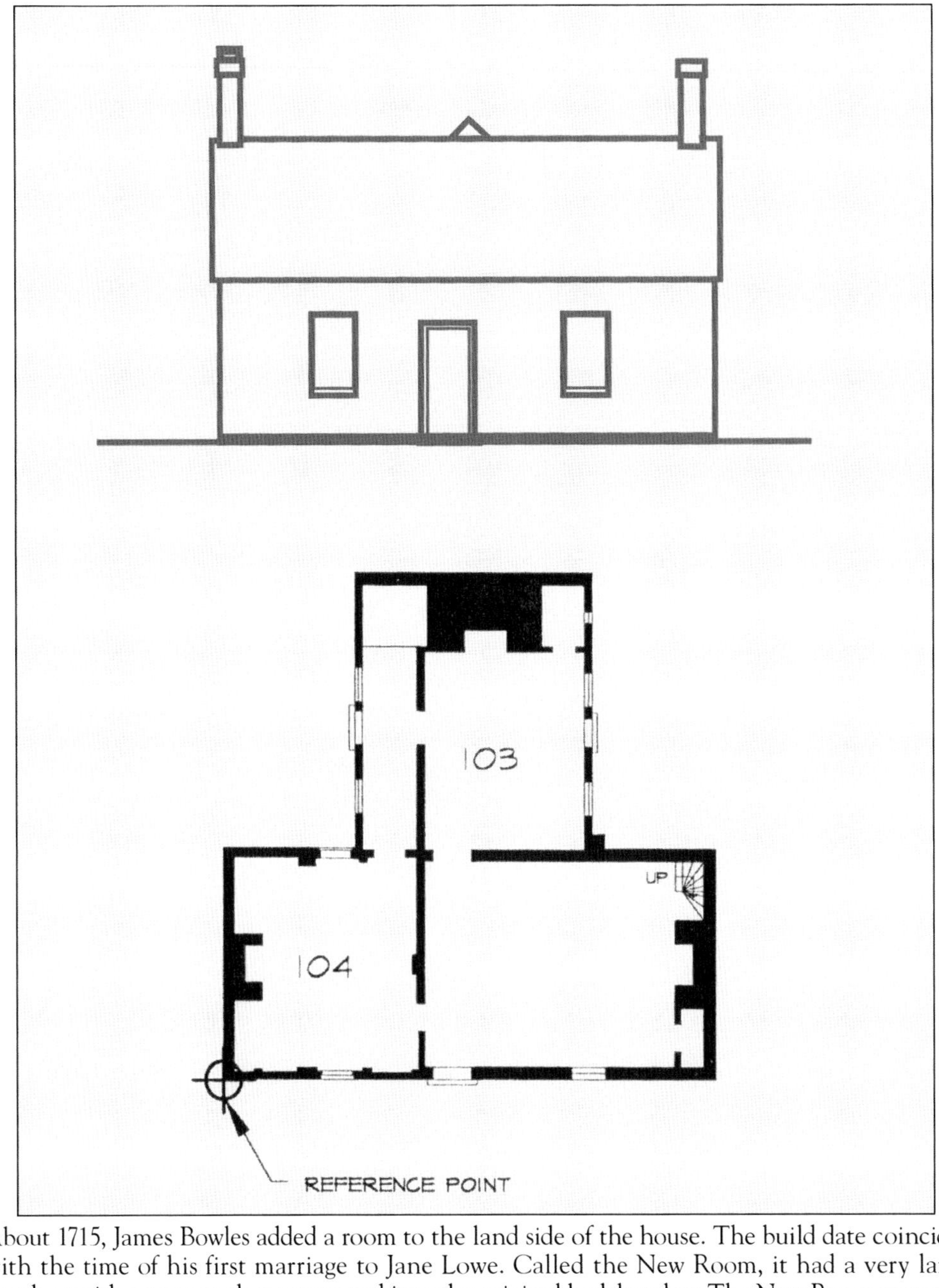

About 1715, James Bowles added a room to the land side of the house. The build date coincides with the time of his first marriage to Jane Lowe. Called the New Room, it had a very large fireplace with a passage that connected it to the original bedchamber. The New Room was used as a dining room, with items such as china punch bowls, cups, saucers, china plates, custard cups, pewter, and a tea table and chairs. The passage was also used for storage and most likely sleeping space for domestic slaves identified as Pegg, Lucy, and Blackwell. The rooms had small chambers above, which were also full of possessions that only the very wealthy could afford. The cellar below had a large hearth, perhaps a laundry, and a place to store large amounts of cider, molasses, and wine. Bowles could afford to import expensive spices such as cinnamon, nutmeg, and pepper and costly books, fabrics, and furniture. A separate room for dining was a sign of growing prosperity and social status.

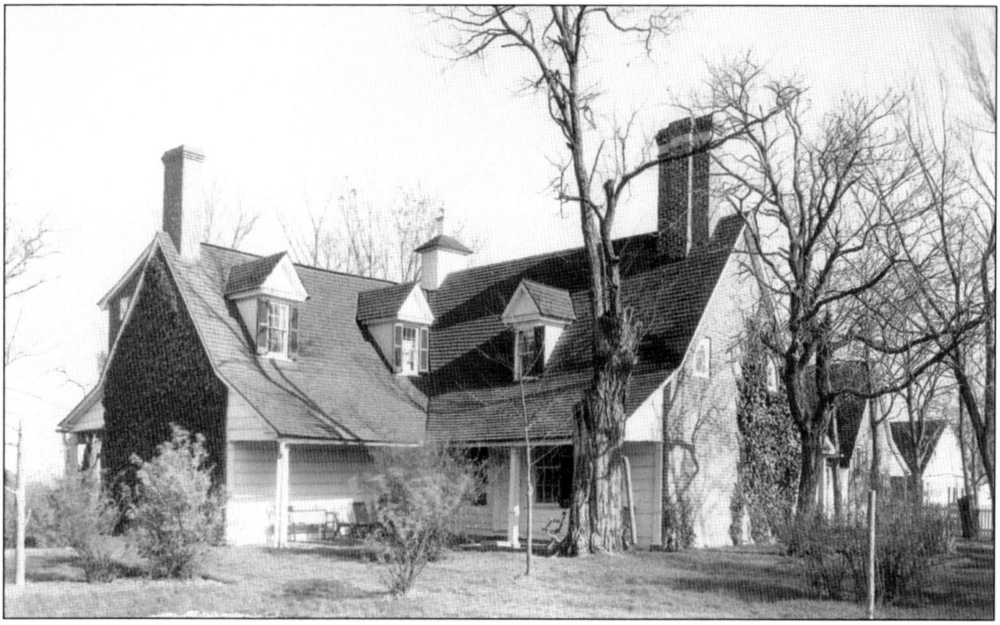

In the 1920s photograph above, the New Room is seen from the garden looking southwest. The three-room Bowles house was a luxury home in St. Mary's County in the early 1700s. Support buildings with foundations were located on the land side at the time. The kitchen and dairy would be in close proximity to the dining room. The interior of the New Room is seen below around 1950. The original hearth was much larger than this opening. To the left above the mantel, the scar where the passageway wall once existed can be seen. The door on the left was the narrow stairway that went from the cellar below to the chamber above. The door on the right opens to a small closet.

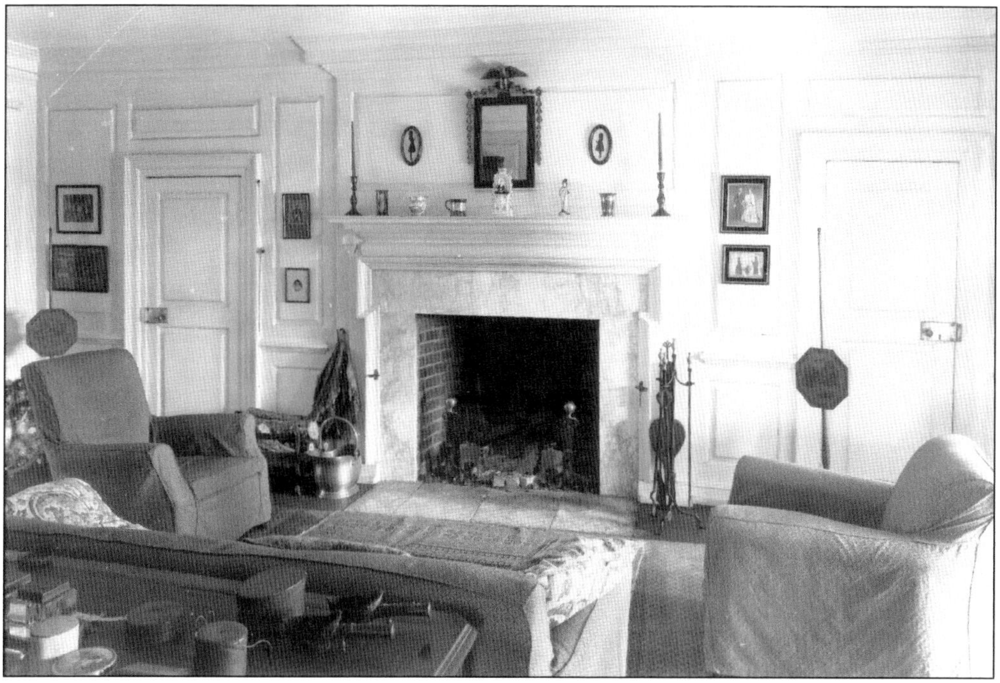

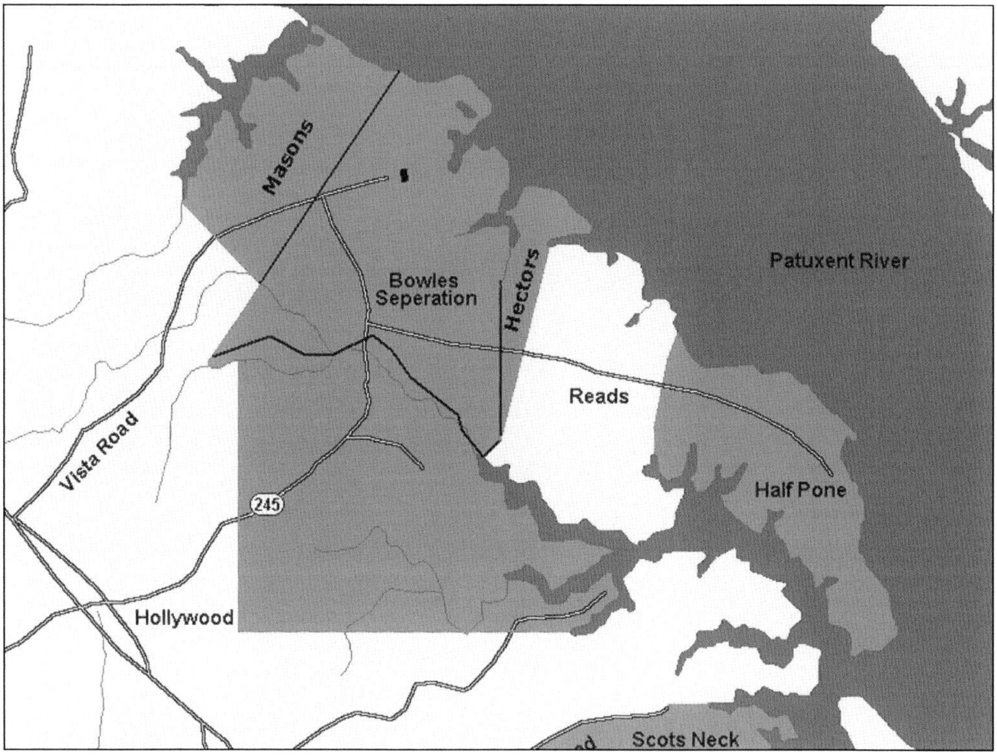

As he expanded his plantation house, James Bowles was also expanding his property. The land surrounding the house remained the home plantation, but he also owned the areas marked as Mason's, Hogg Neck, and Half Pone, all of which had their own outbuildings, livestock, slaves, and equipment. Towerhill and Dick were enslaved carpenters on the home plantation. The dark rectangle on the map designates the plantation house. (Courtesy of Peter Himmelheber.)

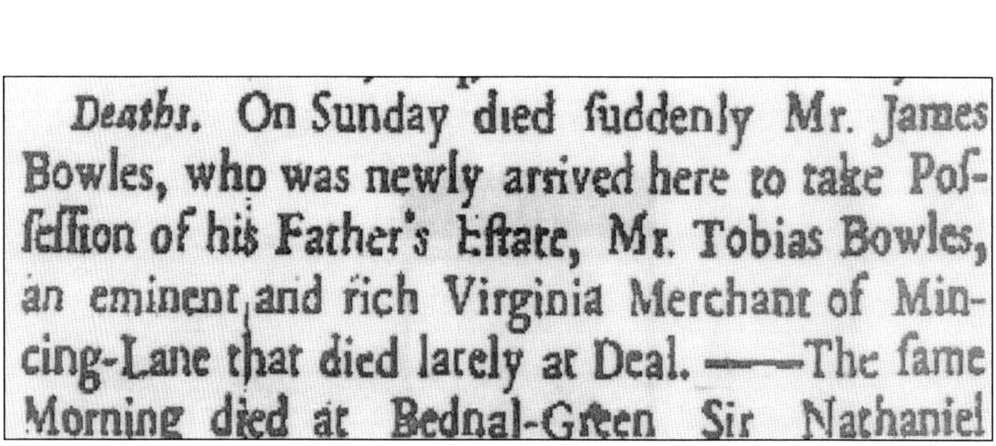

Deaths. On Sunday died ſuddenly Mr. James Bowles, who was newly arrived here to take Poſ-ſeſſion of his Father's Eſtate, Mr. Tobias Bowles, an eminent and rich Virginia Merchant of Min-cing-Lane that died lately at Deal. ——The ſame Morning died at Bednal-Green Sir Nathaniel

In 1727, James Bowles traveled back to England to claim his father's estate, leaving his plantation and family, but he never returned. He died shortly after his arrival, only in his late 40s. He was buried in London. His obituary, seen here, appeared in the *London Journal* on Tuesday, September 2, 1727.

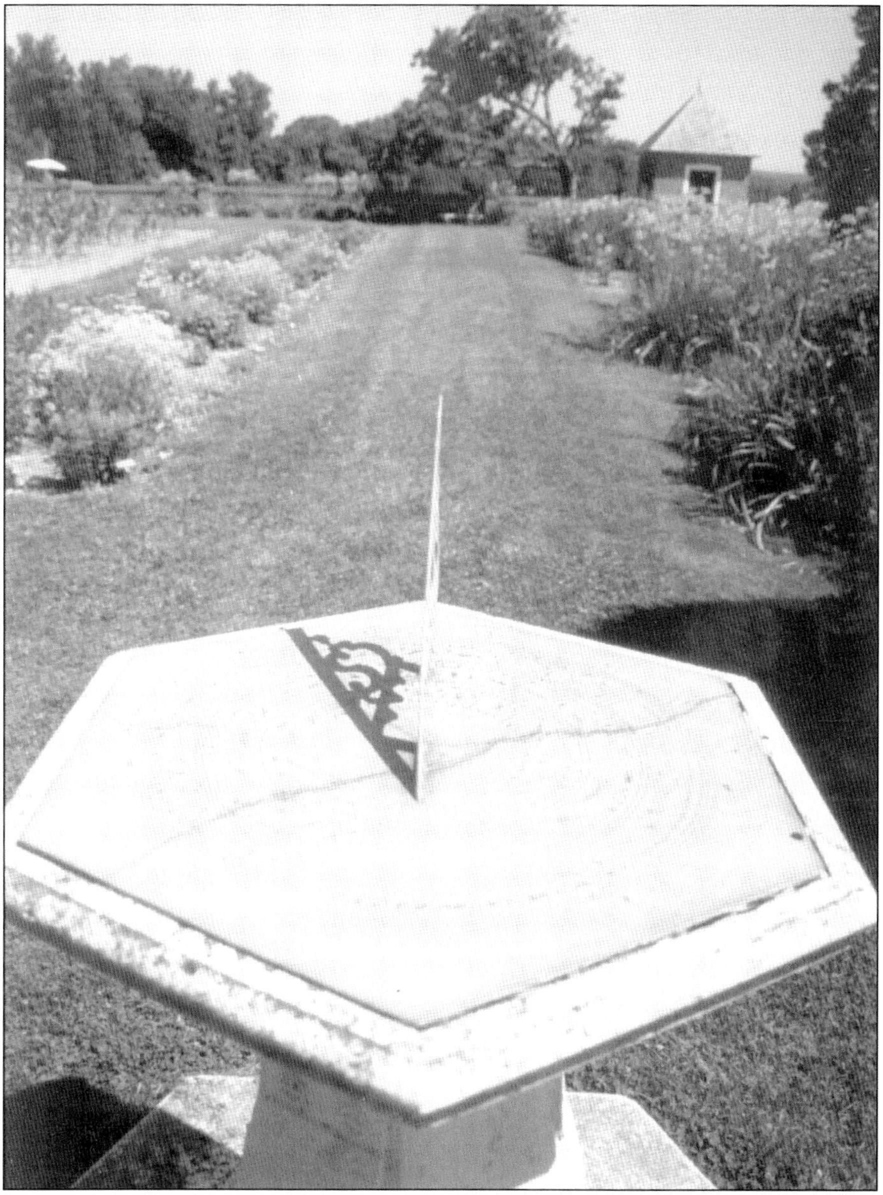

When a master died, there were serious matters to be decided upon that affected all who lived and worked on the plantation. A detailed inventory was made of every possession on the estate, including the slaves. These inventories are valuable documents that provide a wealth of information into the lives of the people on the plantation. Such an inventory was taken in 1727 of the "Goods and Chattles of the Honourable James Bowles, Esq. Deceased." Once the amount of total assets was established, any outstanding debts owed would be paid. Then the will would be proved. Bowles's will was proved both in England and in Maryland. He had written in his will, "To Rebecca, my loving wife, I give you one quarter of the estate mentioned above." Bowles warned his family to divide the estate between them without strife. Rebecca could use the plantation house as she pleased for life. The land was then divided between the sisters, Jane, Eleanor, and Mary, making them very wealthy. Seen here is Sotterley's sundial, in the gardens north of the plantation house near the New Room.

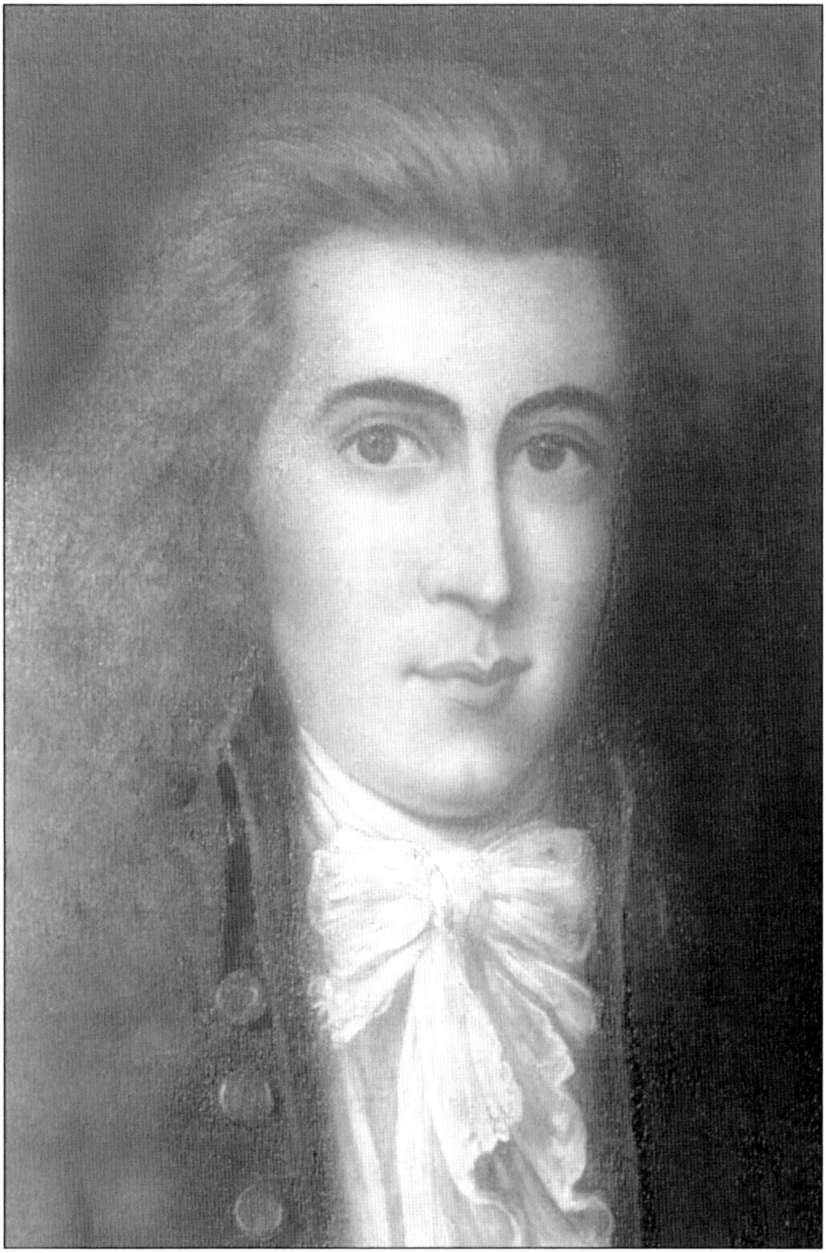

Rebecca Bowles remarried in 1729 to George Plater II, seen here, the son of George Plater and Ann Burford Doyne. The elder George Plater had come from England and served in high government offices, including as attorney general. George Plater II and James Bowles had known each other; in fact, after Bowles's death, Plater signed his will as the registrar of the prerogative court when it was proved in Maryland. Marriages in this period between the upper classes were based on advantageous family connections and wealth, combined with good timing. George Plater II was 35 when he married Rebecca, an acceptable age for men of his class, as men had to secure their educations and professions before marriage. Rebecca had married James Bowles at 16; by 1729, she was a wealthy widow in her mid-20s. It was common for women to marry for the first time between 13 and 16 years of age.

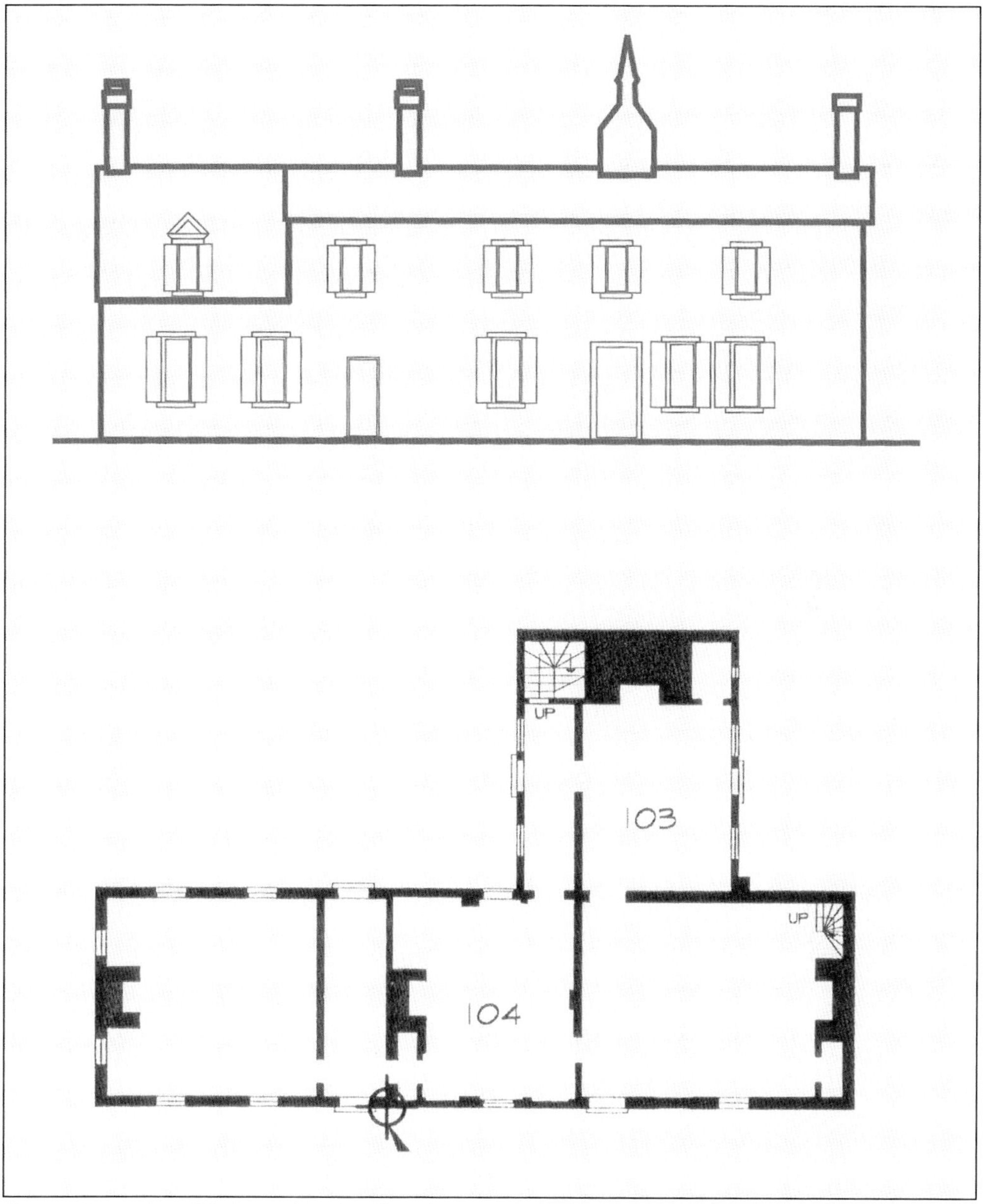

George Plater II and Rebecca Bowles Plater became a wealthy and powerful Maryland couple. Plater paid for the land that had been left to his stepdaughters, growing Sotterley into one of the largest estates in Maryland. He also owned thousands of acres in other Maryland counties and a house in Annapolis that served the next generation as well. He held the position of Naval Officer of the Patuxent, which provided a large stipend. He was also appointed to the governor's council and the upper house. By 1750, Plater had added a formal dining room and a passageway to the southwest end of the house, as seen here. The original bedroom and the New Room were repurposed as the house was raised to a full two stories with adequate bedrooms upstairs. The kitchen was probably relocated at this time, likely somewhere near the kitchen that exists today. Rebecca and George Plater II had three children: Rebecca, Elizabeth, and George III. Rebecca's three daughters from her first marriage, Jane, Eleanor, and Mary Bowles, all married prominent Virginians.

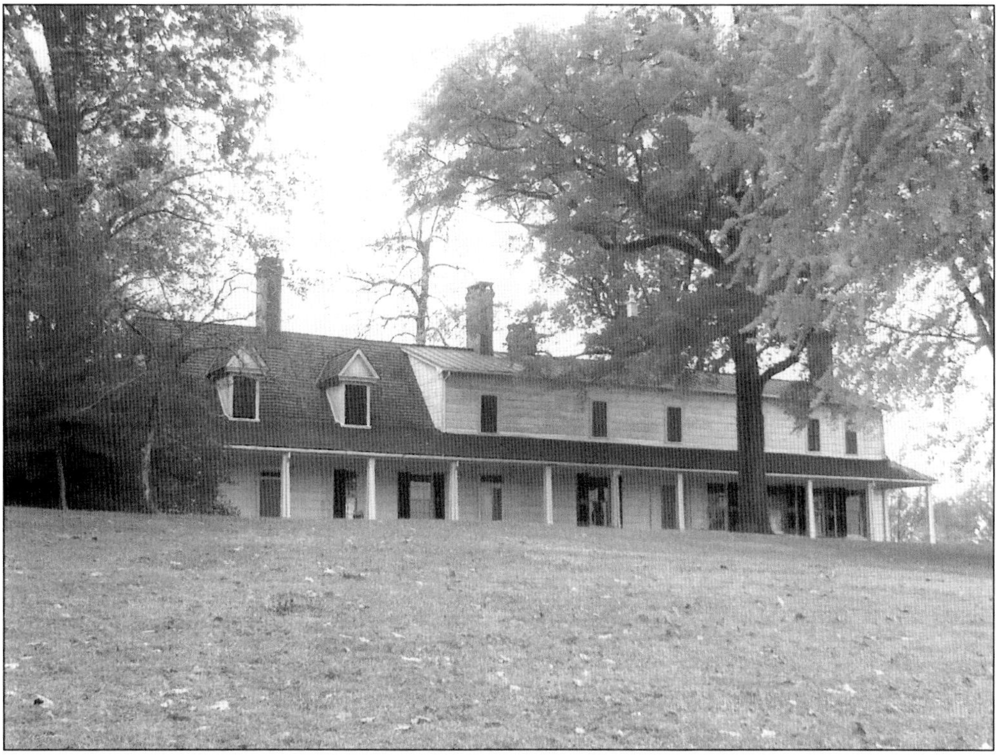

With the Plater II build, Sotterley's plantation house began to take on the iconic shape visitors see from the river side today. The door under the second dormer from the left connects to the Plater dining room passageway. Passageways like these allowed domestic slaves and servants to do their work without being seen. The piazza was added to the house in the late 1760s.

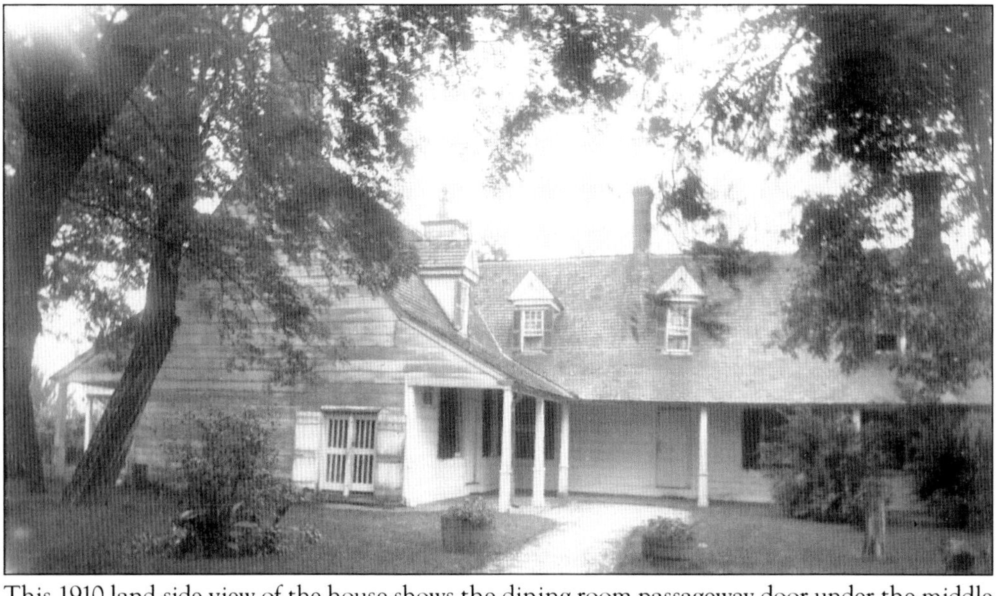

This 1910 land-side view of the house shows the dining room passageway door under the middle dormer and the dining room to the right. The New Room is on the left, with a barred door on the end that opened into the stairwell and the cellar. The porches were added in the 1800s.

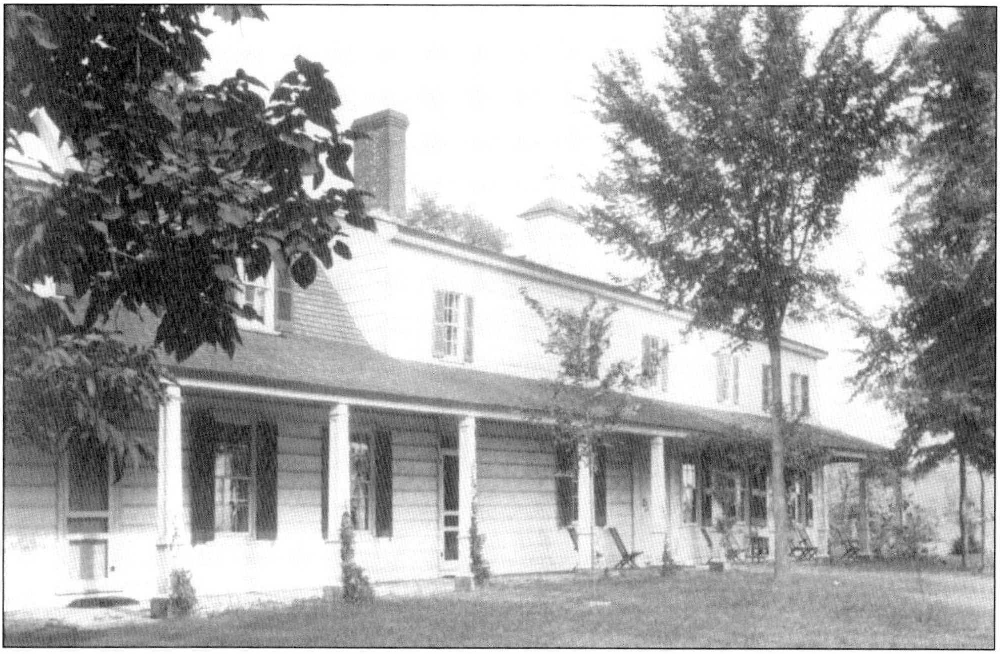

The river-side view of the plantation house above and the photograph of the dining room below were both taken in the 1920s. By 1753, only white males with a freehold of 50 acres or equal worth in sterling were allowed to vote. Catholics were also required to take an oath pledging first allegiance to the British crown, which excluded most from the vote. George Plater II represented this small segment of the population that held high positions, received government appointments with large stipends, made and enforced laws, collected taxes, and discerned the innocent from the guilty. They made trade and economic policy that benefited their interests and the desires of the British crown. Evidence suggests that conditions were harsh for the enslaved at Sotterley. In 1738, two of Plater's slaves, identified as Judy and Pompey, were accused of poisoning the overseer and gardener. They were jailed, tried, and then hanged for the crime. Their sentence of death was decided by the royal governor.

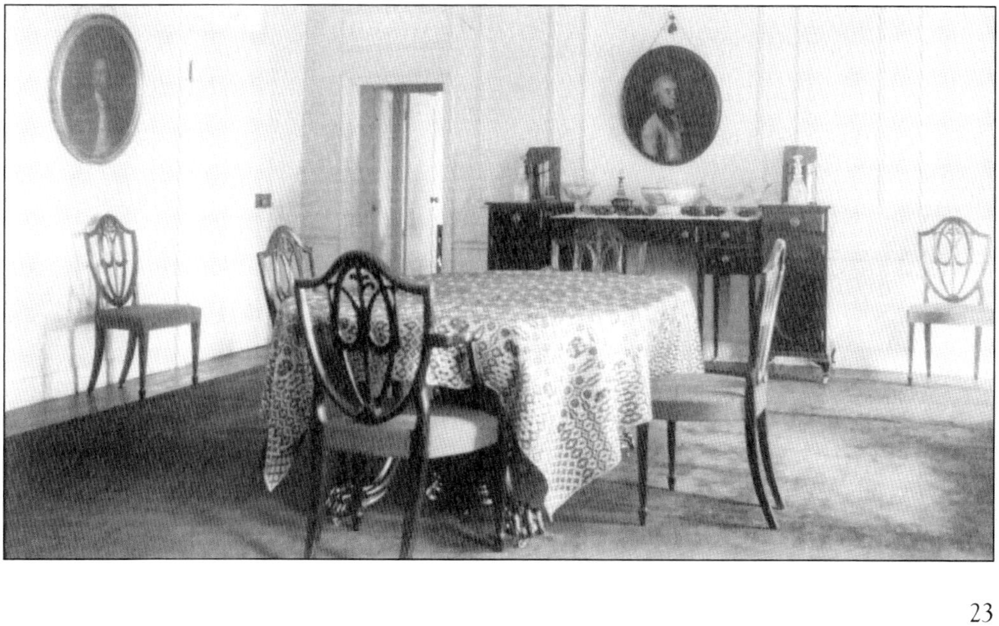

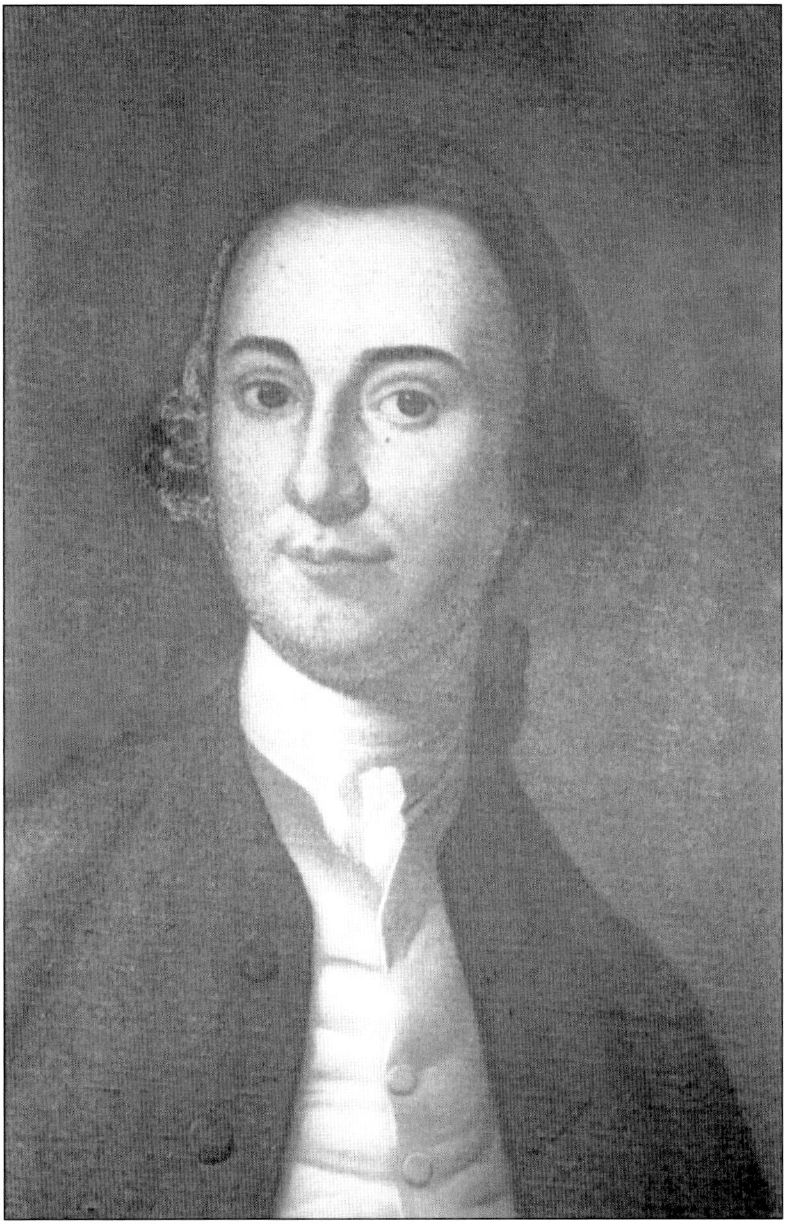

Born in 1735, George Plater III was likely tutored at home in his early years. In 1753, he attended the College of William and Mary in Williamsburg, Virginia. As others of his status and wealth at the college, he was accompanied by an enslaved manservant to see to his daily needs. In 1755, George Plater III, at just 19 years old, inherited Sotterley. At 21, he was elected warden of All Faith Parish. He was also appointed judge of St. Mary's County Court and elected as one of four delegates from St. Mary's County to the lower house of the Maryland assembly in the same year. He served as Naval Officer of the Patuxent and helped establish St. Andrew's Church, serving on the vestry. After the declaration of war with Britain, Plater III served on the council of safety, raising funds and materials to supply the Patriot cause. Wealth and social standing not only meant living as a gentleman, it was also the path to power and responsibility in all social and governmental circles.

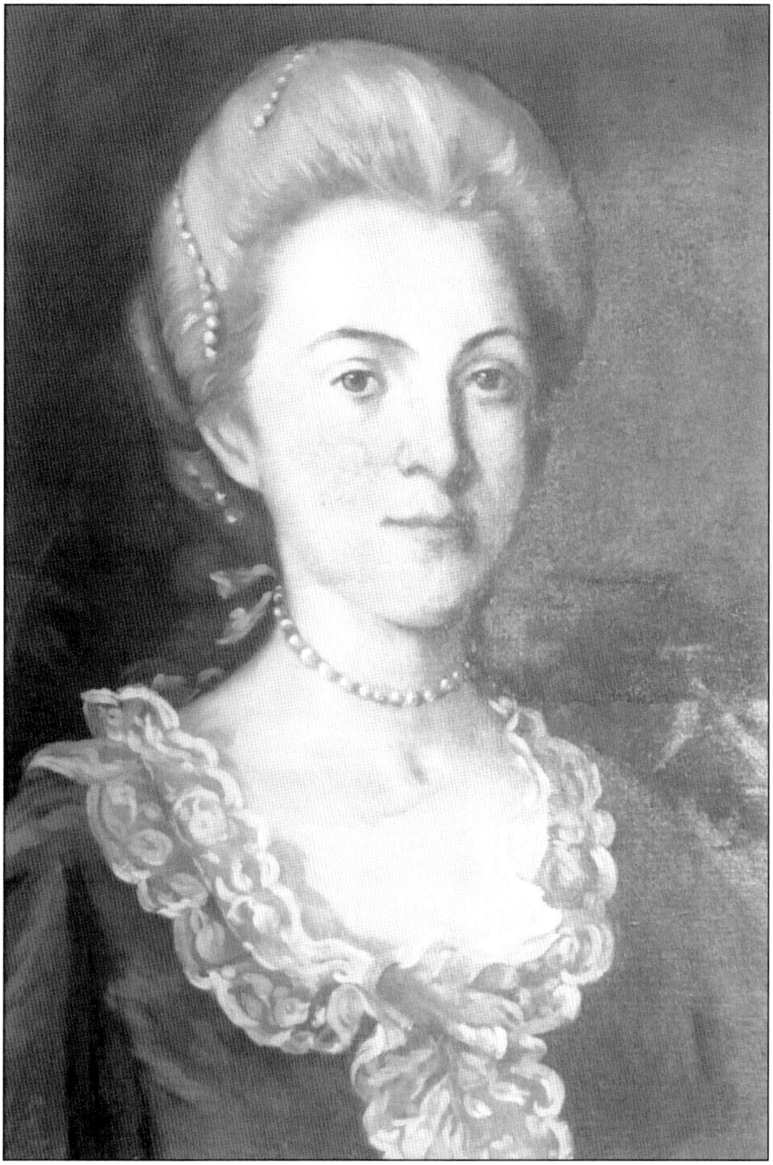

George Plater III's first wife, Hannah Lee, died after 11 months of marriage, probably because she was weakened by childbirth. Tuberculosis was a leading cause of death at the time, especially to anyone in an already weakened condition. James Bowles and four generations of Plater men all had first wives who died. Elizabeth Rousby, seen here, was the second wife of George Plater III. Elizabeth was the daughter of John Rousby and Anne Frisby. The Rousby family was already allied with the Platers, and Elizabeth and George even shared a common grandmother, Anne Burford Doyne Plater Rousby. Elizabeth's stepfather was William Fitzhugh. Not quite 14 when she married in 1764, Elizabeth was, by all accounts, at ease with the social obligations of a gentlewoman. She most likely learned from a tutor at home at Rousby Hall and from her mother. By 1774, Elizabeth had five surviving children: Rebecca, George IV, John Rousby, Thomas, and Ann. She signed her personal correspondence "Eliza," her preferred name among family and friends. She traveled with her husband to Annapolis and Philadelphia and, probably more than anyone else, helped to advance her husband's ambitions. She died in October 1789, not yet 40 years old.

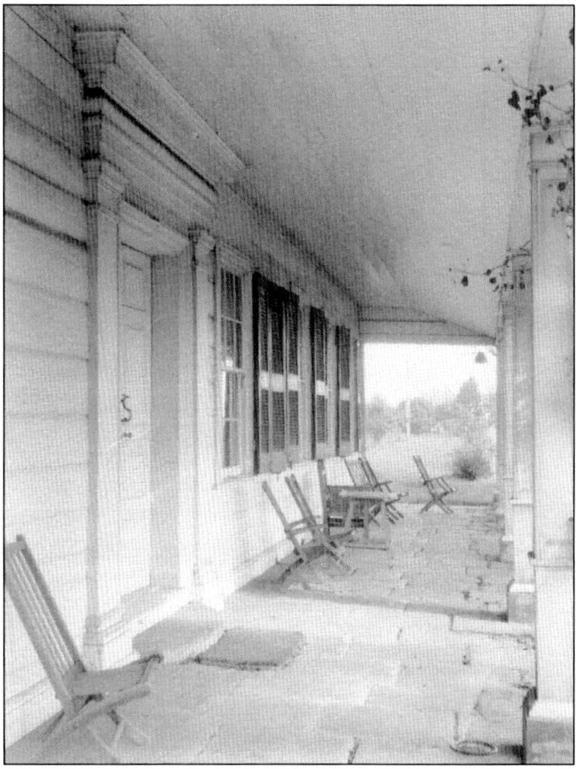

George Plater III transformed Sotterley's plantation house by adding an entry hall. Before that time, the entry door led directly to an owner's living space or a passageway entrance meant for domestic slaves and servants. Guests could now be received in the entry hall by a well-dressed domestic slave and shown to a room to wait for the master's arrival. This entry made the house much more formal while further widening the gap between owners and workers. These photographs show the double-door, river-side entrance, which was considered the front entrance in the 1700s.

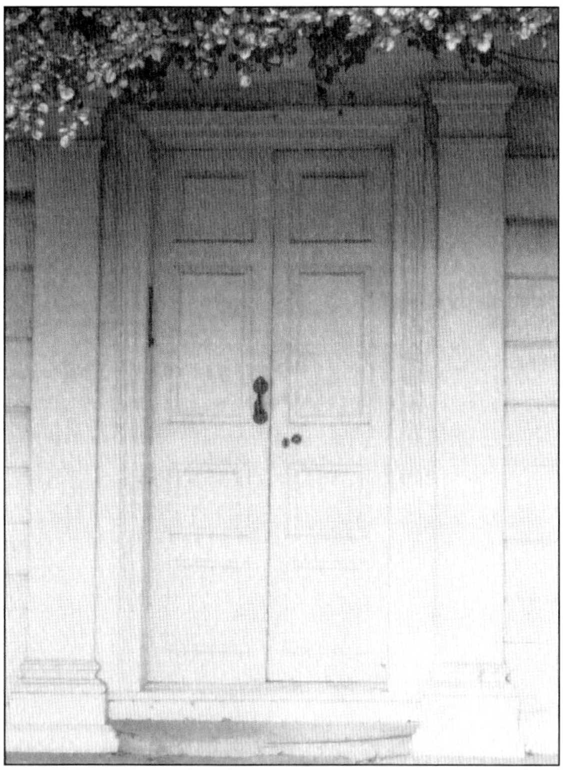

By the late 1760s, Plater had this Chinese Chippendale staircase installed for the entry, one of the earliest examples of this design in the region. Designs by Thomas Chippendale were copied throughout Colonial America and are still popular today. Elegant and beautiful, the basic stair structure is very simple. The woodwork is attributed to Richard Boulton, an expert joiner and carpenter, who was also hired to design interiors for St. Andrews Church, St. Thomas Manor, and All Faith Parish. This photograph was taken in 1910.

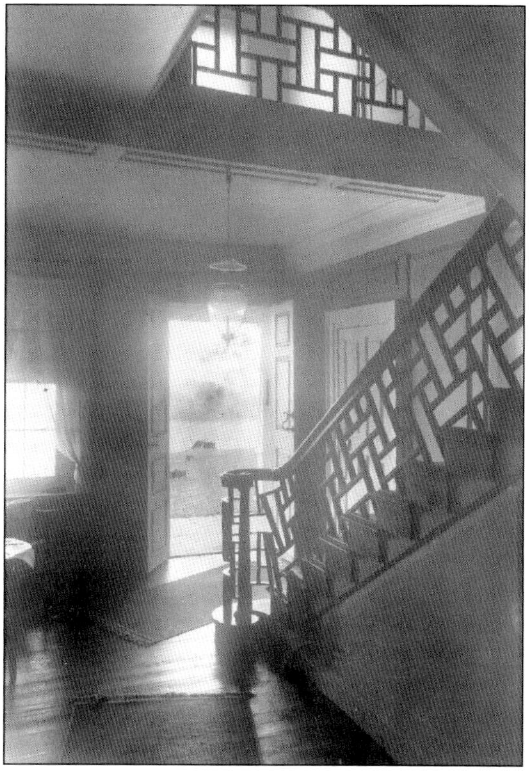

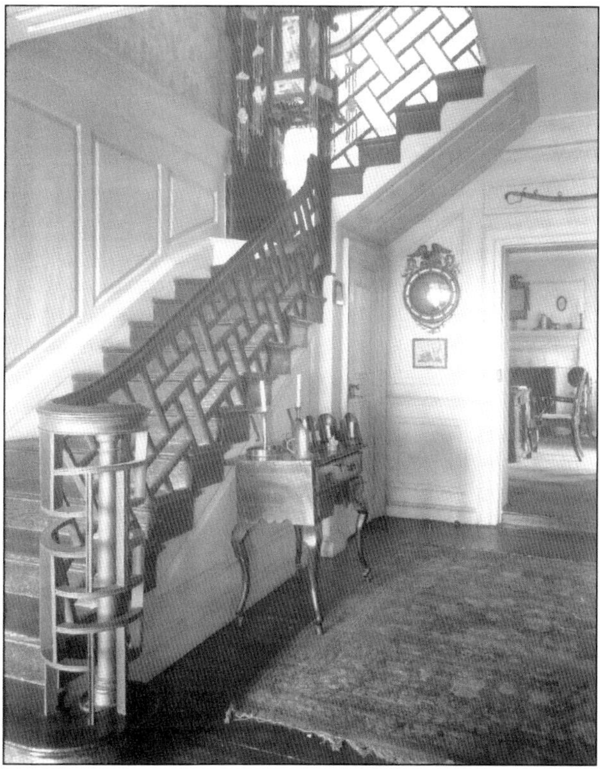

According to surviving correspondence, Richard Boulton was recommended to George Washington by William Fitzhugh, Elizabeth Rousby Plater's stepfather. Washington contracted with Boulton to do interior work at Mount Vernon. Boulton was to have his tools transported to Mount Vernon but did not fulfill the contract, which caused embarrassment for Plater and Fitzhugh and annoyed Washington. In this 1920s photograph, the New Room can be seen through the doorway at right.

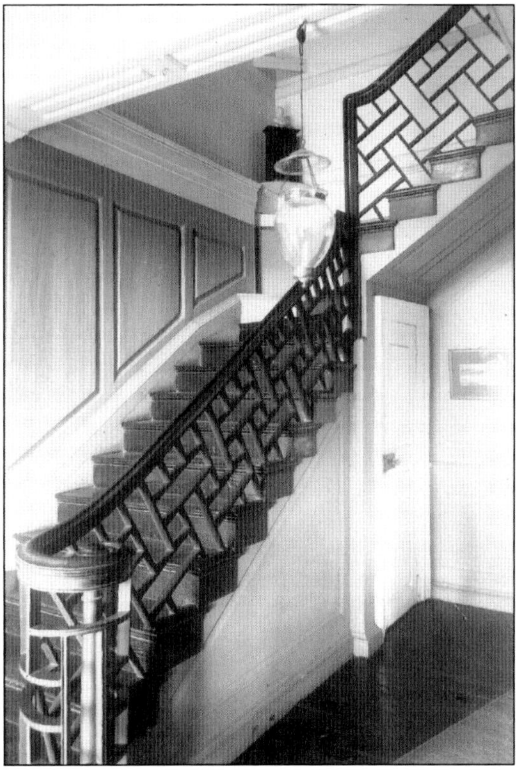

This is another detailed view of the staircase taken in the 1910s. The door under the staircase is a small closet.

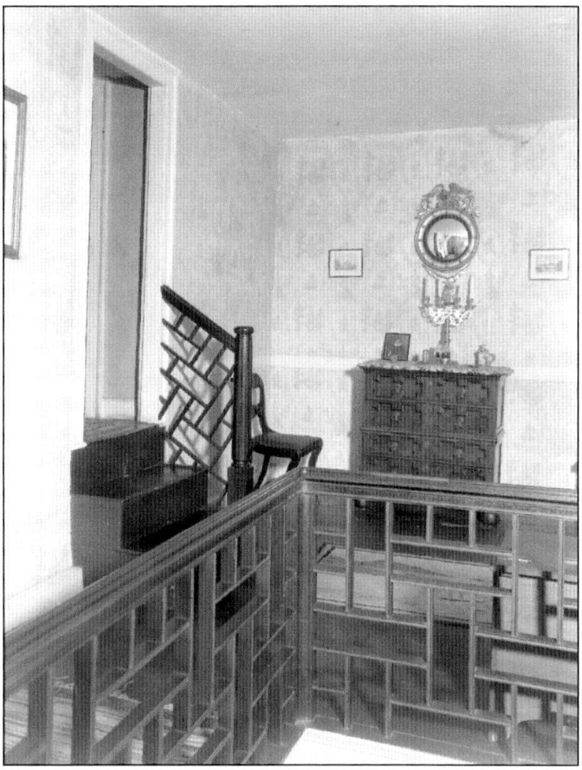

This photograph features the landing residents would see when they reached the top of the staircase. It is large enough for a small sitting area. Note that the latticework continues around the opening and up a few steps to a bedroom above George Plater III's new drawing room.

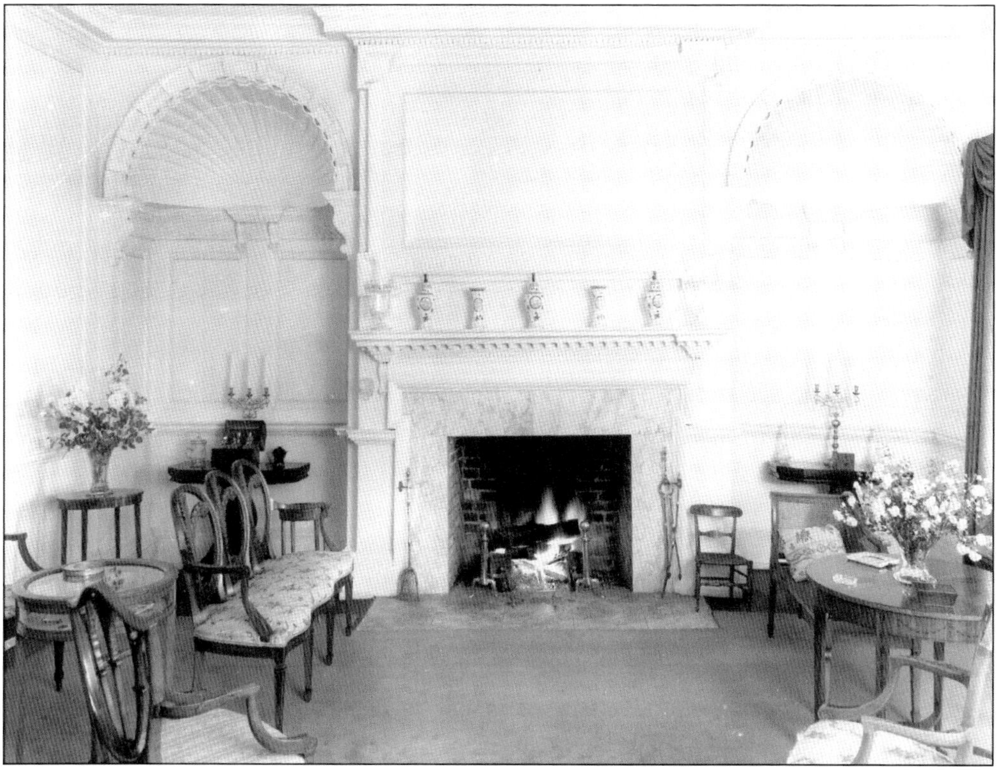

During George Plater III's major building project on the entry hall, he also doubled the size of the original Bowles hall and raised the ceiling. He had Richard Boulton design the shell alcoves. At right, actress Shannon Rose Invanchev stands in front of the alcove wearing an Empire-style dress designed by Leon Wiebers. This room was made to entertain and impress. Greek and Roman motifs were used in the woodwork around the alcoves and mantel, and original 18th-century wood paneling still lines the walls. As the family's wealth increased, rooms were painted in more expensive and stylish colors. Green, grey, blue, and yellow paint was more expensive to make than the red ochre in the original interior. Furnished and painted to suit different owners over the centuries, this remains one of the most beautiful rooms in America.

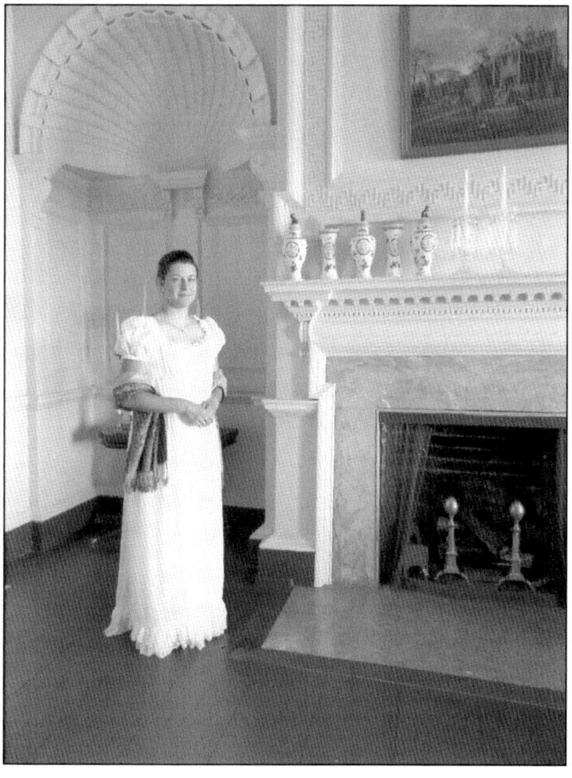

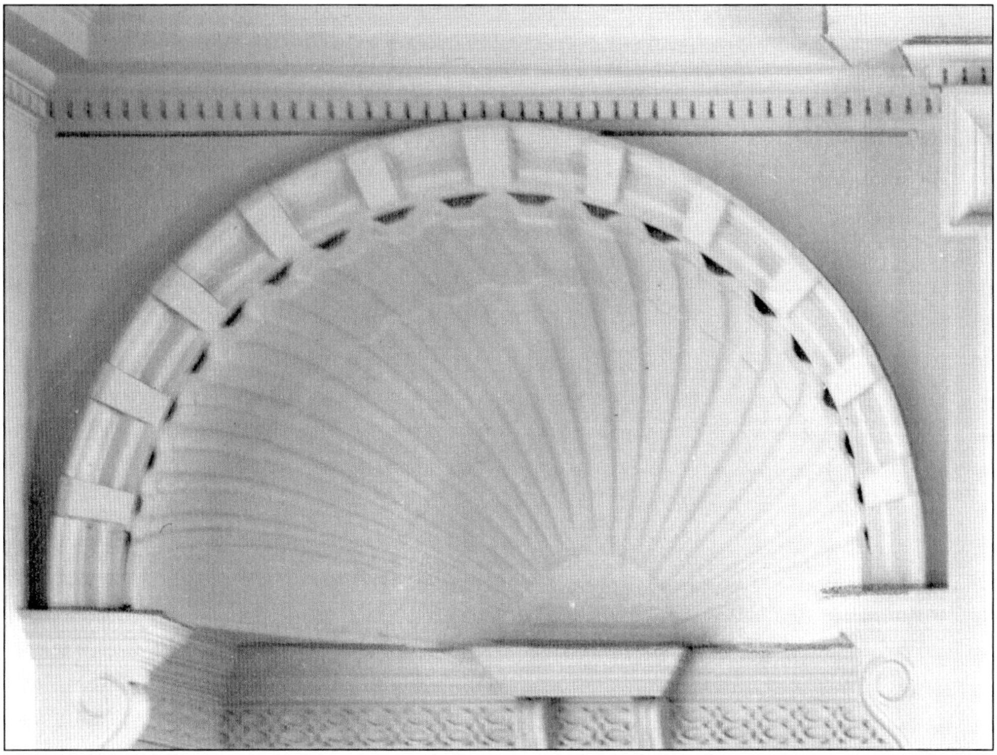

These detailed photographs of the shell alcove (above) and the woodwork over the mantel (below) reveal the fine detailing and beautiful craftsmanship of the talented people that designed and built George and Elizabeth Plater's drawing room. The shell design was made with strips of local wood that were softened, curved, and then layered together to look like one piece. Although designed by Richard Boulton, much of the labor was likely done by skilled enslaved workers. During major construction projects at their plantation house, the Platers probably lodged elsewhere.

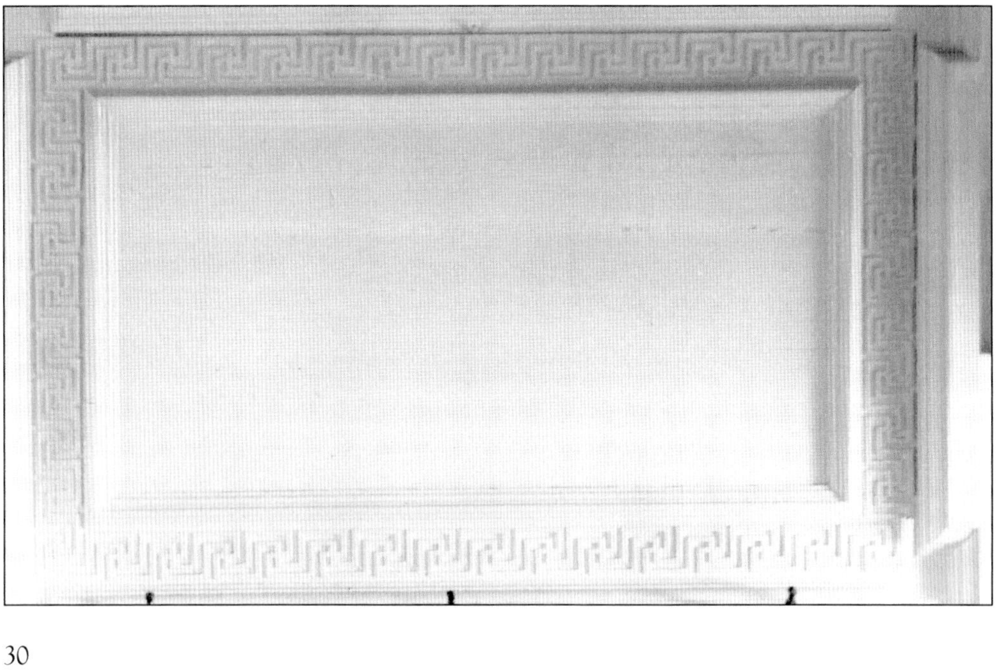

The drawing room's interior door (right) adjoining the entry hall is original to the room. Made of solid wood and finely detailed and finished, it still has the original brass lock and brass-covered rising hinges. Brass locks such as these were ordered and shipped from England, and it sometimes took months for the locks to arrive. Builders at Sotterley would not know ahead of time which way the doors would need to swing open. When the box arrived, the locks were put on the doors, sometimes upside-down like this one. A 1930s exterior view of the double-door entryway is seen below. The door opened to reveal the grand staircase.

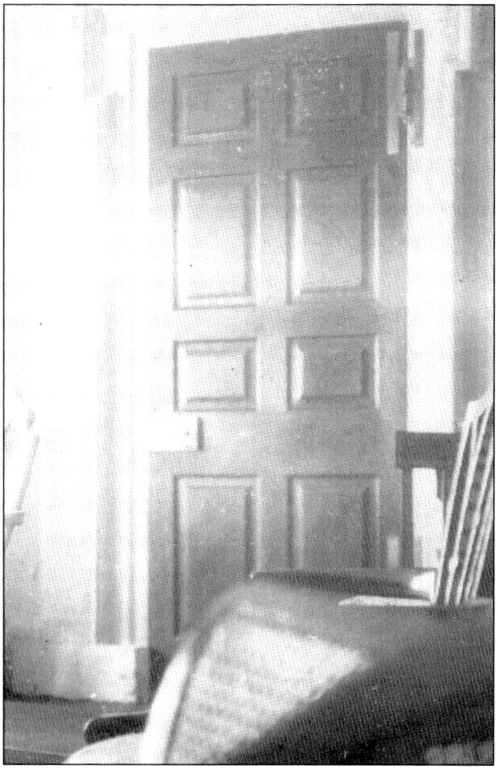

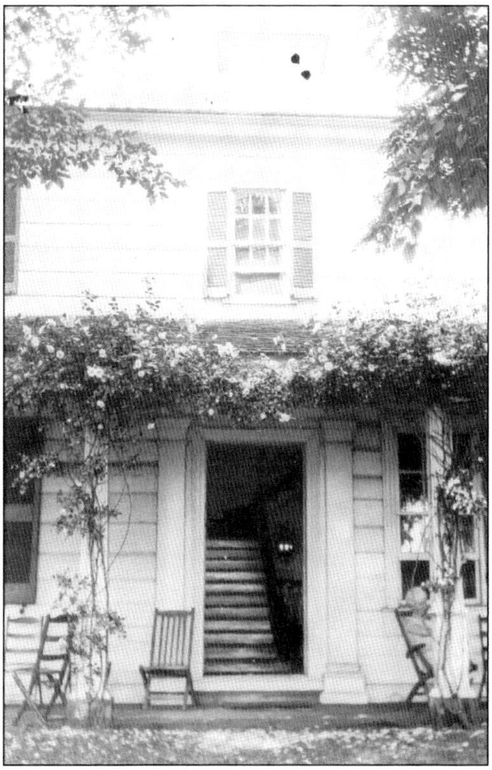

Sotterley, September 29, 1786.

On the first day of November next, will be offered for sale, at the subscribers seat in St. Mary's county, on Patuxent river,

SEVERAL young negro women, boys, and girls. Credit will be given, on bond and good security. Those negroes are sold for no fault, but the proprietor is overstocked.

GEORGE PLATER.

The advertisement above was placed by George Plater III in 1786. It announces a slave sale that is to take place at Sotterley on November 1. The enslaved people would not know this was coming until overseers gathered them before the sale. It was after planting season, and Plater probably did not want to feed, clothe, and house so many slaves through the winter. After the American Revolution, it became more difficult for planters with large estates to maintain their land and wealth. The enslaved lived in constant fear of days like this. Women and children, sold away from their husbands, wives, or parents, were looked over by traders and neighbors searching for a good bargain. Slaves were first brought to Sotterley via the Patuxent River, but the river also provided food and sometimes an escape route to freedom. Sotterley Creek (below) is just a short walk down the hill from the plantation house.

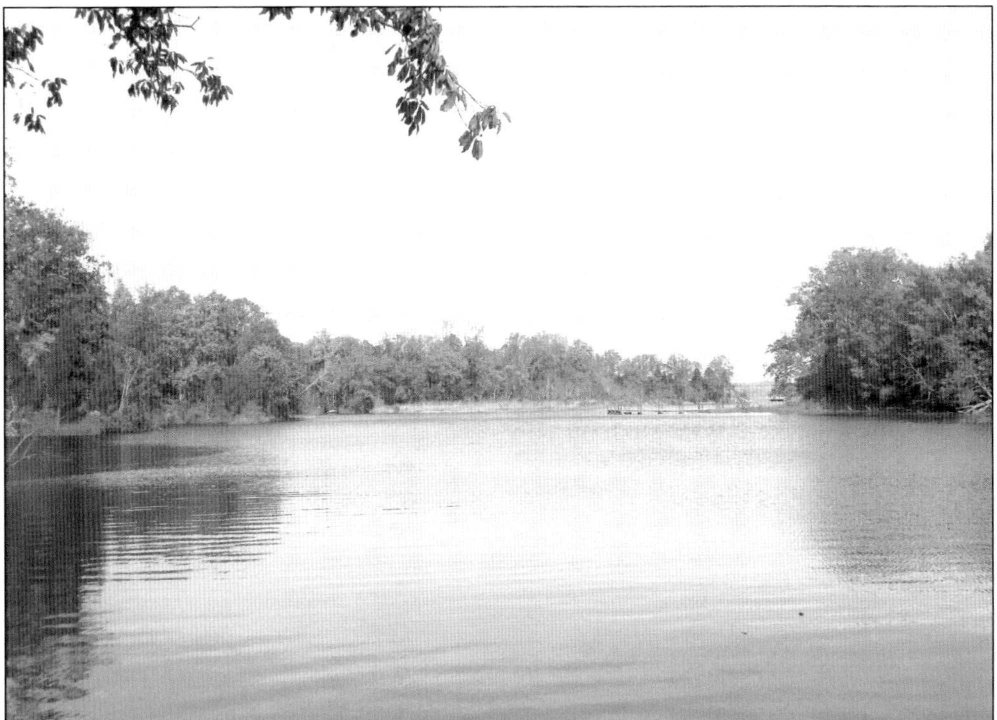

Sotterley, March 6, 1791.

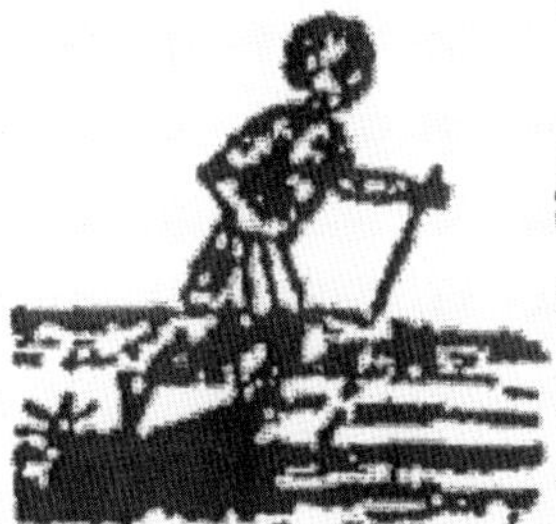

RAN away from the ſubſcriber, living in St Mary's county, on the 19th of laſt month, a likely young negro man named JOE, about 18 or 20 years of age, near ſix feet high, well made, and very black, has a ſoft mode of ſpeech, and inſinuating manners; had on a country cloth jacket and breeches, oſnabrig ſhirt, yarn ſtockings, and common negro ſhoes. Whoever will ſecure him, ſo that I may get him again, ſhall be paid EIGHT DOLLARS. 4w

GEORGE PLATER.

George Plater III placed the advertisement above on March 6, 1791, offering a reward for the capture of an escaped slave named Joe. He could speak well, which made him valuable to his master. "Insinuating manners" was a form of resistance, meaning he would tell his master one thing but do or feel something else. Joe had escaped on a sloop and ended up in a jail on the Eastern Shore of Virginia. There he gave a false name and presented a forged letter stating his free status. He finally gave up his master's name because he knew if he was not returned to Sotterley, the jailer could sell him to an even worse situation. Joe was again in the newspaper in the advertisement (below) in 1793. Gov. George Plater III died in February 1792, and George Plater IV was the owner of Sotterley by this time, but Joe had evidently been sold twice since 1791, first to Uriah Forrest in Georgetown, George Plater III's son-in-law, and then to John Linthicum in Montgomery County, whom Joe subsequently escaped from. Repeat runaways often became more trouble than they were worth to their masters, and Joe was determined to be free.

Five Pounds Reward.

RAN AWAY from the ſubſcriber, on the 31ſt ult. a Negro Fellow named JOE, a ſtout, well made fellow, about 25 years old, 5 feet 11 inches high; he was formerly the property of George Plater of St. Mary's County, Maryland, and lately belonged to Colonel Forreſt of George-Town, of whom I purchaſed him.—Whoever takes up the ſaid Negro and ſecures him ſo that I get him again, ſhall receive the above reward, and if brought home, or to Montgomery County Gaol, a reaſonable compenſation.

JOHN LINTHICUM.

Seneca, Montgomery County, Maryland, September 3d, 1793.

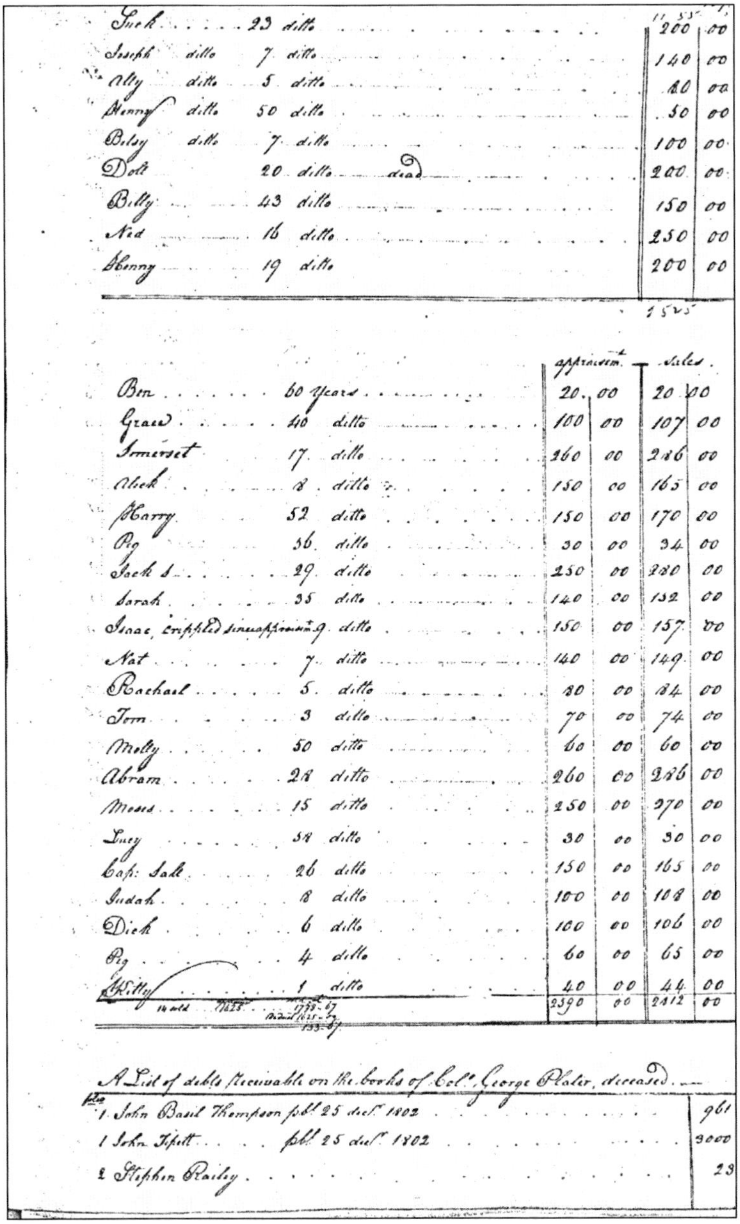

Suck		23 ditto	200 00
Joseph	ditto	7 ditto	140 00
Alty	ditto	5 ditto	80 00
Henny	ditto	50 ditto	50 00
Betsy	ditto	7 ditto	100 00
Doll		20 ditto dead	200 00
Billy		43 ditto	150 00
Ned		16 ditto	250 00
Henny		19 ditto	200 00

		appraisem.t		sales	
Ben	60 Years	20	00	20	00
Grace	40 ditto	100	00	107	00
Somerset	17 ditto	260	00	286	00
Aleck	8 ditto	150	00	165	00
Harry	52 ditto	150	00	170	00
Peg	56 ditto	30	00	34	00
Jack S	29 ditto	250	00	280	00
Sarah	35 ditto	140	00	132	00
Isaac, crippled since appraisem.t	9 ditto	150	00	157	00
Nat	7 ditto	140	00	149	00
Rachael	5 ditto	80	00	84	00
Tom	3 ditto	70	00	74	00
Molly	50 ditto	60	00	60	00
Abram	28 ditto	260	00	286	00
Moses	15 ditto	250	00	270	00
Lucy	58 ditto	30	00	30	00
Cap: Sall	26 ditto	150	00	165	00
Judah	8 ditto	100	00	108	00
Dick	6 ditto	100	00	106	00
Peg	4 ditto	60	00	65	00
Kitty	1 ditto	40	00	44	00
		2590	00	2412	00

A List of debts Receivable on the books of Col.o George Plater, deceased.

1	John Basil Thompson pbl.e 25 dec.r 1802	961
1	John Tifett pbl.e 25 dec.r 1802	3000
2	Stephen Railey	23

In 1792, George Plater III died within months of becoming governor. Sotterley was then divided between his three sons, with George Plater IV keeping a vast estate and the acreage around the plantation house. The third-wealthiest man in St. Mary's County, George Plater IV married Cecilia Bond in 1795. They had one son, George Plater V, before Cecilia died. George Plater IV then married Elizabeth Somerville, and they had one daughter, Ann. In 1802, both George IV and Elizabeth died. Within 10 years of receiving his inheritance, George Plater IV had accumulated a large amount of debt. A portion of the George IV inventory, the original of which is housed in the Maryland State Archives, is seen here. Slaves were listed here along with all the other property and possessions and could be sold, collected as payment for debts, or willed to different family members. George Plater IV had 64 slaves. His brother John Rousby Plater served as the master of Sotterley and managed the estate until his young nephew George Plater V came of age.

John Rousby Plater was a long-standing Maryland delegate and a judge for the orphan's court in St. Mary's County. As with other Federalists that believed in a strong central government, he was against the trade embargo declared by Thomas Jefferson in 1807 in retaliation to the British habit of commandeering US ships. He was also against going to war with the British, as he feared it would devastate trade and the region's economy and leave southern Maryland unprotected against overwhelming British forces. His fears were realized when what is now known as the War of 1812 was declared. By 1813, the British had blockaded the Chesapeake Bay. British ships sailed up the Patuxent River, burning farms and taking food and supplies from the residents. In June 1814, in the days during and after the Battle of St. Leonard's Creek, which is within sight of Sotterley's plantation house, British forces landed at Sotterley and burned a tobacco barn where about 300 militiamen had assembled. On June 14, the British confronted John Rousby Plater. They spared Sotterley's plantation house but did something that was perhaps even more devastating to him: offered freedom to his slaves. The map above traces the route taken by the British on their way to Washington, DC. Below, a facsimile of one page from the claim for reparations made by John Rousby Plater for the 49 slaves he lost in 1814 listed first and last names, ages, and sometimes occupations of the escaped slaves. The original document is housed at the National Archives. By 1826, the British had paid John Rousby Plater approximately $280 per slave taken. (Above, courtesy of FCIT.)

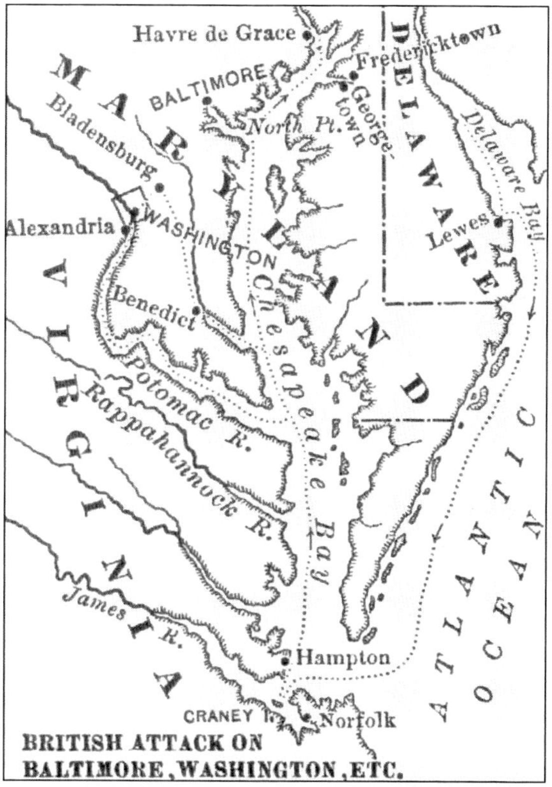

BRITISH ATTACK ON BALTIMORE, WASHINGTON, ETC.

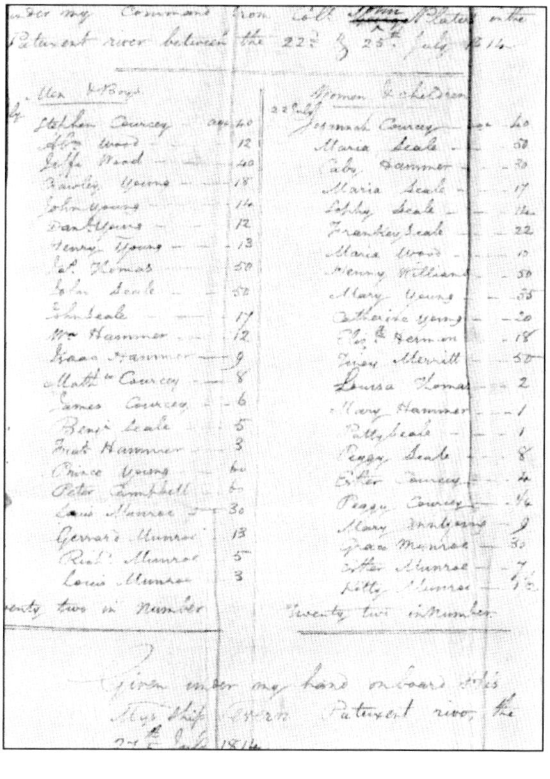
under my Command from Col. John Plater on the Patuxent river between the 22d & 25th July 1814.

Men & Boys	age	Women & Children	
Stephen Courcey	40	Jemimah Courcey	40
[illegible] Wood	12	Maria Seale	50
Jeffe Wood	40	Caby Hammer	30
Hawley Young	18	Maria Seale	17
John Young	14	Sophy Seale	14
Danl. Young	12	Frankey Seale	22
Henry Young	13	Maria Wood	10
[illegible] Thomas	50	Henny William	50
John Seale	50	Mary Young	35
Thos. Seale	17	Catharine Young	20
Wm. Hammer	12	Eliz. Herman	18
Isaac Hammer	9	Tiney Merrill	50
Matthew Courcey	8	Louisa Thomas	2
James Courcey	6	Mary Hammer	1
Benj. Seale	5	Patty Seale	1
Frank Hammer	3	Peggy Seale	8
Prince Young	60	Ester Courcey	4
Peter Campbell	6	Peggy Courcey	[illegible]
Louis Munroe	30	Mary [illegible]	9
Gerrard Munroe	13	Grace Munroe	30
Richd. Munroe	5	Ester Munroe	7
Louis Munroe	3	Kitty Munroe	[illegible]
[T]wenty two in Number		Twenty two in Number	

Given under my hand on board His Majs. Ship [illegible] Patuxent river, the 2[illegible] July 1814.

SOTTERLEY FOR SALE.

INTENDING to remove to the Western Country, I will offer, at public sale, on Wednesday, 3d day of July next on the premises, the whole of my landed estate, containing about 4000 acres. This estate is situated immediately on the river Patuxent, about equidistant from each extreme end of St. Mary's county,. and is as desirable a farm as any in Maryland. Upon a view, these lands will sustain the high estimate that may be attached to them abroad; thereof, it is hoped, those at least at a distance unacquainted with the estate, who may be inclined to realise their surplus funds, will view the premises previous to the day of sale, as there is seldom such a farm offered at auction.

The estate is susceptible of being divided into several fine farms, which will be done, or sold entire, as may best suit purchasers.—Part of the purchase money will be required to be paid down, when a good and sufficient title will be shewn, and further terms made on the day of sale. Sale to commence at 12 o'clock. GEORGE PLATER.

When the British took 49 Sotterley slaves in the summer of 1814, they offered freedom to anyone that would leave and join them, not just the able-bodied young men, but also whole families. Over 700 Maryland slaves took advantage of this offer. The Munroe, Coursey, and Seale families all left with the British. Peregrine Young, James Bowie, Joseph Wood, and Ignatius Seale helped other slaves escape from Sotterley and the surrounding area. They knew the land and the people and were invaluable to the British. After their initial escape, they were taken to places like Tangier Island, where they boarded other ships. Some died on these ships and were separated from their families. Eventually, most were taken to Halifax, Nova Scotia, were they lived in crowded and disease-ridden barracks with inadequate clothing for the harsh weather and were resented by Halifax residents. Some had received a small parcel of land in Nova Scotia by 1815. Others, like James Bowie and Joseph Wood, were taken to Trinidad. They were given land for their service in the Colonial Marines. When George Plater V came of age and took charge at Sotterley, he had an inadequate labor force, with only 19 slaves in 1820, and inherited debt. This advertisement offers Sotterley for sale. George Plater V sold Sotterley in 1822 and, according to this notice, was planning to go west.

Two

Family and Freedom
1823–1909

Walter Hanson Stone Briscoe was from a long line of Maryland's founding families when he married Emeline Dallam in 1826. That same year, Emeline and her stepsister Lydia Barber inherited 1,000 acres. In 1828, the land was divided by court decree, with Lydia receiving 600 acres and Emeline receiving 400 acres and the plantation house. Lydia married Chapman Billingsley. Chapman and Walter Briscoe were lifelong friends, business partners, and community leaders. The Briscoe house was full, as they had 13 of their own children, as well as girls from the boarding school they started, who lived in the house most of the year. Along with the farm, Dr. Briscoe had a busy medical practice and was a respected member of the community. Walter and Emeline owned Sotterley longer than any other single family.

Sotterley was a network of cultures and communities whose fates were dependent on one another. The slaves of the Billingsleys and the Briscoes were connected, with members of the same families owned by each master. Hilry Cane was a skilled plasterer owned by Billingsley. His wife and children were owned by Briscoe. Other enslaved families had members owned by different masters as well, including the Edwards, Barnes, and Plowden families. Enslaved domestics living in the house and in quarters near the plantation house would have been a common sight.

The Briscoes recognized marriages and kinships in their enslaved communities. This recognition, however, did not protect enslaved families from the realities of their status as property. The Briscoes participated in the domestic slave trade, which meant family members could be sold away at the whim of their master, depending on labor needs and economic conditions at the time. Tax records and the oral tradition of a Cane descendant, Agnes Kane Callum, corroborates this, with episodes when the Cane children were lined up to be looked over by traders that came to the house.

Life changed drastically for all with the passage of the Fugitive Slave Act in 1850, and the next 10 years leading up to the Civil War. Pres. Abraham Lincoln prevented Maryland from seceding from the Union. This left Marylanders, such as the Briscoes at Sotterley, who were loyal to the Confederate cause, living behind enemy lines.

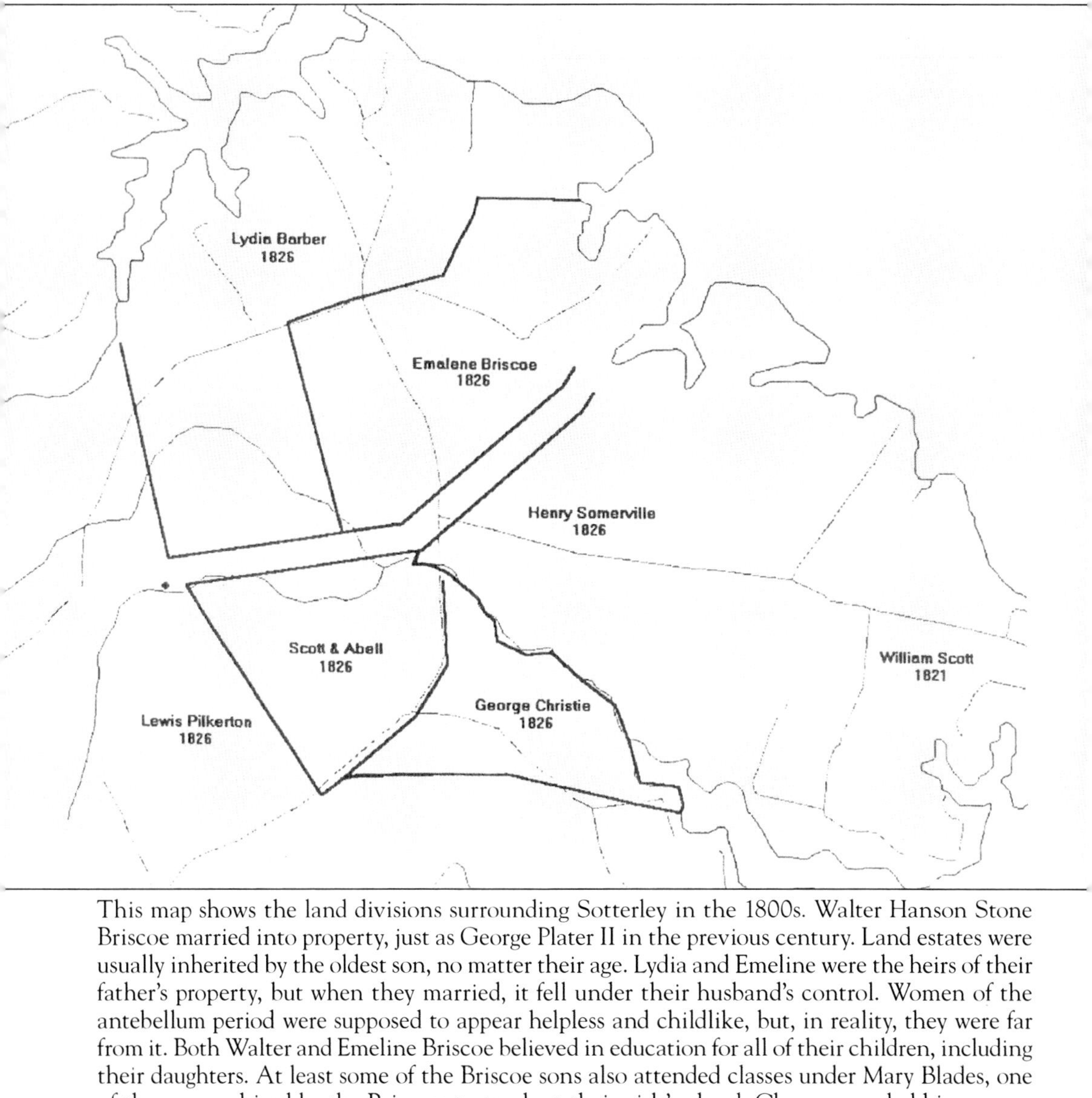

This map shows the land divisions surrounding Sotterley in the 1800s. Walter Hanson Stone Briscoe married into property, just as George Plater II in the previous century. Land estates were usually inherited by the oldest son, no matter their age. Lydia and Emeline were the heirs of their father's property, but when they married, it fell under their husband's control. Women of the antebellum period were supposed to appear helpless and childlike, but, in reality, they were far from it. Both Walter and Emeline Briscoe believed in education for all of their children, including their daughters. At least some of the Briscoe sons also attended classes under Mary Blades, one of the women hired by the Briscoes to teach at their girls' school. Classes were held in a room somewhere in the front of the property, most likely in what is now called the north gatehouse. By this time, the orientation of the plantation house had changed, and the road side of the house was now considered its front. Dr. Briscoe added on to his land estate with the purchase of Half-Pone farm. As his land increased, so did the number of slaves he owned. Steamboat travel had replaced the tall ships by 1830, carrying goods to market and people to and from St. Mary's County. Sotterley's steamboat landing, at the end of Sotterley Wharf Road, was a busy port and community meeting place for the next 100 years. (Courtesy of Peter Himmelheber.)

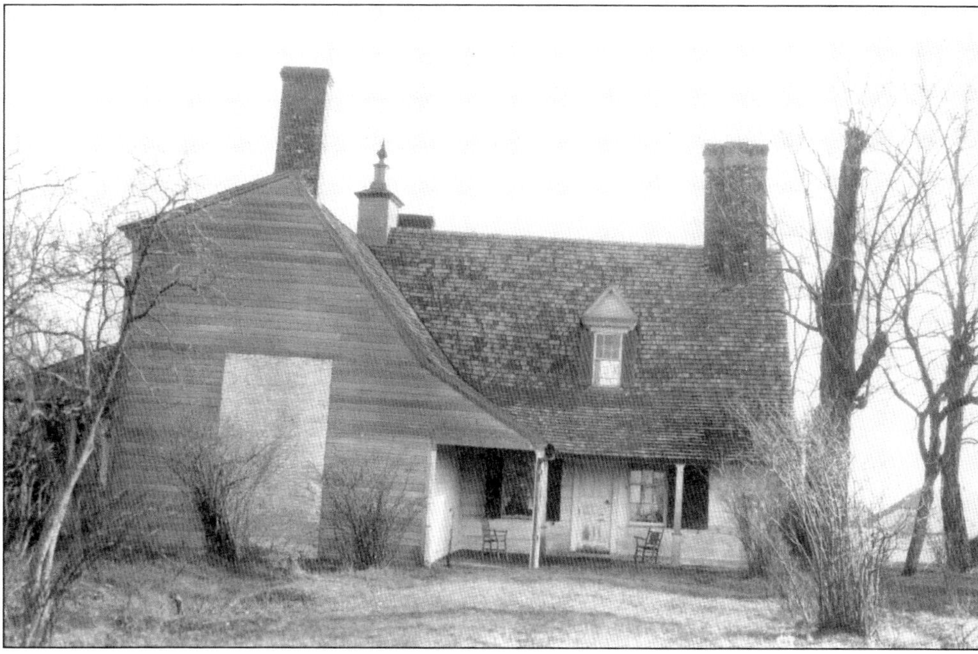

The plantation house, as it looked in the 1800s, is seen here from the garden looking southwest in 1910. The north side of the New Room and drawing room wing is visible. Note that the house is covered with wooden siding, not brick, and that the bedroom above the drawing room does not yet have dormer windows.

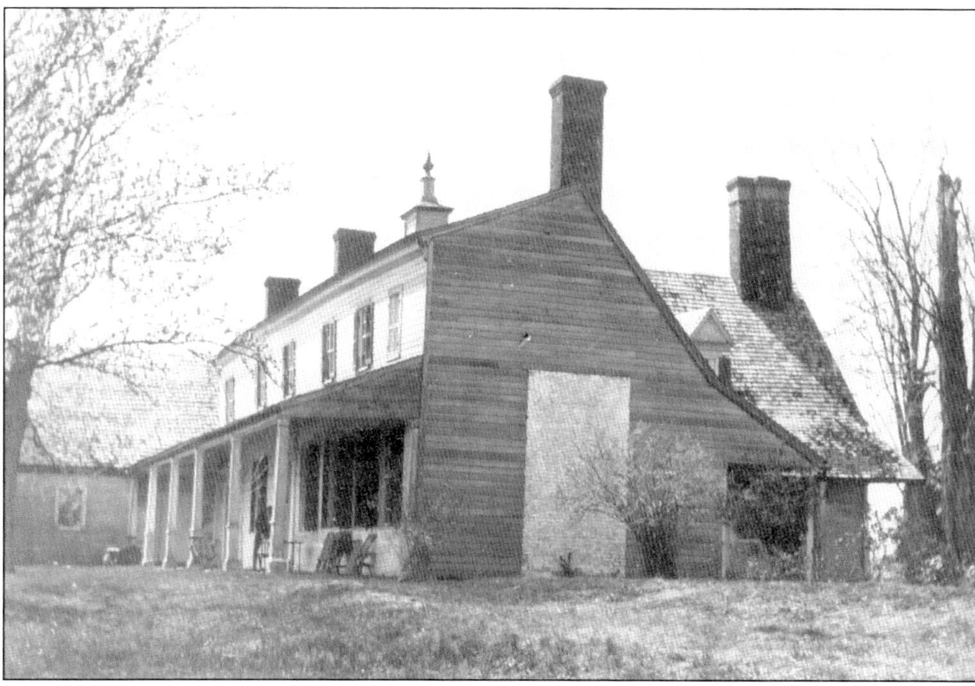

Looking to the southeast from the river side, this photograph shows the kitchen that was attached to the house just past the dining room passageway door. This kitchen, often referred to as the Briscoe kitchen, was added sometime in the early 1800s.

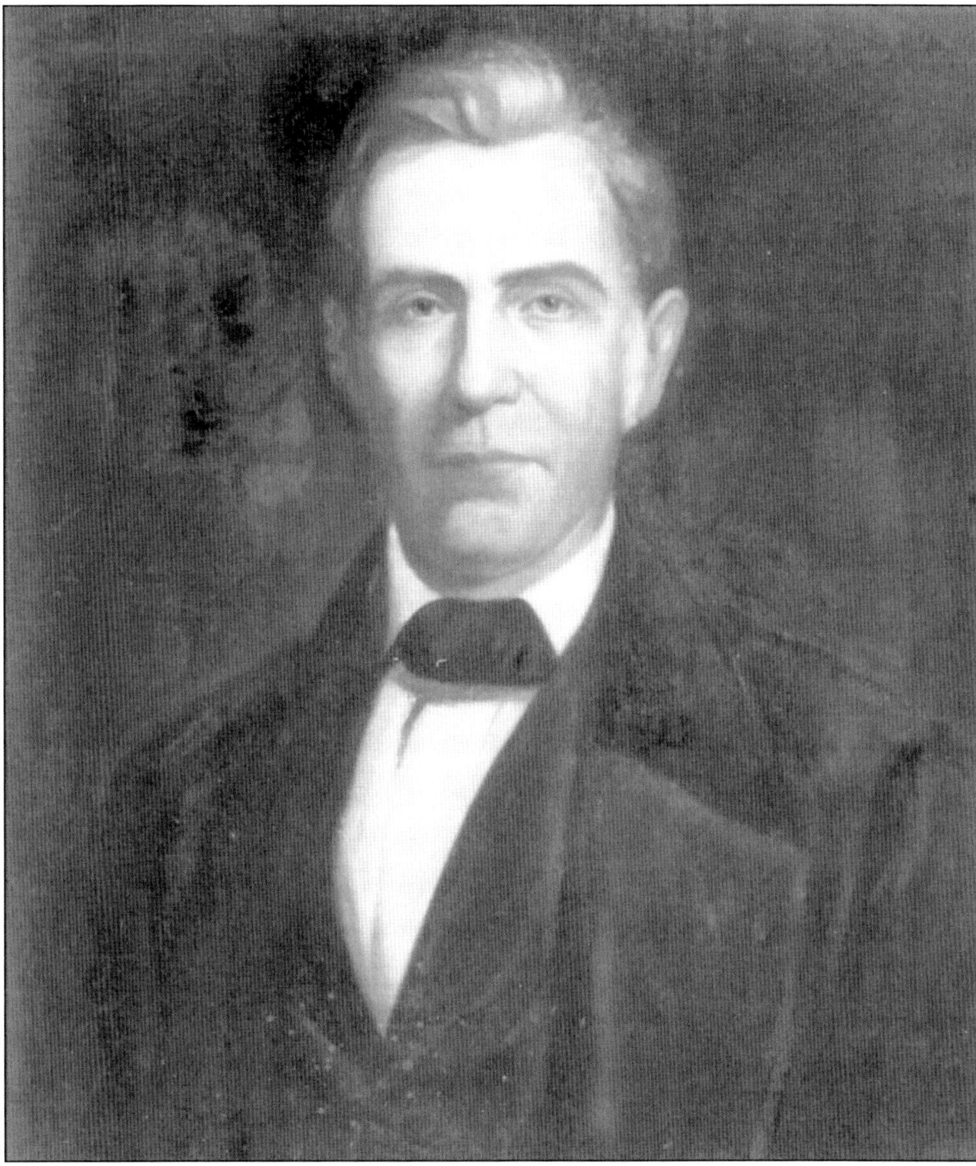

These portrait reproductions of Dr. Walter Hanson Stone Briscoe and Emeline Dallam Briscoe (opposite) were donated by a visiting Briscoe descendant of their oldest daughter, Margaret. Walter looks to be in his early to mid-50s, which would date these portraits sometime between 1850 and 1855. He graduated from the school in Charlotte Hall and then learned to practice medicine from Dr. N.R. Smith. He purchased pews one and two at St. Andrew's Church and served on the vestry there for over 50 years. In 1850, he listed the value of his real estate at $18,000. On the farm, he grew wheat, then the major cash crop, as well as some tobacco, corn, and cotton. He also raised hogs and sheep and kept horses and oxen. He rode in a carriage driven by an enslaved coachman to house calls and was highly respected by his family and his community. Unlike the Platers, who had many legal documents, court proceedings, and newspaper accounts of their lives, Dr. Walter Hanson Stone Briscoe is conspicuously absent from this kind of attention, as he led a privileged yet quiet family life and was at peace with his neighbors. He would need this quiet resolve in the turbulent years to come.

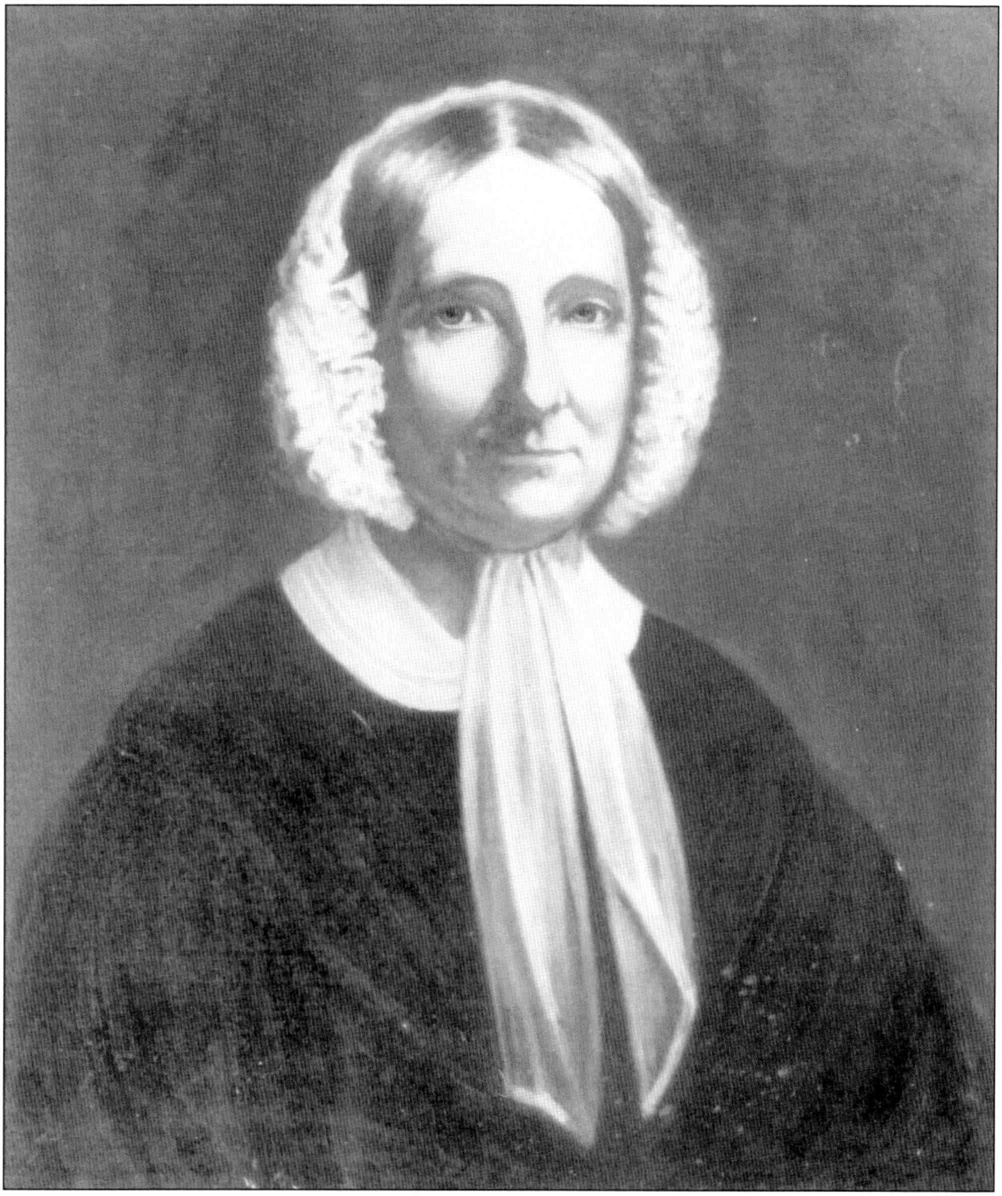

Emeline Wellmore Dallam Briscoe was born in Philadelphia to John Dallam and Emeline Wellmore in 1809. Her husband, Walter, was eight years her senior. After Emeline's father died, her mother married Thomas Barber, who owned Sotterley for just a few years before his death in 1826. Emeline was 16 when she married, and until her mid-40s, her life was a constant cycle of pregnancy, childbirth, and nursing, as she had 13 children. Women in the 1700s and 1800s were active during pregnancy and would appear socially as long as their health permitted, altering their clothes as needed. For most women, childbirth was still traditionally a woman's domain, with relatives and midwives in attendance. In 1850, there were 20 family members, teachers, and boarders living in the plantation house, including Walter and Emeline, 11 of their children, four girls aged 11 to 16, a woman of 45, and two women in their 60s, one of whom, Mary Blades, was hired to teach for the Briscoes. In 1850, the Briscoes' oldest living child, Margaret, was 20 years old. Emeline's youngest child was yet to born.

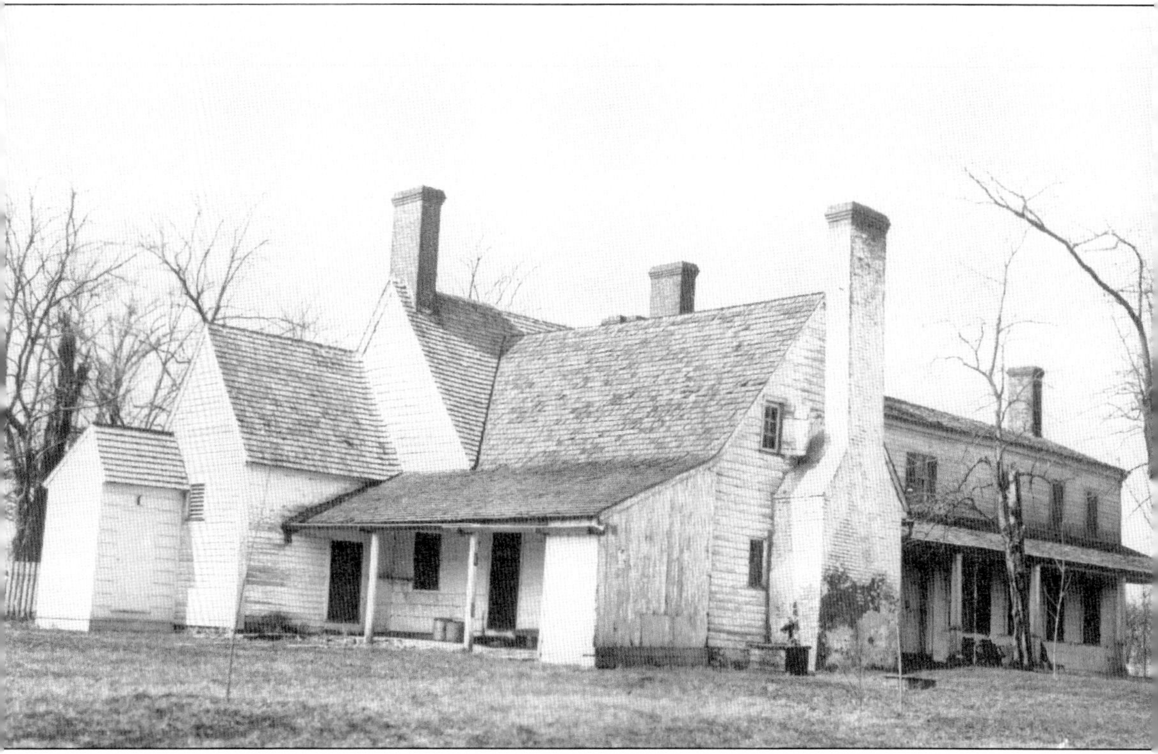

In this view of the back of the Briscoe house kitchen, note the water pump by the chimney, the attached larder on the house with a door, the covered porch with storage, and a passage door to the opposite side. The second-floor kitchen window can also be seen. One could enter an upstairs room of the house from the second floor of the kitchen. The only access to the rest of the house from this room was a ladder stair that most likely ended in or near the dining room passageway. Enslaved domestics would have lived, worked, and served in these spaces. At some point in the mid-1800s, the ladder stair was closed off, perhaps coinciding with emancipation. According to oral tradition, the Briscoe slaves would line up in this back covered area by the kitchen to receive their rations of fatty pork and corn meal every Saturday afternoon.

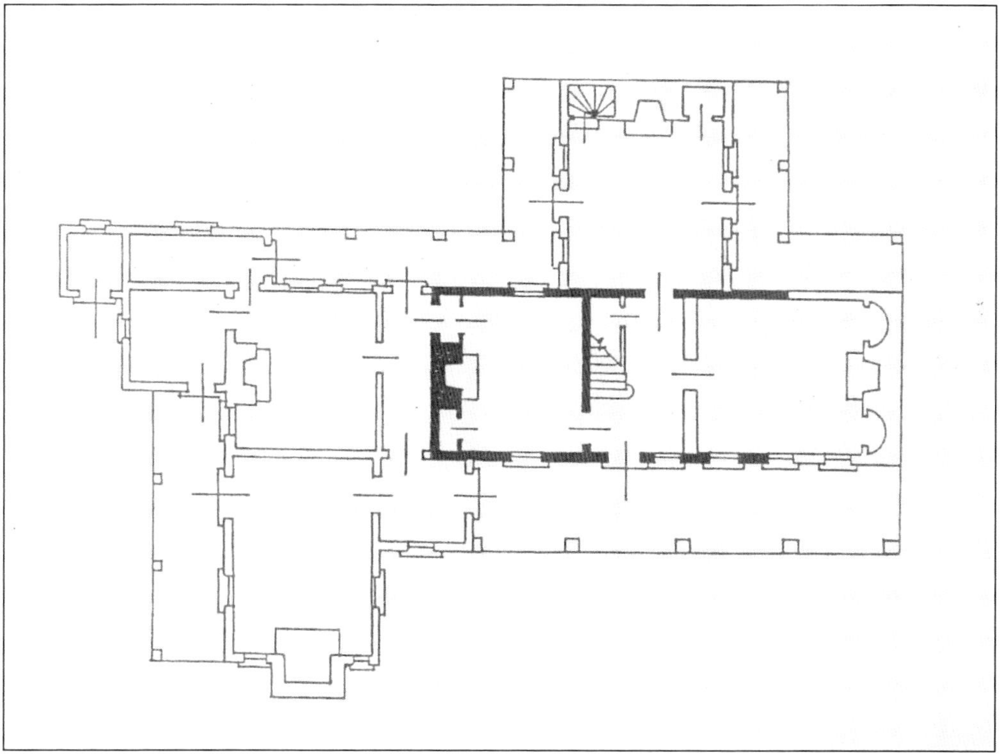

This floor plan of the Briscoe house of the 1800s has the original two-room Bowles house in bold outline. An 18th-century vaulted larder was attached to the dining room, which opened to the covered outside area of the kitchen. There was also another passage from the dining room to the road side with access to the porch. Tracing the patterns of passageways and exits, the enslaved domestics that served the Briscoes could prepare and serve meals to 20 residents with only a few servers actually seen in the dining room.

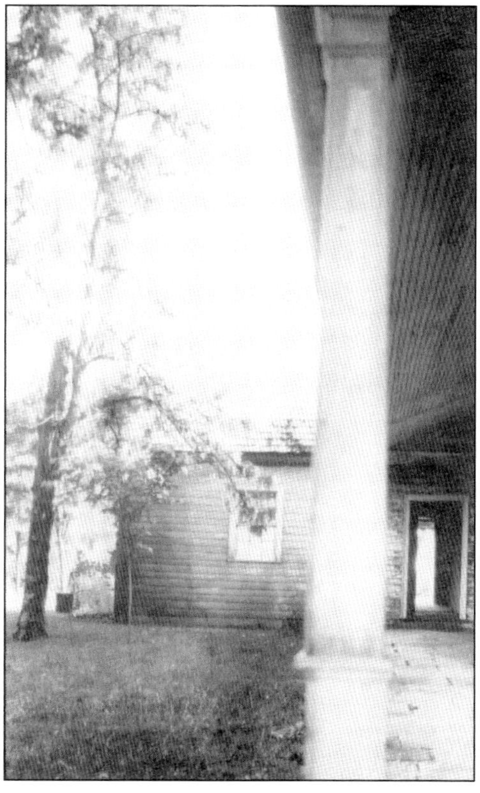

This 1910 photograph shows the Briscoe kitchen passage looking from the north end of the river-side stone portico. When the Briscoes lived here, enslaved cooks worked all day, every day to prepare food for the residents. Good cooks were considered valuable servants. It took hard work, timing, and management skills for food to go from farm to table. Laundry for the household was also a continuous task, requiring soaking, washing, rinsing, drying, starching, and ironing. Heating water meant keeping a burning fire in all seasons and 12-to-14-hour days of backbreaking work.

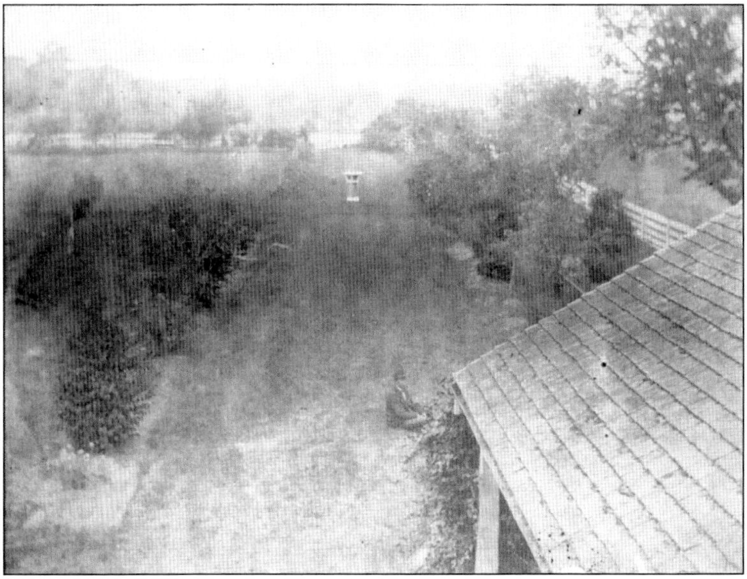

This late-1800s photograph looks north toward the garden from the second floor of the New Room, showing the sundial in the center. The garden area is surrounded by white fencing and the necessary, or brick outhouse, is totally obscured by overgrowth. A young boy is sitting on the ground near the house, wearing a cap, coat, and bow tie.

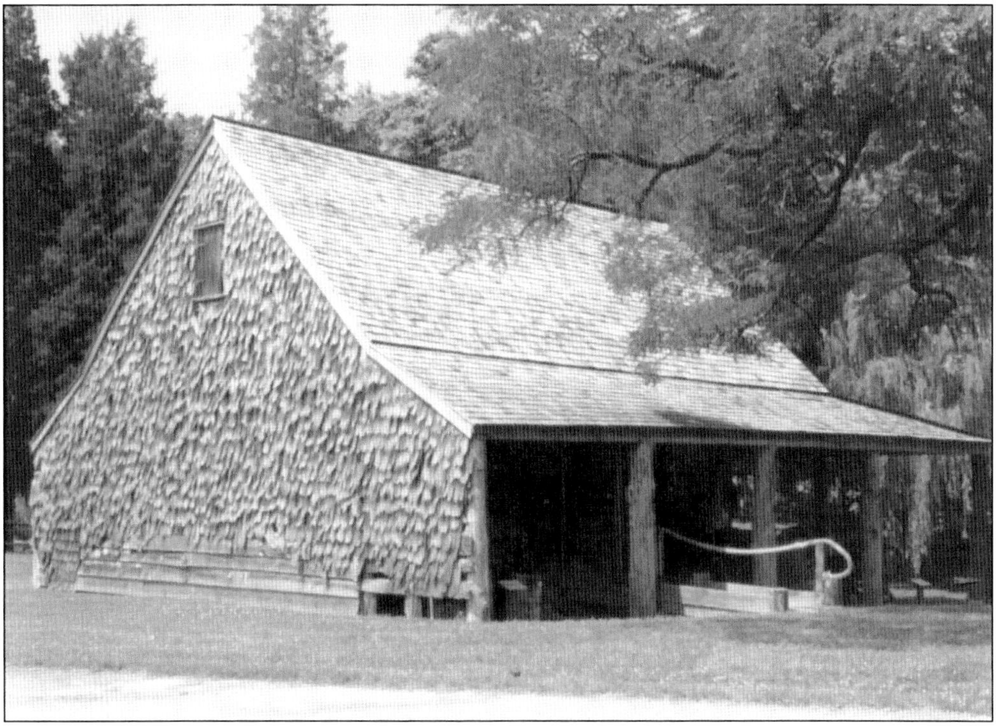

Called the Corn Crib, this structure was built with repurposed wood in the 1800s and used as a storehouse for grain to keep away moisture and rodents. Sotterley Plantation has always been dependent on the people that labored on its land. Men, women, and children worked year-round planting, tending, harvesting, and processing crops from sunrise until sundown, six and sometimes seven days a week. Enslaved children were working a full day sometimes by the age of eight. Skilled workers, both enslaved and free, such as blacksmiths, joiners and carpenters, coopers, plasterers, brick masons, stonemasons, wheelwrights, and those skilled in animal husbandry, were highly valued and were part of the workforce at Sotterley Plantation for its entire history.

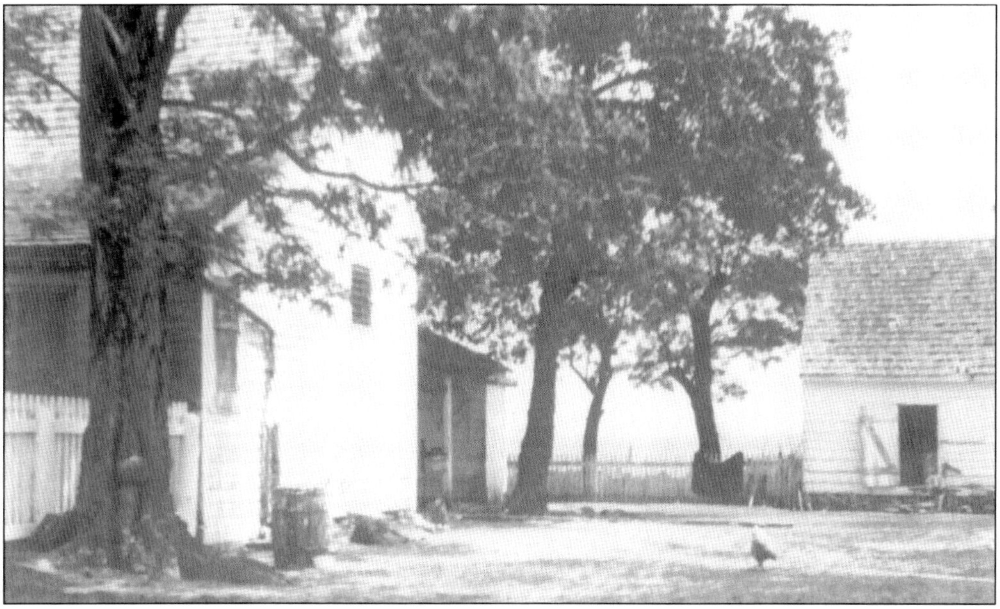

The enslaved population of Sotterley in the 1800s was quartered in various locations on the plantation surrounding their work. Sometimes, families were allowed to live together in one location. Hilry Cane, a skilled plasterer owned by Chapman Billingsley, was allowed to quarter with his wife and children at Sotterley. After Cane was purchased by Chapman Billingsley, Cane's wife, Mariah, and four of their children, including an infant, Frank Cane, did not bring the price needed when auctioned on the block in Leonardtown, Maryland. Within a year, Dr. Briscoe purchased Mariah and her children for over $500. Mariah was a skilled laundress, although workers often had several duties. She died after four years at Sotterley. Hilry Cane then married 15-year-old Alice Elsa Bond, another Sotterley laundress and spinner. They had 12 children. The quarter above, on the south side behind the plantation house, was demolished in 1910, soon after these photographs were taken. The photograph below shows the same structure in full view. It looks almost identical to Sotterley's existing slave cabin, except for the added structure attached to the right. Enslaved domestics working in and for the plantation house would have been housed here. After slavery was abolished, African American families continued to occupy these dwellings and work as servants well into the 1900s.

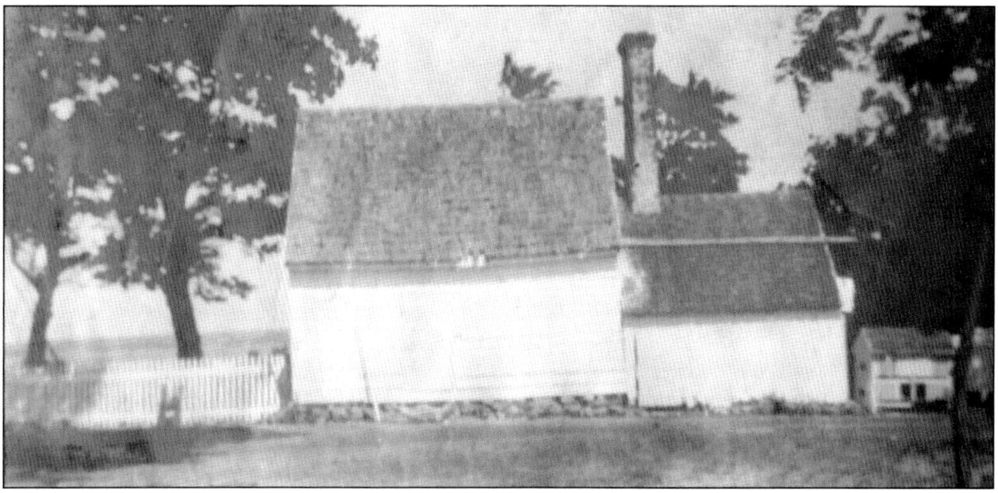

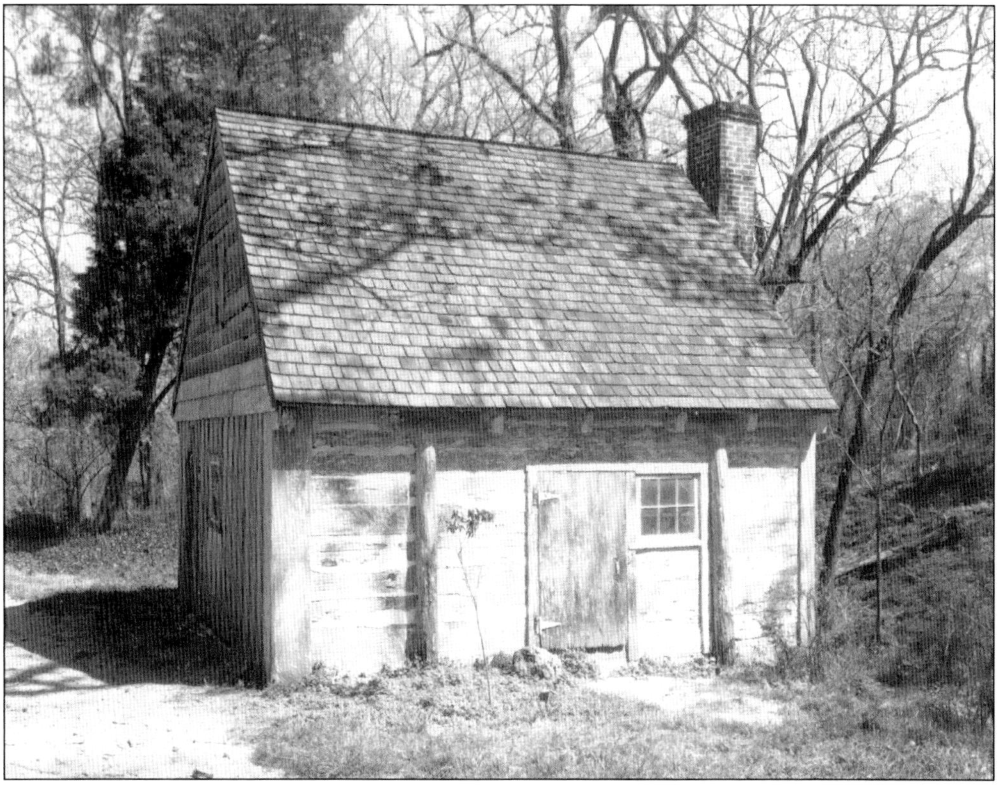

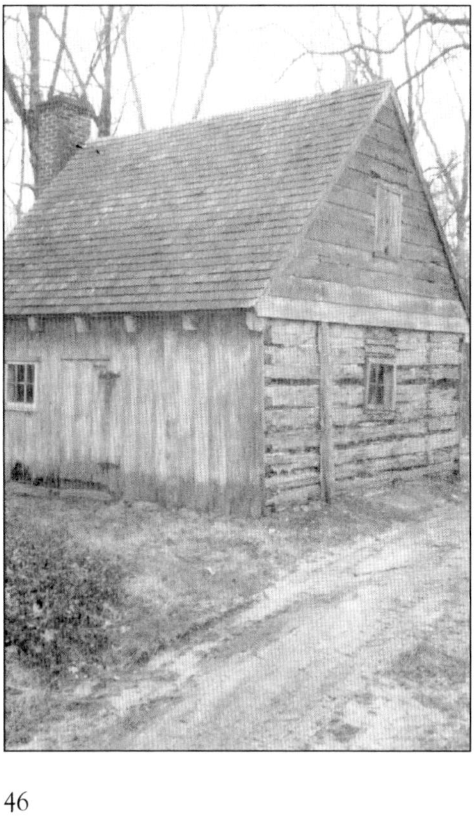

Sotterley Plantation's only surviving slave cabin, seen in both these photographs, is down the hill and to the southeast of the plantation house on Rolling Road. It measures 16 feet by 18 feet with a loft and was made of sewn and hewn pine logs, square-notched at the corners. The outside walls were also supported by earthfast cedar posts attached with wooden pegs. It has a brick chimney and two wooden doors. The windows were added after emancipation. Clay and hog's hair, along with other similar materials, were used as chinking between the logs. In summer, the chinking was removed to let in air. In the fall, it was replaced to keep out the cold wind. Today, the exterior is covered by white wooden panel siding to preserve the structure. An enslaved family of skilled and domestic laborers would have lived in this cabin. The Cane family alone included 18 people, compared to the 20 people that lived in the plantation house in 1850. In 1910, a woman named "Aunt" Nannie Williams and at least three of her relatives were still living in this cabin. This fact, along with the cabin's location and distance from the main house, probably saved it from destruction.

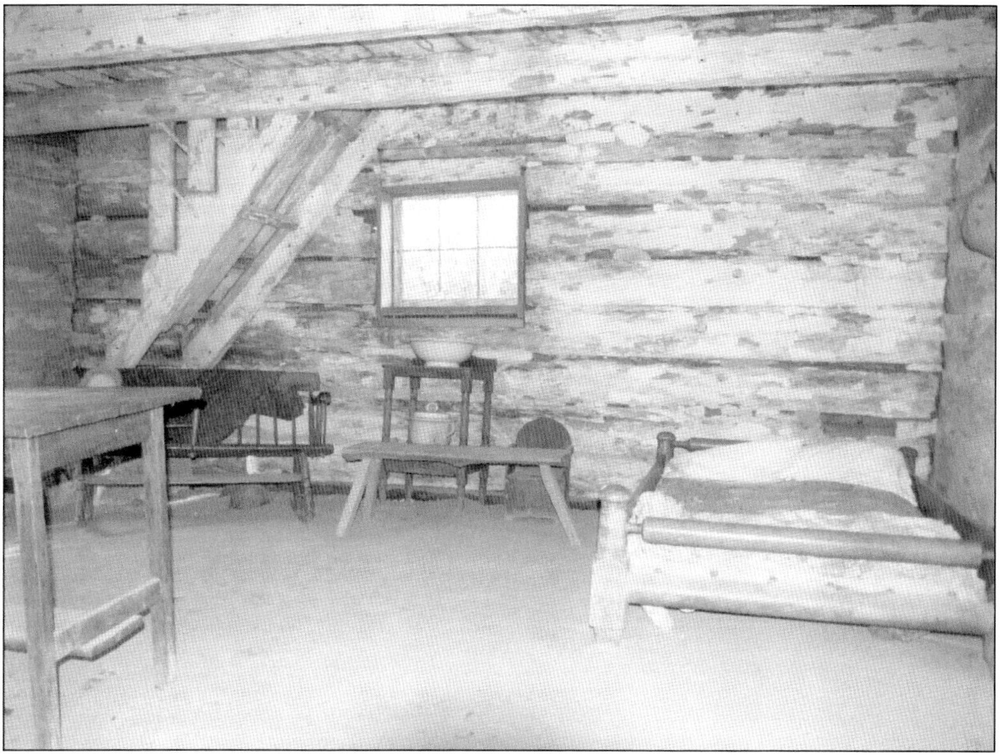

The interior view of Sotterley's existing slave cabin above shows the window and staircase that were added after emancipation. Originally, ladder stairs at opposite corners of the cabin led to the loft for sleeping. The floors were hard-packed clay. Pots and utensils for cooking and eating, ongoing work on clothes, tools for survival, and perhaps a few sticks of furniture made from scraps would have been inside. Grain sacks stuffed with corn husks or feathers would have sufficed for a bed on the ground for most. Homemade musical instruments, dolls, and toys were created. The hearth (below) would contain a one-pot meal that included any small game caught in a trap the night before to supplement the rations given by Dr. Briscoe, along with freshwater fish and seafood from the brackish water of the creeks along the Patuxent River.

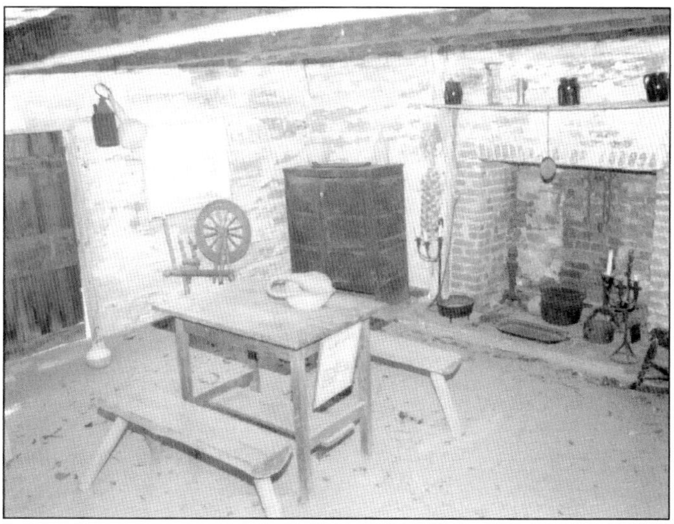

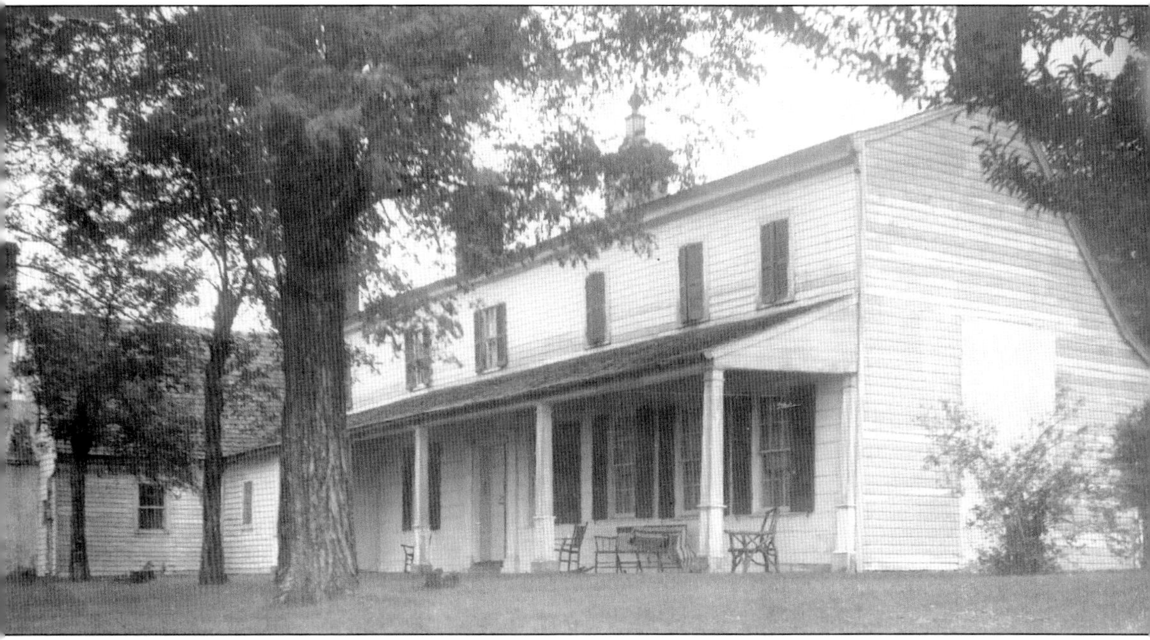

The river-side dining room windows were obscured by the kitchen passage at the Briscoe house. Missing from this photograph from 1910 are all of the animals, people, and activity that would have been seen in this yard in the 1800s. There are no brick exteriors on the house except for the chimneys. Sotterley's plantation house has survived war, raids, and storms. It is miraculous that it was not burned or destroyed by the ravages of time or development.

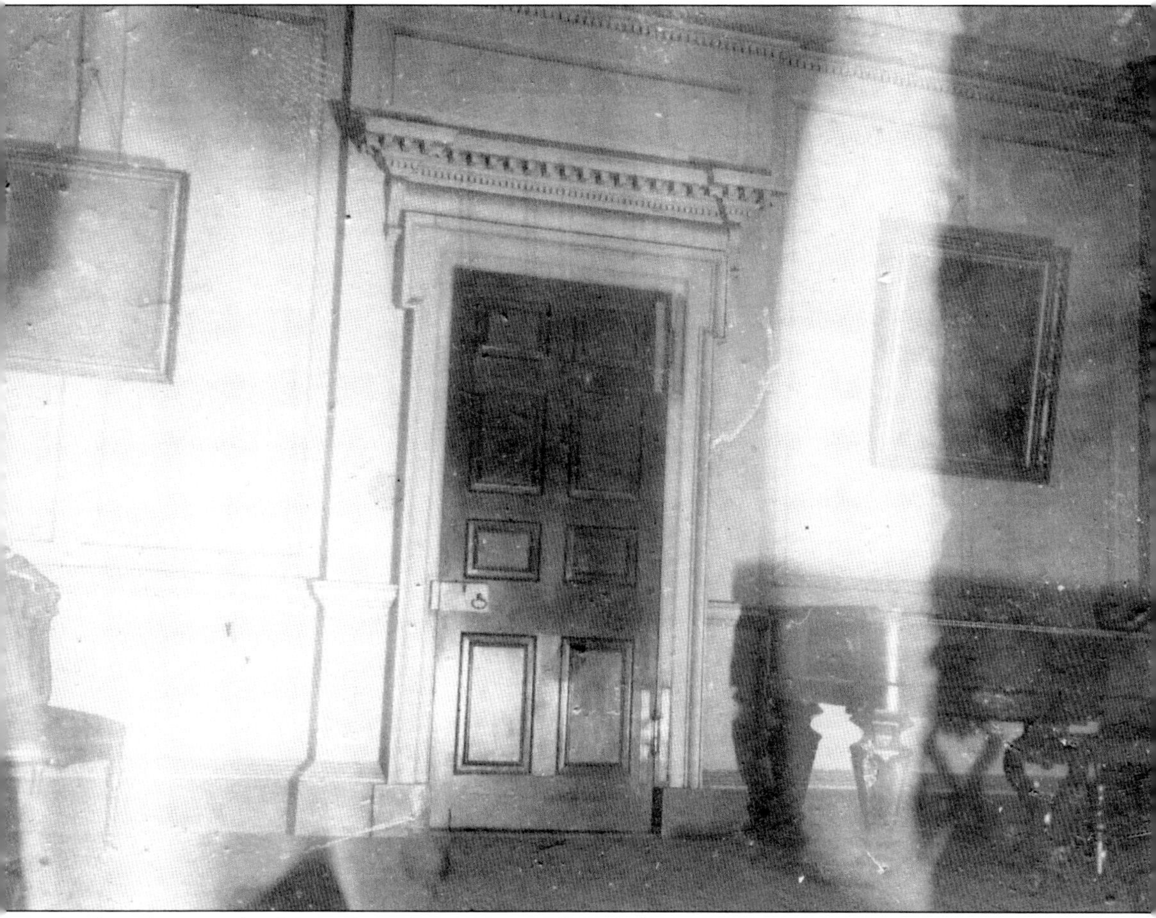

In this photograph of Sotterley's drawing room from before 1910, a Victorian parlor stove heats the room. Sometime in the late 1800s, parlor stoves were installed in hearths throughout the house in order to distribute heat more efficiently. Five beautiful stoves still remain in the upstairs rooms. Mantels were painted black sometime during the Briscoes' ownership. This view of the drawing room entrance shows an Empire Revival–style square grand piano to the right. These heavy instruments were very popular in the 1800s. Residents enjoyed music played by family members or hired musicians for dances, parties, and their evening entertainment. The plantation house was a beloved home for its owners, lived in and cared for by different families and their servants for over three centuries.

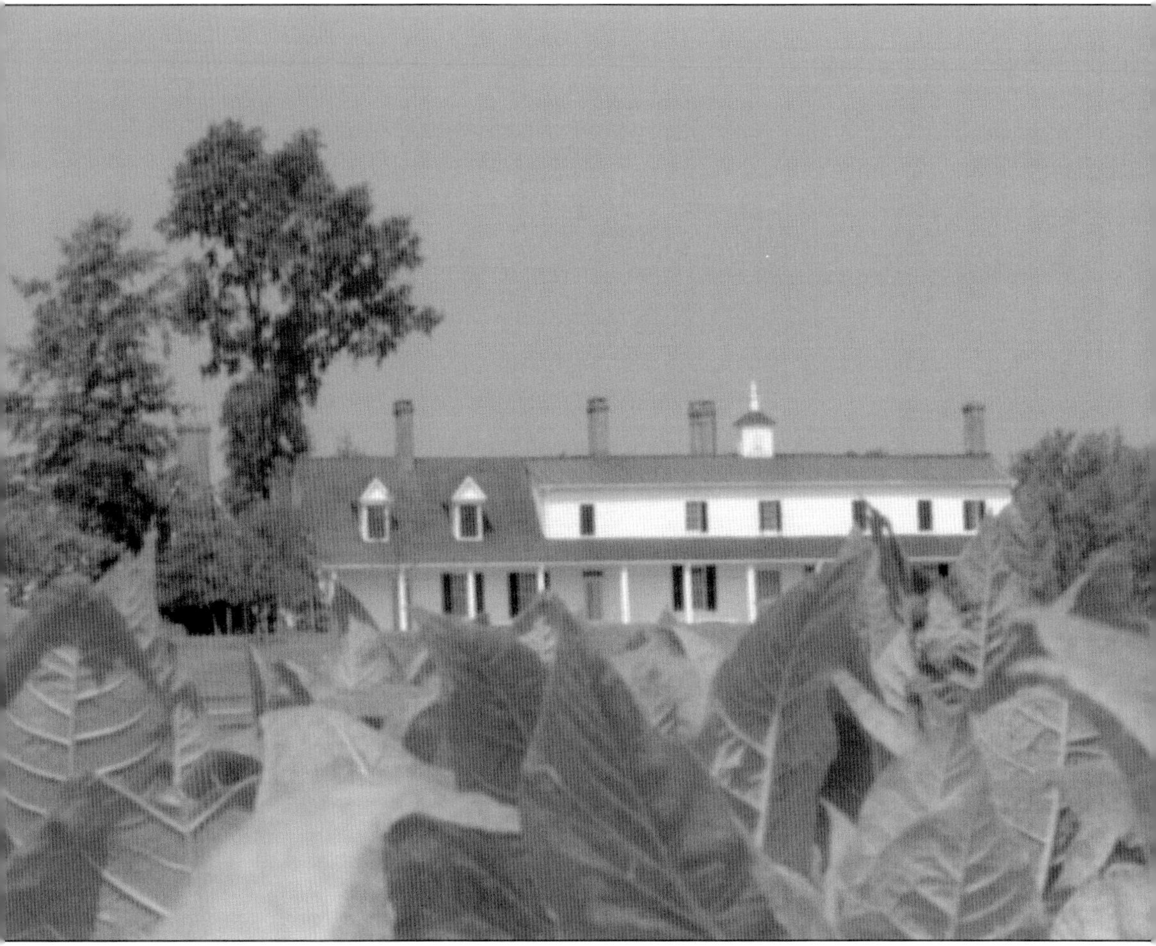

With the election of Abraham Lincoln, lines were divided between North and South. Border states like Maryland, along with Delaware, Kentucky, and Missouri, remained in the Union. Southern Maryland planters, including Dr. Walter Hanson Stone Briscoe, were Confederate sympathizers and tried desperately to hang on to their way of life. With the outbreak of war, three of Walter and Emeline Briscoe's sons, Chapman, Henry, and David, went to Richmond and joined the Army of Virginia. All three enlisted in the 1st Maryland Infantry. In southern Maryland, life became dangerous for African Americans, both free and enslaved. The jail in Leonardtown was full of runaways fleeing north, and even free blacks could be rounded up and sold into slavery. After President Lincoln signed the Emancipation Proclamation in Washington, DC, on January 1, 1863, there was what was described as a "stampede" of slaves leaving St. Mary's County. When the United States finally allowed African Americans to serve in the Union, recruitment of enslaved men up and down the Patuxent River began with the promise of compensation to slave owners. Sotterley's plantation house is seen with Maryland tobacco.

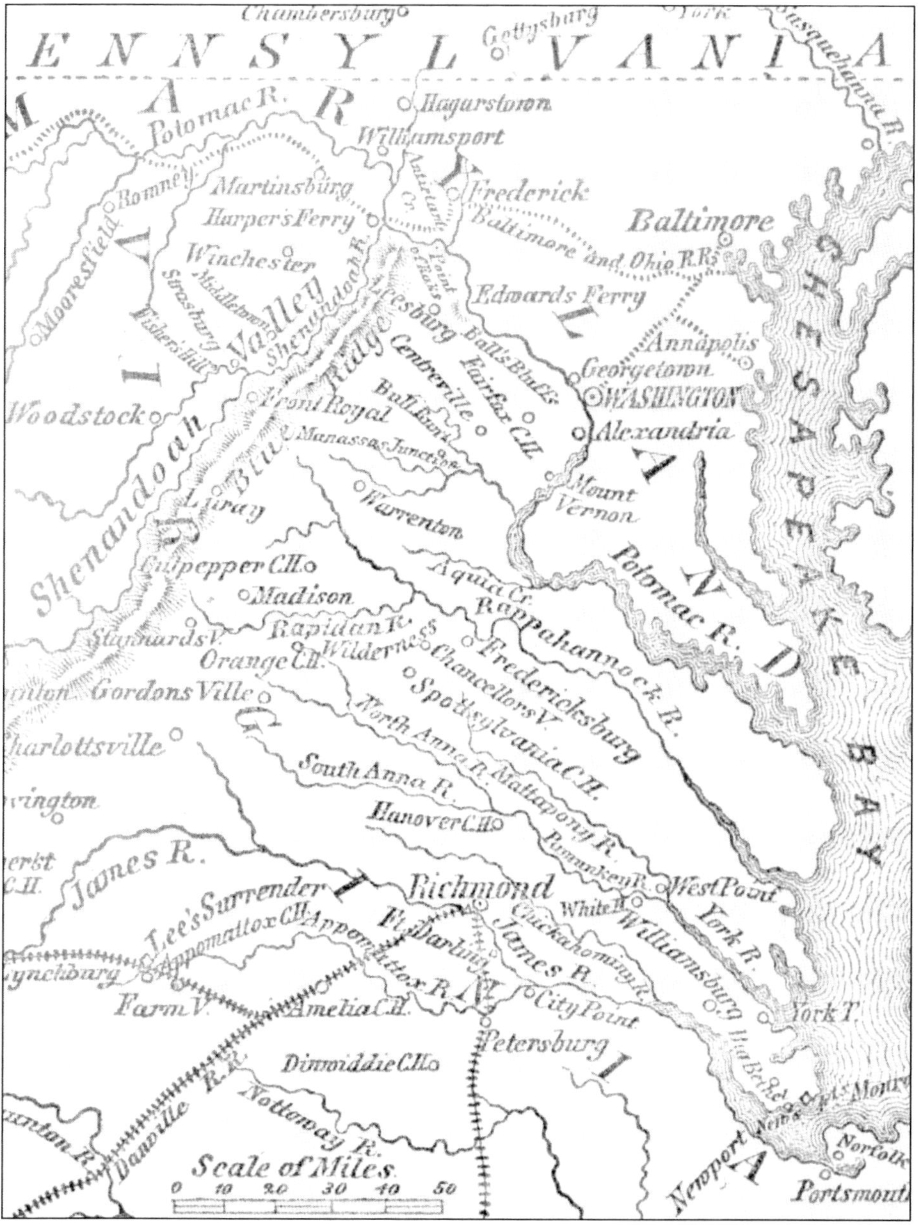

St. Mary's County, a peninsula bordered by the Chesapeake Bay and the Patuxent and Potomac Rivers, was a hotbed of hostility after Abraham Lincoln was elected. After the Battle of Gettysburg, Pennsylvania, the government stationed Union troops in St. Mary's County and established a prison camp for captured Confederate soldiers. Thousands of Confederate soldiers died at Point Lookout Prison before the war's end. The remnants of the fort and memorials of this prison camp can be visited today at Point Lookout State Park. Union troops occupied St. Mary's County, and some plantation owners resisted with force. Others, like Dr. Briscoe, kept a low profile but helped with Confederate wounded and with rounding up runaway slaves. One of the Briscoes' younger sons, James, was questioned and roughed up by Union soldiers after being accused of trying to supply the enemy. This map shows the bloody battlegrounds of Virginia. Sotterley is near the "N" in Maryland. The Briscoes, and everyone at Sotterley, had much at stake. (Courtesy of FCIT.)

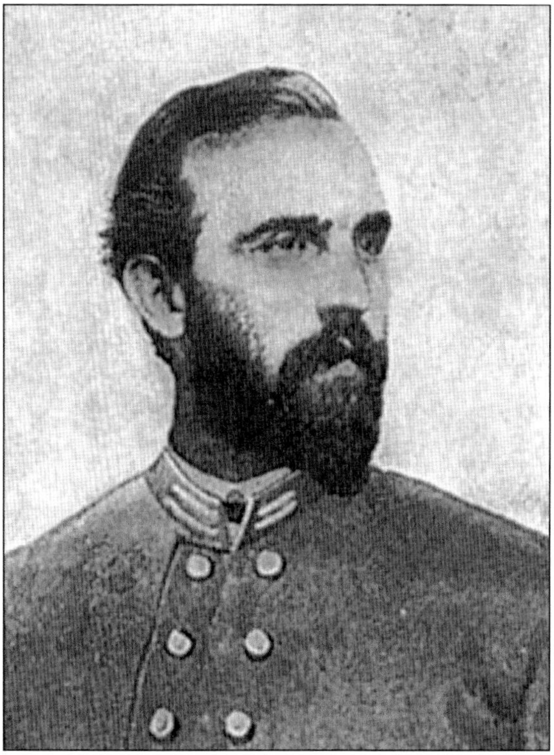

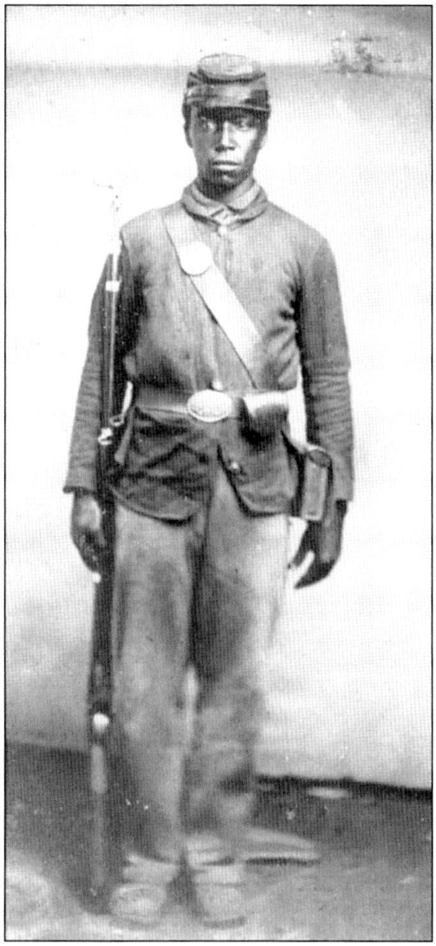

Chapman Briscoe served as a sergeant in the 1st Maryland Infantry, while his brothers David and Henry began as privates. When the unit was dissolved, Chapman got a job as a clerk in Richmond. Henry and David Briscoe joined other units. Lt. David S. Briscoe (above) served in the 43rd Battalion, Virginia Cavalry. One of Dr. Briscoe's slaves was enlisted into Company I, 7th Regiment, United States Colored Troops (USCT), on October 29, 1863. The name on his enlistment card was George W. Briscoe. He was 26 years old and was still considered Dr. Briscoe's property until Maryland emancipated their slaves in 1864. Many soldiers like George were enlisted with their owner's name. Documents after the war, however, reveal that George's real name was George W. Barnes. He is listed as a farmer. He was mustered in at Camp Stanton, near Benedict, Maryland. Camp Stanton was ridden with disease, and many did not live through the first winter. George traveled with his unit up and down the eastern seaboard, participating in battle, performing manual labor, and setting up camps. The 7th suffered heavy casualties. No known photograph of George W. Barnes is known to exist. This photograph shows an unidentified USCT soldier. (Courtesy of the National Archives.)

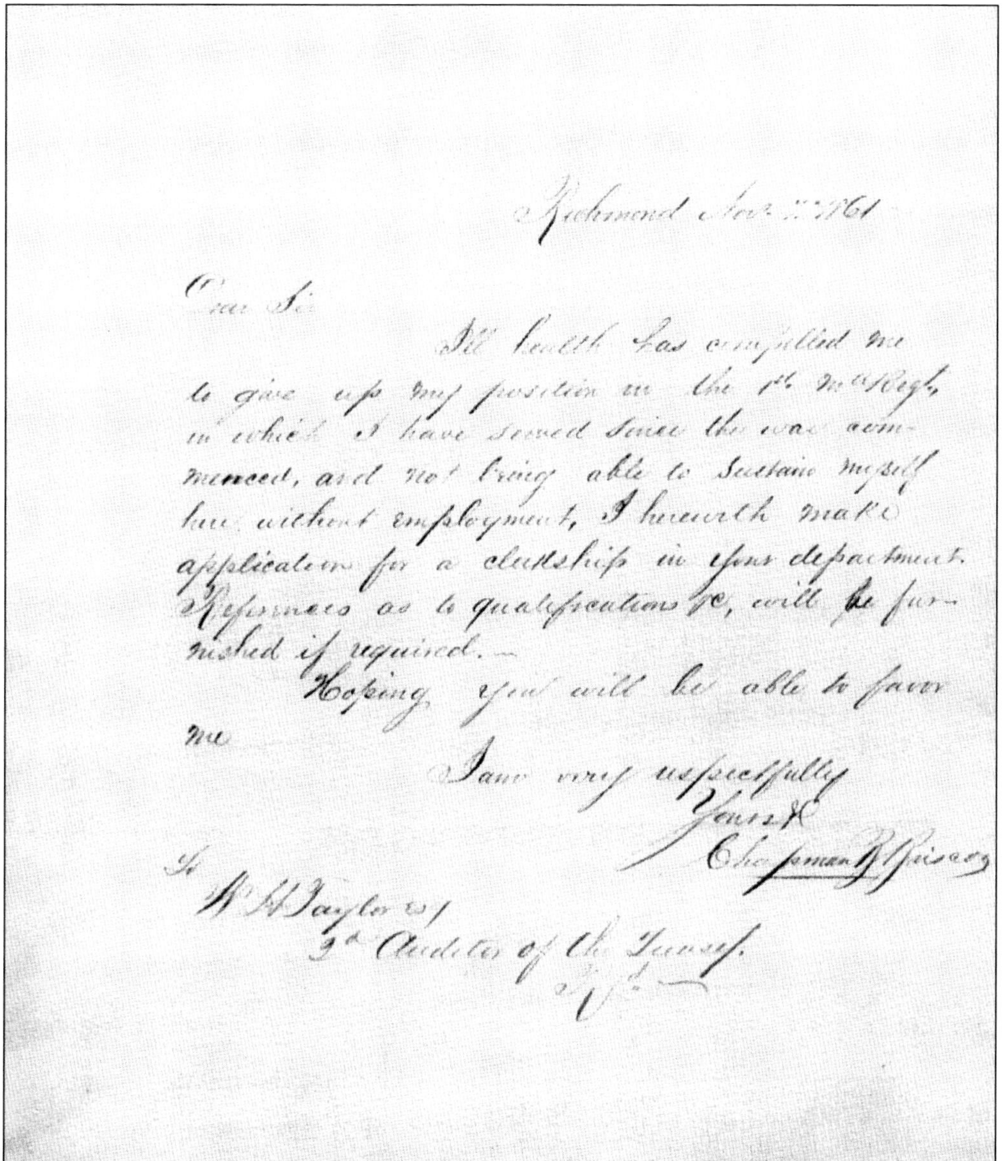

Richmond Nov. [illegible] 1861

Dear Sir

Ill health has compelled me to give up my position in the 1st Md Regt, in which I have served since the war commenced, and not being able to sustain myself here without employment, I herewith make application for a clerkship in your department. References as to qualifications &c, will be furnished if required.—

Hoping you will be able to favor me

I am very respectfully
Yours &c
Chapman B Briscoe

To W. H. Taylor Esq
3d Auditor of the Treasury
C.S.

This letter from Chapman Billingsley Briscoe is a request for a clerkship in Richmond. During his time in the 1st Maryland Infantry, he became seriously ill and resigned his position. In his letters of recommendation, he was given high praise and assurances of his character based on his family's status and good name. He received the position. Chapman married in Richmond and remained there after the war. Rampant disease at home and on the battlefield was a common enemy during the Civil War.

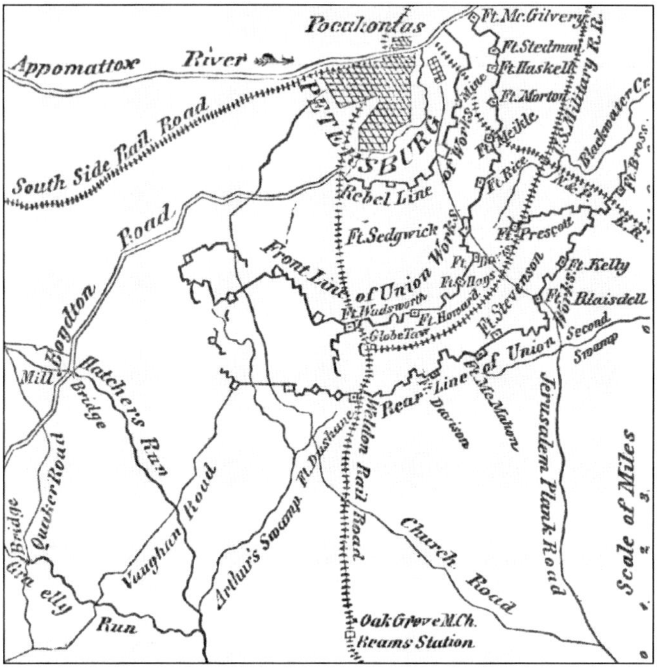

Walter and Emeline Briscoe's son Henry served at Petersburg, Virginia. Lt. Henry Briscoe, an assistant surgeon in Wise's Brigade of the 76th Virginia Regiment, was wounded at Petersburg in the summer of 1864 as shown on the muster card on the right from the National Archives. The siege of Petersburg lasted for nearly nine months, culminating in battle on April 2, 1865, and a Union victory. This left Richmond open to invasion and led to the collapse of the Confederacy. All three Briscoe sons survived the war. The 7th Regiment USCT also served at Petersburg, which included George W. Barnes (Briscoe). (Above, courtesy of FCIT.)

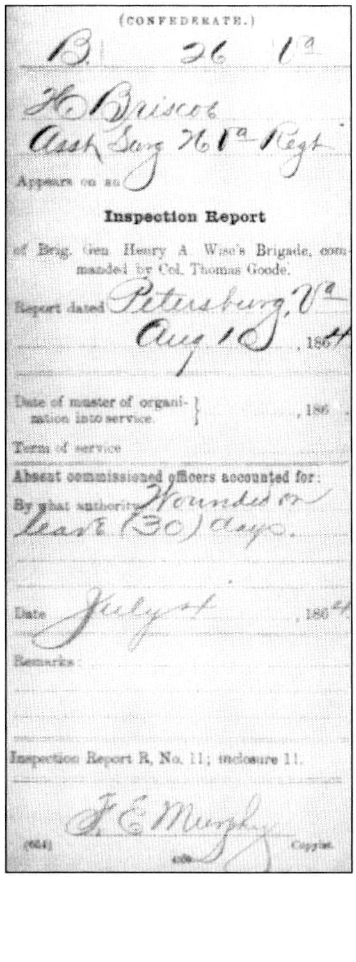
(CONFEDERATE.)

B. 26 Va

H. Briscoe
Asst Surg 76 Va Regt

Appears on an

Inspection Report

of Brig. Gen Henry A. Wise's Brigade, commanded by Col. Thomas Goode.

Report dated Petersburg, Va
Aug 18, 1864

Date of muster of organization into service , 186

Term of service

Absent commissioned officers accounted for:

By what authority Wounded on leave (30) days.

Date July 1st, 1864

Remarks:

Inspection Report R, No. 11; inclosure 11.

F. E. Murphy

(664) Copyist.

After the war was over, George W. Barnes went with his unit by steamship to the Mississippi Delta. From there, the 7th Regiment USCT was assigned to guard duty in Indianola, Texas. A cholera epidemic broke out in the city, and George died there a free man on October 18, 1866. The next day, the 7th returned to Baltimore, where the unit was disbanded. A pension claim from his widow, made in 1867, listed the name George W. Briscoe as an alias, with his actual name, Barnes, written underneath. George's muster card at Camp Stanton (right) was dated November 5, 1863. Rolling Road at Sotterley Plantation (below) leads to the slave cabin and Sotterley Creek. George was one of many brave men who would never see home again.

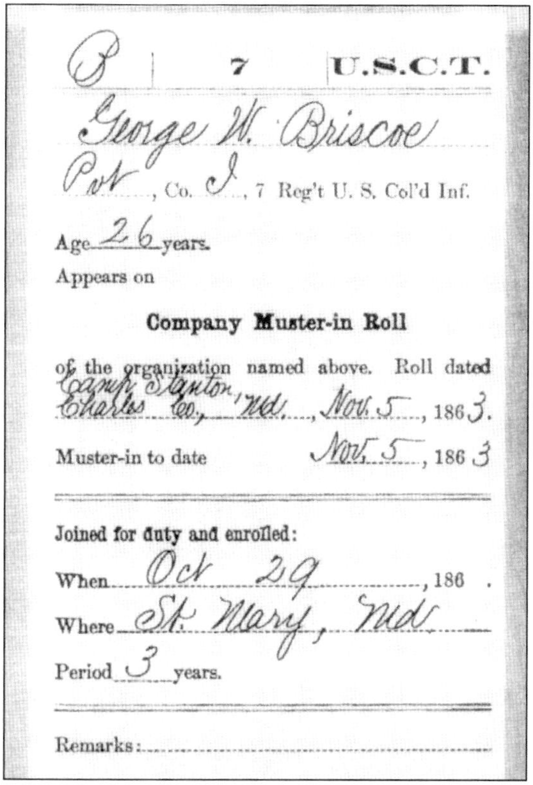
B | 7 | U.S.C.T.

George W. Briscoe
Pvt, Co. I, 7 Reg't U. S. Col'd Inf.

Age 26 years.

Appears on

Company Muster-in Roll

of the organization named above. Roll dated
Camp Stanton, Charles Co., Md., Nov. 5, 1863.

Muster-in to date Nov. 5, 1863

Joined for duty and enrolled:

When Oct 29, 186 .

Where St. Mary, Md.

Period 3 years.

Remarks:

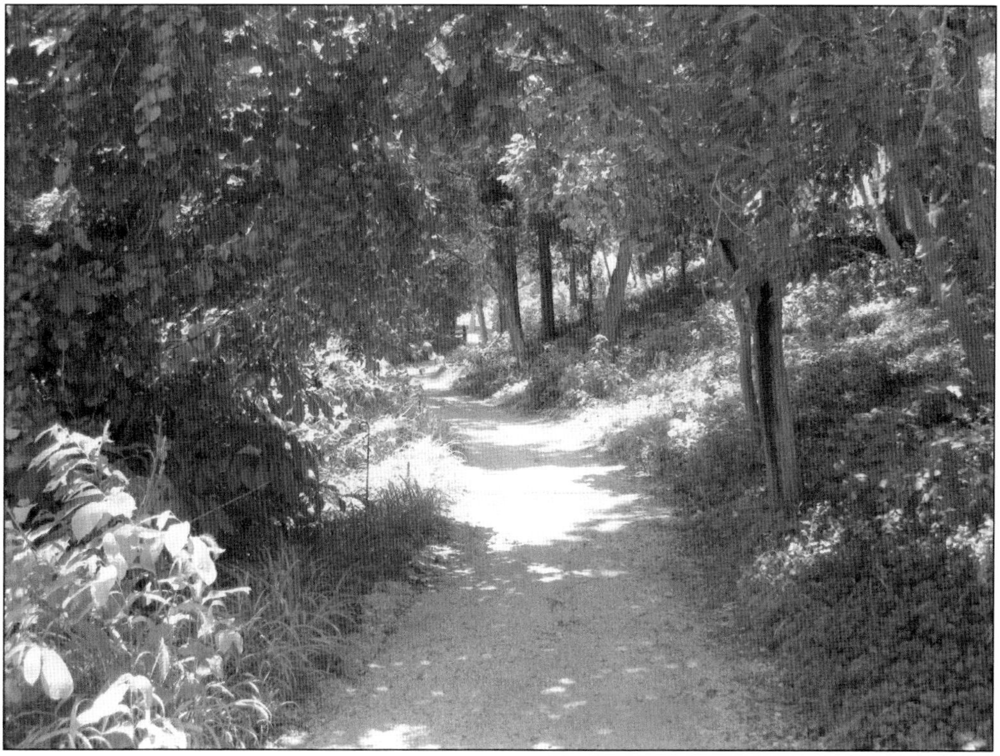

OWNER Dr. Walter H. Briscoe

DATE April 16, 1869

Name Of Slave		Sex	Age	Emancipated by State of Maryland	Remarks
Harris	Edwards	M	15	Nov. 1, 1864	
George	Cane	M	20	" " "	
Frank	Cane	M	17	" " "	
Alfred	Edwards	M	17	" " "	
Thomas	Millard	M	17	" " "	
Horace	Millard	M	12	" " "	
Samuel	Edwards	M	17	" " "	
Charles	Medley	M	2	" " "	
George W.	Biscoe	M	26	" " "	
Dick	Brown	M	33	" " "	
Robert	Plater	M	37	" " "	
James	Millard	M	48	" " "	
Hamilton	Steward	M	49	" " "	
Alex	Medley	M	52	" " "	
Leanda	Edwards	M	52	" " "	
William	Barnes	M	52	" " "	
Temperance	Cane	F	18	" " "	
Matilda	Cane	F	22	" " "	
Alice	Cane	F	16	" " "	
Eliza	Cane	F	14	" " "	
Sarah	Cane	F	12	" " "	
Charlotte Ann	Biscoe	F	14	" " "	
Mary	Edward	F	21	" " "	
Marie	Millard	F	23	" " "	
Mary Jane	Wilson	F	13	" " "	
Henny	Cane	F	20	" " "	
Ann Delia	Barnes	F	21	" " "	
Georgeann	Barnes	F	19	" " "	
Cecelia	Edwards	F	19	" " "	
Susan	Guyther	F	22	" " "	
Ellen	Cane	F	24	" " "	
Rebecca	Brown	F	24	" " "	(324,325)
Martha Ann	Wilson	F	28	" " "	
Nellie	Plowden	F	29	" " "	
Alice	Cane	F	31	" " "	
Henrietta	Hall	F	27		L-Feb. 28, 1863
Presella	Edwards	F	38	" " "	
Eliza	Mason	F	38	" " "	
Mary Ann	Millard	F	47	" " "	
Louise	Mason	F	52	" " "	
Henrietta	Barnes	F	58	" " "	
Cecelia	Plowden?	F	52	" " "	

Maryland finally emancipated its slaves by state constitutional amendment on November 1, 1864. The Civil War ended, but, even years later, slave owners who had lost their property and their labor force had not given up hope of being compensated by the federal government for their losses. Much like today, getting compensation from the government required paperwork. To receive such compensation, slave owners in Maryland recorded all slaves they still owned on November 1, 1864. This record, known as the Slave Statistics, contains these lists submitted in 1869. When Agnes Kane Callum was conducting research into her family's history, she used her family's oral traditions, census reports, and the Slave Statistics from 1869 at the Maryland State Archives in Annapolis. As she researched, she made an index of all slave owners in St. Mary's County and the people they listed as having owned in 1864. Among the list were her ancestors at Sotterley Plantation. Her ancestor Hilry Cane was owned by Chapman Billingsley but lived with the rest of his family at Sotterley, owned by Dr. Walter Hanson Stone Briscoe.

OWNER Dr. Walter H. Briscoe

DATE April 16, 1869

Name		Sex	Age	Emancipated by State of Maryland	Remarks
Andrew	Brown	M	6	Nov. 1, 1864	
Edgar	Guyther	M	28	" " "	
Frank	Guyther	M	2	" " "	
Hilry	Cane	M	1	" " "	
Alex	Plowden	M	2	" " "	(325)
Francis	Millard	M	6	" " "	
Margaret	Brown	F	3	" " "	
Rebecca	Wilson	F	1	" " "	
Catherine	Barber	F	21	" " "	
Mary A.	Barber	F	2	" " "	No. of Slaves #53
Jeff	Johnson	M	1	" " "	
				Col. Chapman Billingsley-Owner April 16, 1869	
Harris	Rustin	M	15	Nov. 1, 1864	
Frank	Medley	M	11	" " "	
McKelvey	Rustin	M	16		E-Oct. 1, 1863
Harrison	Rustin	M	20	" " "	
Baley	Rustin	M	30		E-Dec. 15, 1863
Mortimer	Rustin	M	28		E-Mar. 10, 1864
Charlotte	Ann Rustin	F	20	Nov. 1, 1864	
Mary	Medley	F	36	" " "	
Mollie	Medley	F	15	" " "	
Grace	Medley	F	14	" " "	
Alex	Medley	M	12	" " "	
Edgar	Medley	M	10	" " "	
George	Medley	M	8	" " "	
Lewis	Medley	M	6	" " "	
Matilda	Medley	F	4	" " "	
Infant	Medley	F	4mO	" " "	
Jeff	Johnson	M	20	" " "	
Alfred	Lyles	M	24	" " "	
Lee	Edwards	M	36	\	E-Dec. 15, 1863
Hilry	Cane	M	46	" " "	
Thomas	Plowden	M	57	" " "	
Infant	Upton	F	6m	" " "	
Martha	Steward	F	18	" " "	
Eva	Steward	F	16	" " "	
Mimie	Steward	F	14	" " "	
Jane	Plowden	F	50	" " "	(326)
Charity	Lyles	F	52	" " "	
Eliza	Plater	F	54	" " "	
Rose Anna	Rustin	F	54	" " "	
Nace	Hawkins	F	68	" " "	
Henry	Bush	M	17	" " "	E-Nov. 1, 1864
Chap	Turner	M	10		E-Nov. 1, 1864
Infant	Turner	M	18mo	" " "	No of Slaves #33

After Agnes Kane Callum conducted her research, she donated the index and other information to the Maryland State Archives for future generations. A copy of the pages listing the slaves of Dr. Briscoe and Chapman Billingsley are seen here. The index lists the name, age, sex, date emancipated, and other details about each slave. Slave owners in Maryland did not receive compensation for emancipated slaves. In 1864, some of those emancipated left Sotterley and never returned. Some families, like the Canes, stayed on at Sotterley as tenants and earned wages for similar work to what they done as slaves. By the time of the 1880 census, Cane and his family had moved from Sotterley to their own home in Hillville, several miles north. Agnes Kane Callum has been a constant supporter of Sotterley's educational mission. She served on Sotterley's board of trustees and is now a trustee emerita.

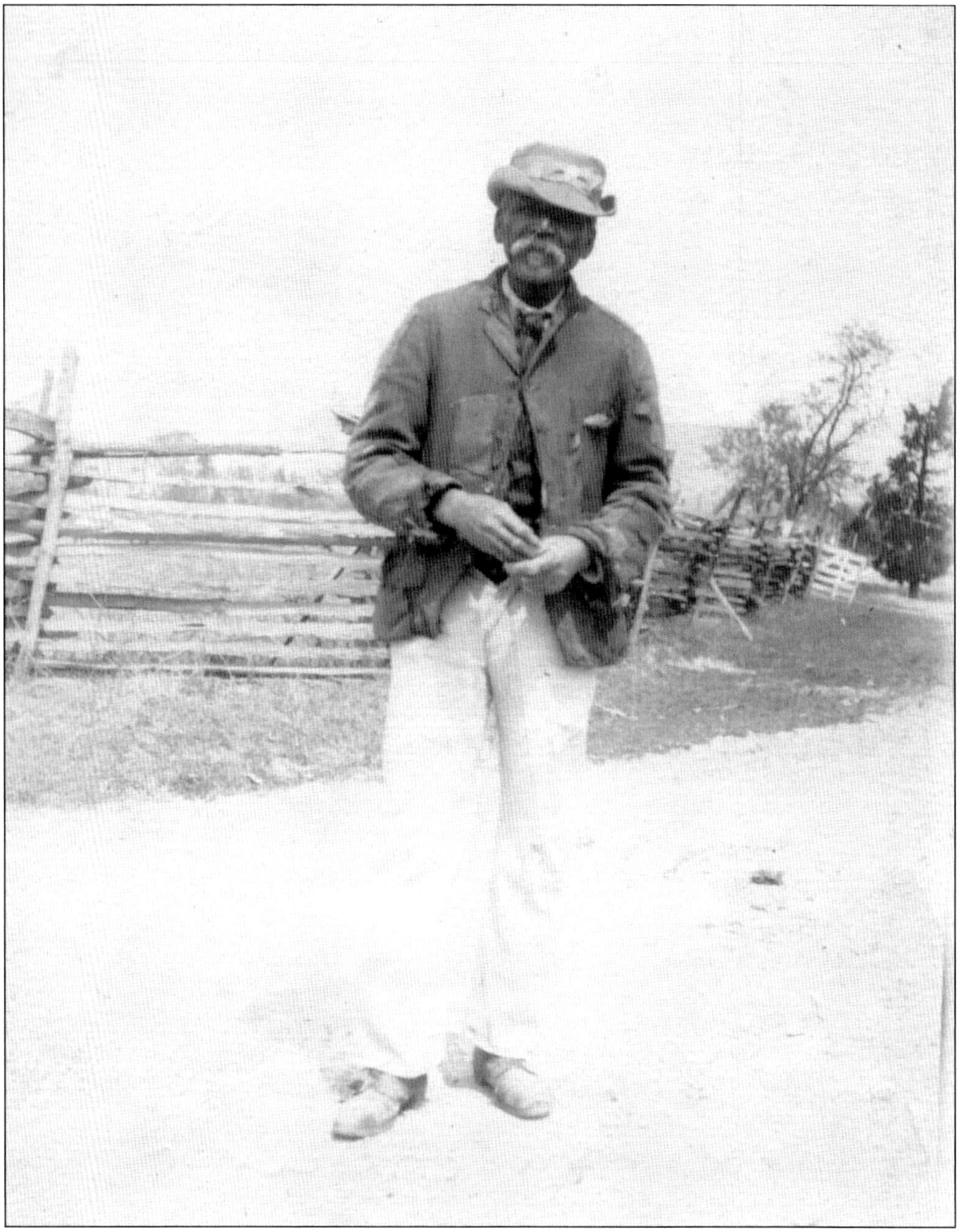

Alfred Edwards (above) was a slave at Sotterley Plantation and was emancipated in 1864 at the age of 17. His father, Lee Edwards, was owned by Chapman Billingsley, and his mother, Priscilla, was owned by Dr. Briscoe. In 1910, Alfred was living in old Billingsley slave quarters with his wife, Alice, and seven of their children and grandchildren. He died in the early 1930s. After Dr. Briscoe's death in 1885, the farm was managed by his son Walter Hanson Stone Briscoe Jr. Emeline died in 1887. Walter Jr. then moved from Sotterley, and Rev. James Briscoe purchased his parents' farm at auction. When he died, he left Sotterley to his daughter Elizabeth and his son James Jr. Elizabeth and her husband, J.D. Cashner, bought out her brother's half of the estate and owned Sotterley by 1904.

Walter Barber and his wife, Harriet, lived at Sotterley as workers for the Cashners. They had seven children born at Sotterley, and they lived near Steer Horn Neck Road. Life was difficult for many in St. Mary's County, as discrimination and segregation were the norm and few economic opportunities or schools were available for African Africans. Migration of African Americans after the Civil War brought the ancestors of Sotterley's labor force of the 20th century.

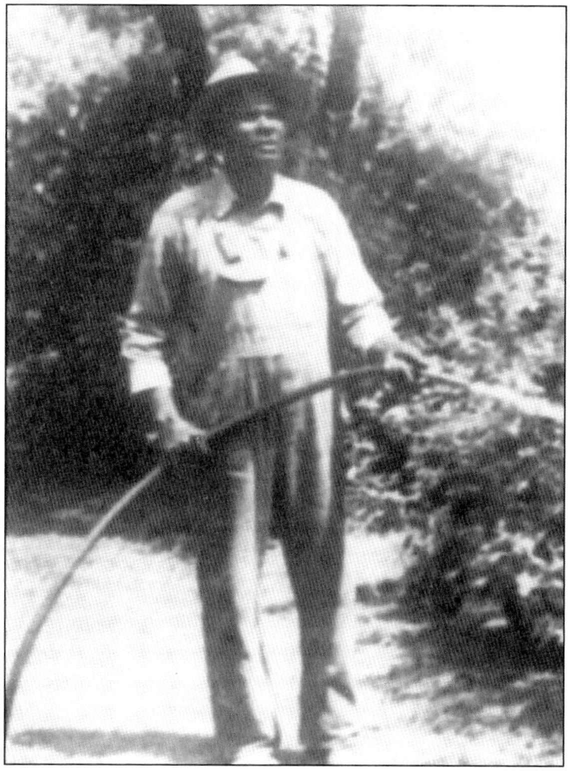

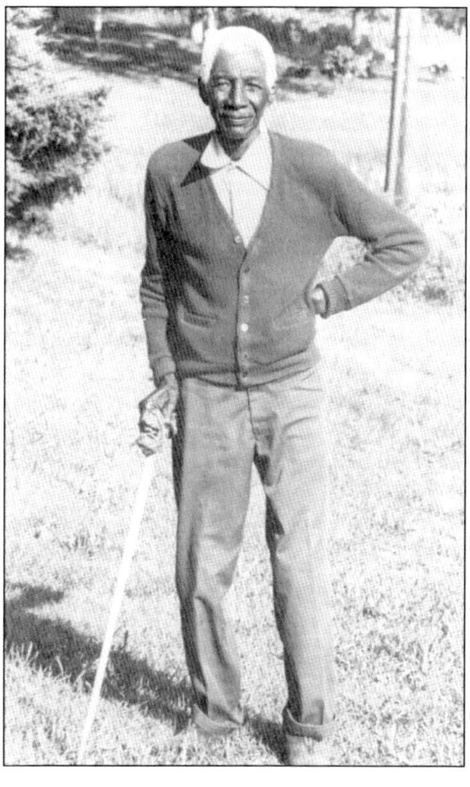

James Scriber and his wife, Nettie, lived at Sotterley in former slave quarters off Old Sotterley Wharf Road. The Scribers had 16 children born at Sotterley and they sharecropped on the Cashner farm. Scriber's grandfather had migrated to Maryland from Georgia after the Civil War.

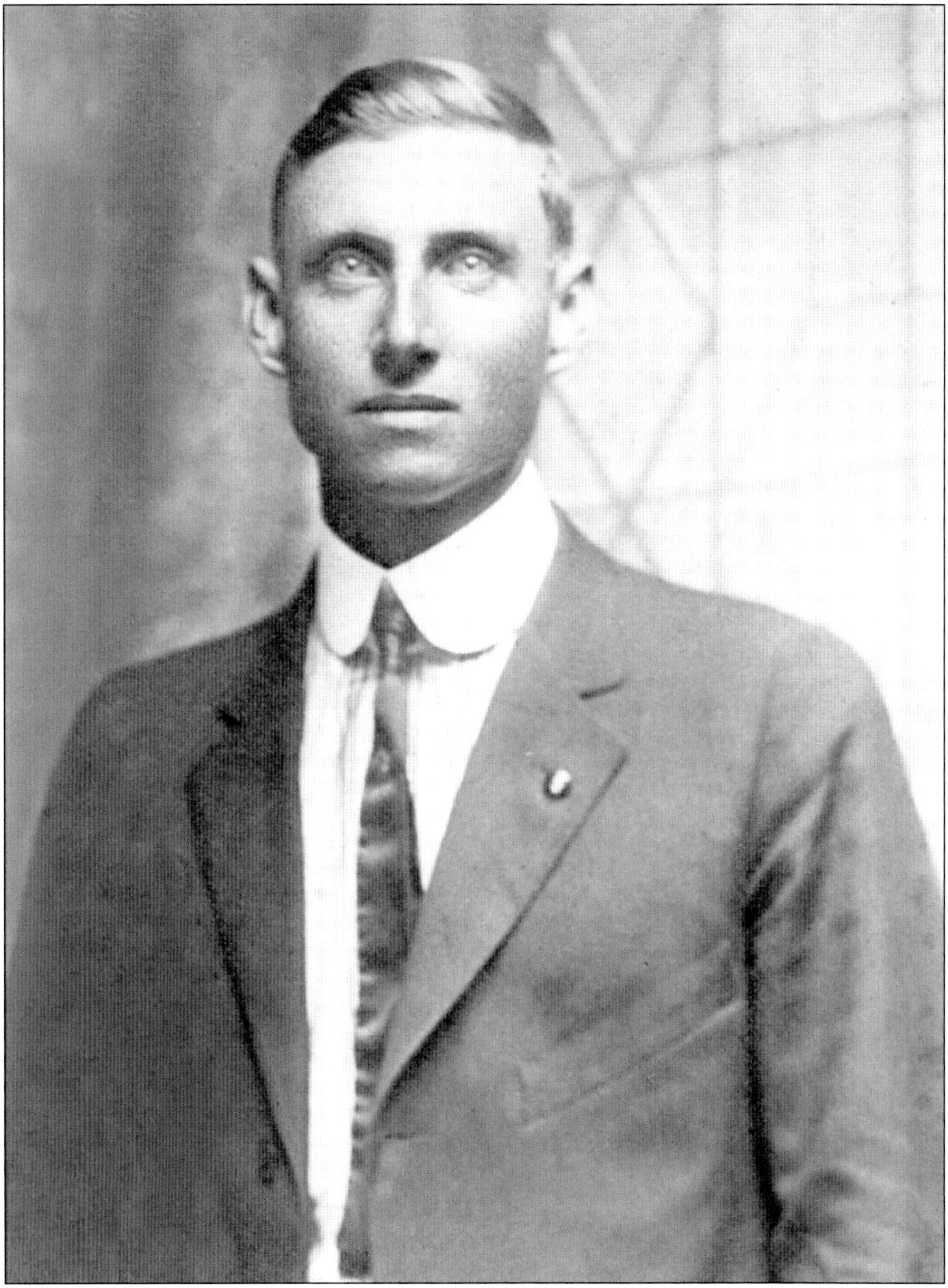

Charles Knott was born in 1884 in St. Mary's County. Economic times were hard and jobs were scarce in the early years of the 1900s. In 1910, J.D. Cashner was looking to fill a farm manager's position for the new owner of Sotterley, Herbert Satterlee. Knott was hired and spent the next 50 years in the position. Generations of the Barber, Scriber, and Knott families formed an efficient, tight-knit farming community, working and serving Sotterley's owners for nearly 80 years.

Three

Vision and Revival 1910–1947

Beginning with the US centennial in 1876, a wave of renewed patriotism spread through the country. At the same time, industrialization and new innovations with little or no government regulation or taxes were creating a class of some of the wealthiest citizens in American history. The Gilded Age brought large waves of eastern European and Catholic Irish immigrants to America, and as the era came to an end, major social change threatened, with the continued struggles for women's suffrage and racial equality. Out of this developed what is now called the Colonial Revival period. Men with unimaginable disposable wealth, like Rockefeller, Vanderbilt, and Dupont, began purchasing and restoring 18th-century estates or creating large European-style manor houses, often building whole communities around them.

When Herbert Satterlee heard that Sotterley Plantation was finally for sale, he made plans to visit the property. He had heard about Sotterley from his cousin Henry Yates Satterlee, the bishop of the Episcopal Diocese of Washington, DC. St. Andrews Church, in St. Mary's County, was part of the diocese, and the owners of Sotterley in the 1700s and 1800s had served on the vestry of the historical church. The bishop realized that the Satterlee family might have a connection to Sotterley and informed his wealthy cousin.

Tracing one's ancestry to Revolutionary War figures and European nobility became a favorite pastime for the upper class during the Colonial Revival period. Herbert Satterlee believed he was descended from the Sotterleys of the 13th century, who had built the ancient Sotterley estate in Suffolk, England, the namesake of Sotterley Plantation. He also believed he was related to the Playters, the ancestors of the Platers, who had owned and named Sotterley Plantation. This belief, combined with his patriotic zeal, his interest in 18th-century restoration, and the financial means to pursue his interests, motivated Herbert Satterlee to buy Sotterley Plantation in 1910.

Satterlee had a vision to restore the plantation to its 18th-century glory, although this nostalgia sometimes romanticized and overlooked some of the realities of that period in history. Satterlee also restored farming operations and expanded Sotterley to 1,000 acres in order to support crops, livestock, orchards, gardens, and a community of people to work and care for the revived Sotterley Plantation.

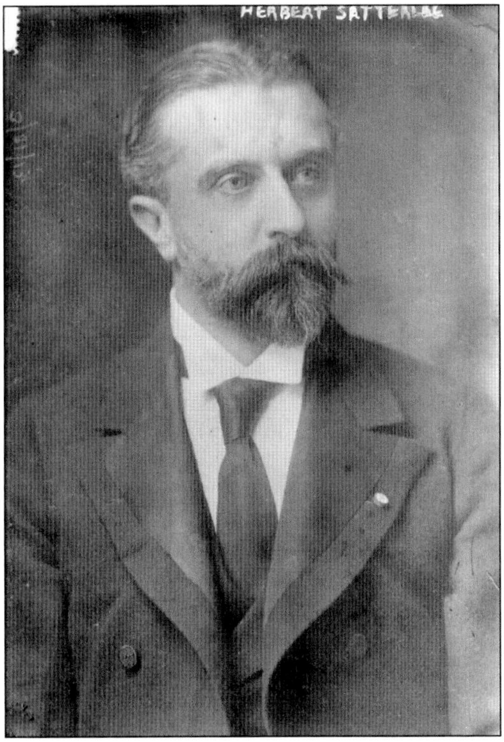

Herbert Livingston Satterlee was born to Sarah Wilcox and George Bowen Satterlee in New York City in 1863. On the 10th anniversary of his father's death, Herbert wrote a melancholy letter to his wife, missing and remembering his father. His parents instilled in him a love of family and the conservative ideals of the day. Herbert received his law degree from Columbia University in 1885 and practiced commercial and corporate law. He founded the law firm Satterlee & Canfield in 1894. His clients included prominent and influential business leaders. He also represented Mark Twain and suggested the name General Motors for the automobile company he helped incorporate. The law firm Herbert Satterlee founded still exists in New York into the 21st century, as Satterlee, Stevens, Burke & Burke, LLC.

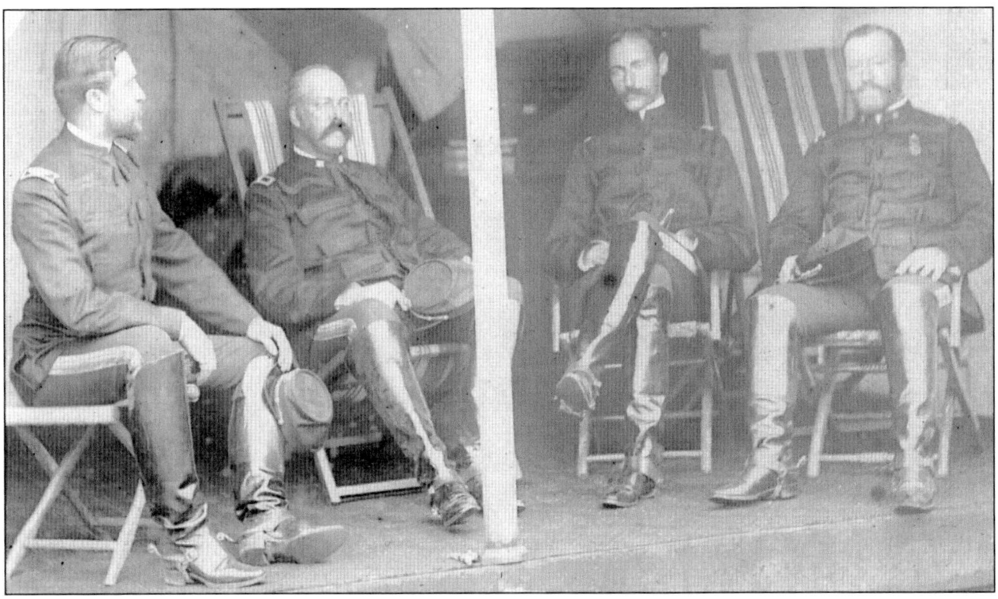

Herbert Satterlee served in the Spanish-American War with the New York State Naval Militia. This 1885 photograph shows, from left to right, Col. Herbert L. Satterlee, Gen. Edward Hayes, Col. John Jacob Astor IV, and Gen. M.O. Terry. Colonel Satterlee was 32 years old in 1885. General Hayes was a decorated soldier who served in several American conflicts, including the Civil War. General Terry served as the surgeon general of New York. John Jacob Astor IV, the heir to the famous Astor fortune, is probably best known as a wealthy passenger who perished on the *Titanic* in 1912.

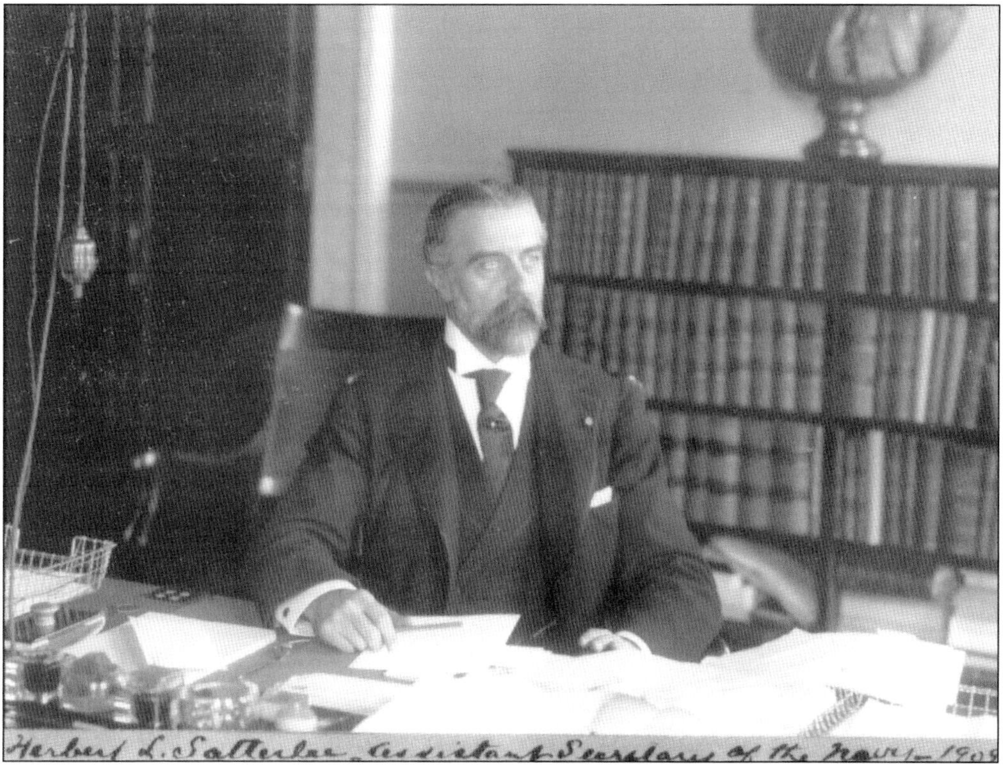

Herbert Satterlee served as the assistant secretary of the Navy for the last months of Pres. Theodore Roosevelt's administration, from December 1908 to March 1909. Satterlee also helped to establish the Navy Reserves and served on the board of visitors for the Naval Academy in Annapolis. His passion for the Navy was evidenced by his collection of nautically themed art and objects.

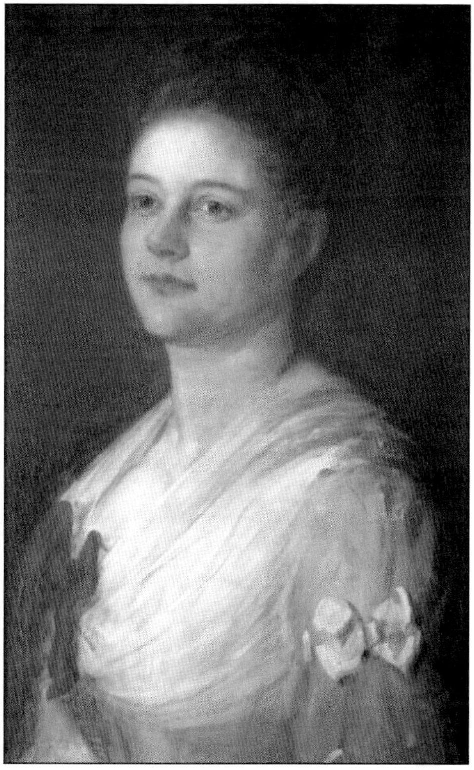

Louisa Pierpont Morgan, born in New York in 1866, was the oldest daughter of John Pierpont Morgan and Francis Louisa Tracy. Louisa was trained and educated as a woman of high society to marry and have a family, entertain, travel, and support philanthropic causes. Louisa was one of four children, with brother, John "Jack" Jr., and two sisters, Juliet and Ann. Louisa Morgan married Herbert L. Satterlee in 1900. The most important event of the New York social season that year, the wedding gifts alone were worth millions of dollars. By 1901, the Satterlee's first daughter, Mabel, was born, followed by another daughter, Eleanor, in 1905. This portrait of Louisa at 18 years of age is part of Sotterley's collection.

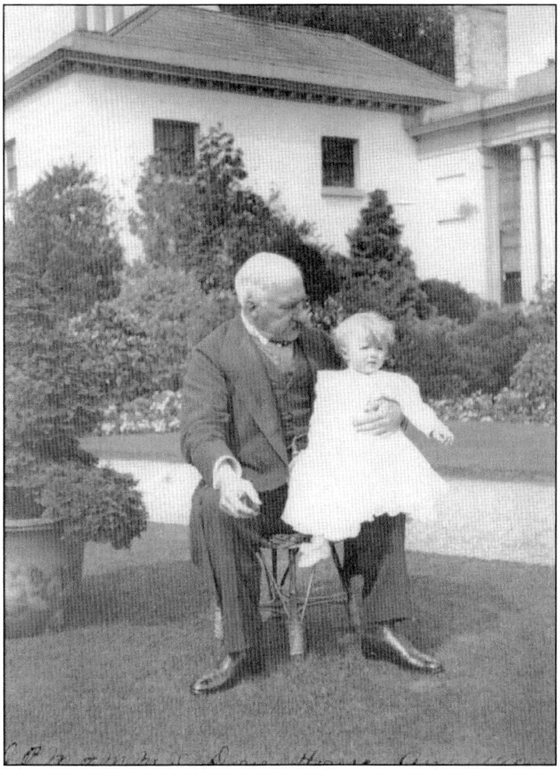

Mabel Satterlee is seen here sitting on the lap of her grandfather John Pierpont Morgan in 1902 at Dover House, the Morgan estate in London. J.P. Morgan was a famous financier and banker who bought and merged companies to create General Electric and US Steel. He also owned several shipping companies, including the White Star Line. In an age before the breakup of business monopolies, stock market regulation, or income taxes, J.P. Morgan was one of the wealthiest men in American history.

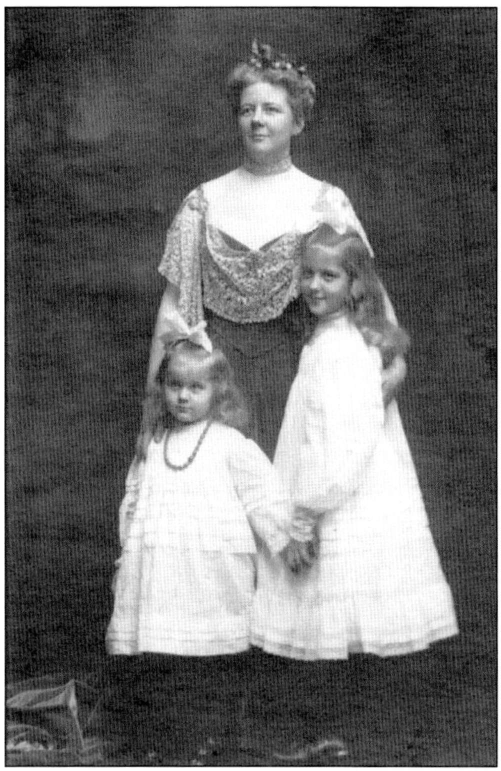

Louisa Pierpont Morgan Satterlee is seen here with her two daughters, Eleanor and Mabel. Elite New York families like the Satterlees would vacation several months a year, traveling to vacation resorts or other homes in Europe and America. Sometimes, the family would travel separately. Wealth did not make the Satterlees immune to tragedy, however. Eleanor suffered with a dangerously high fever as a young child, and her parents feared for her life.

Henry Yates Satterlee, the first bishop of the Episcopal Diocese of Washington, DC, helped to plan and establish the National Cathedral. He first made his cousin Herbert Satterlee aware of Sotterley Plantation and their possible family connection with it. Bishop Satterlee died in 1908.

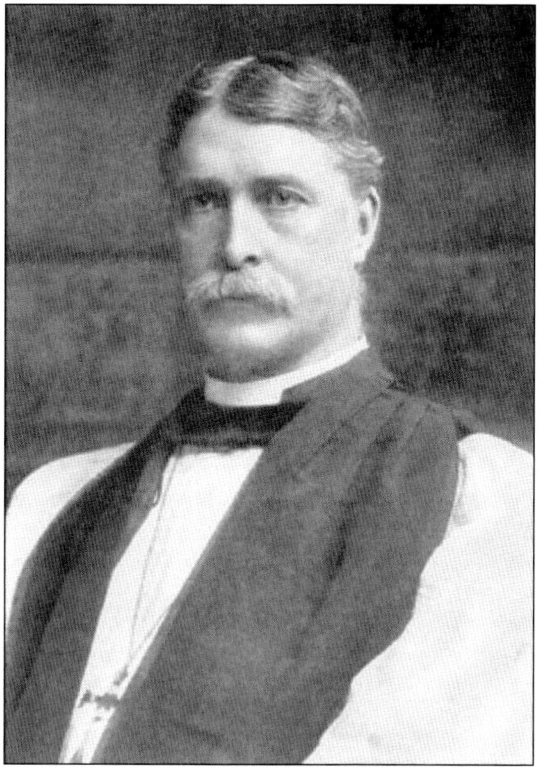

St. Andrews Episcopal Church has always been intertwined with Sotterley's people and history. George Plater III was one of its founding members and supporters, serving on the vestry. Dr. Walter Hanson Stone Briscoe served on the vestry in the 1800s and is buried in the family plot in front of the church. The interiors of St. Andrews were designed by Richard Boulton, who also did much of Sotterley's finer woodwork, including the alcoves and staircase. It was while visiting St. Andrews that Bishop Satterlee first heard about Sotterley Plantation.

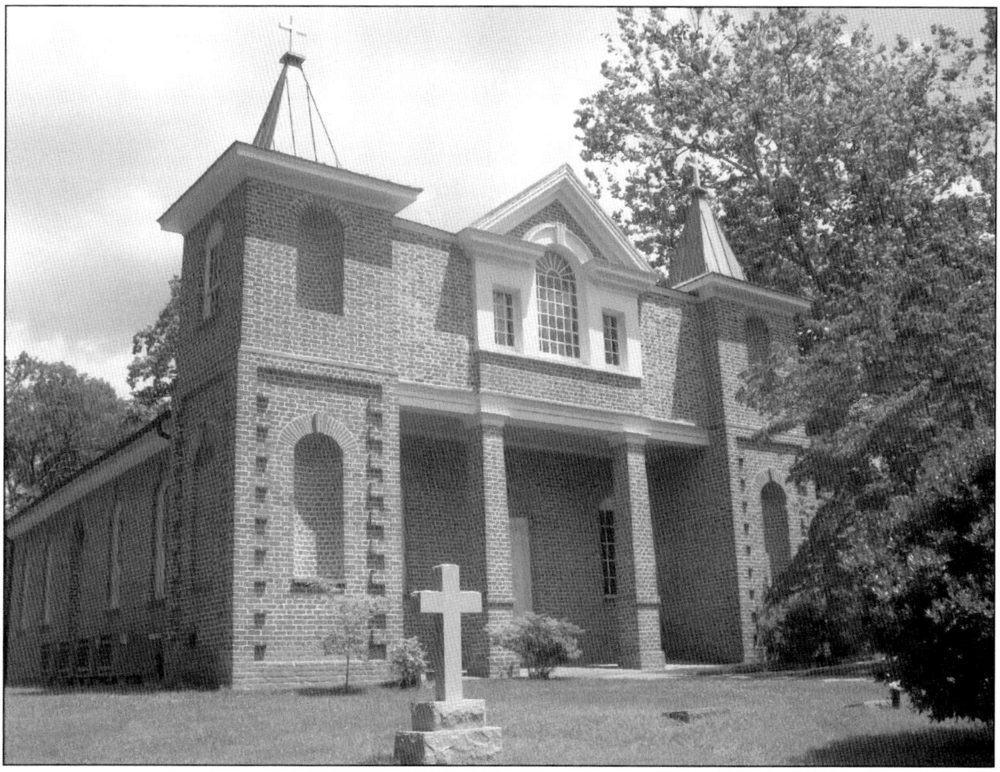

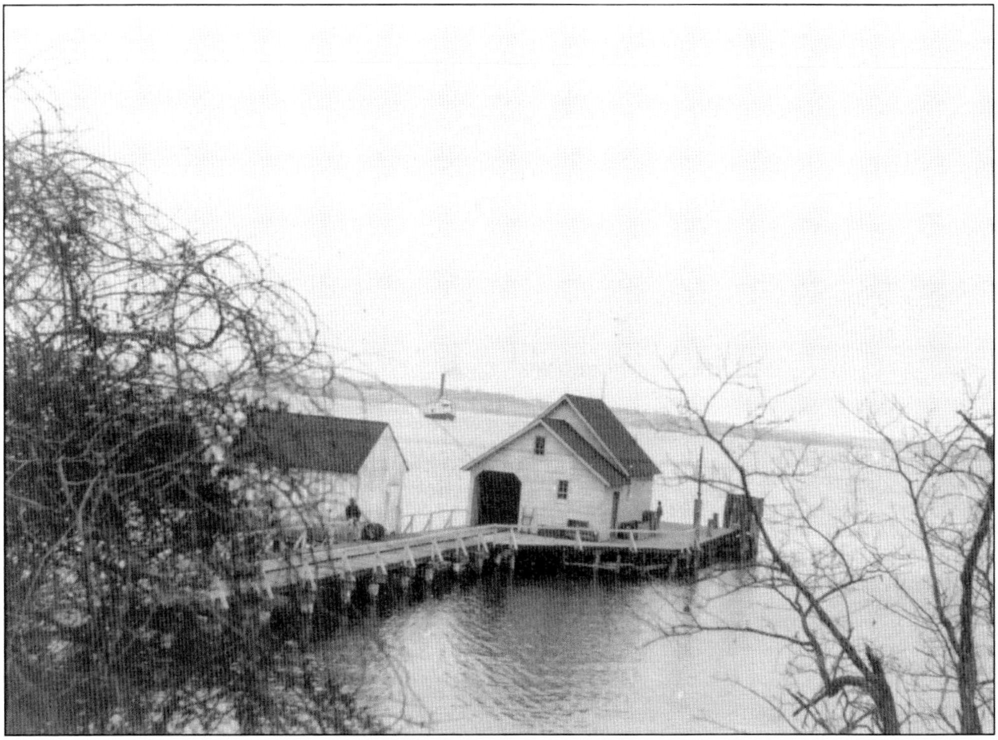

Once Herbert Satterlee received the news that the Cashners were ready to sell Sotterley, he planned a trip to purchase the property. He had visited previously in 1906, but by 1910, the Cashners had fallen on hard times and needed to sell. The Satterlees often arrived by steamboat at Sotterley Wharf. The wharf is seen here in the 1930s with a ship in the distance coming in to port.

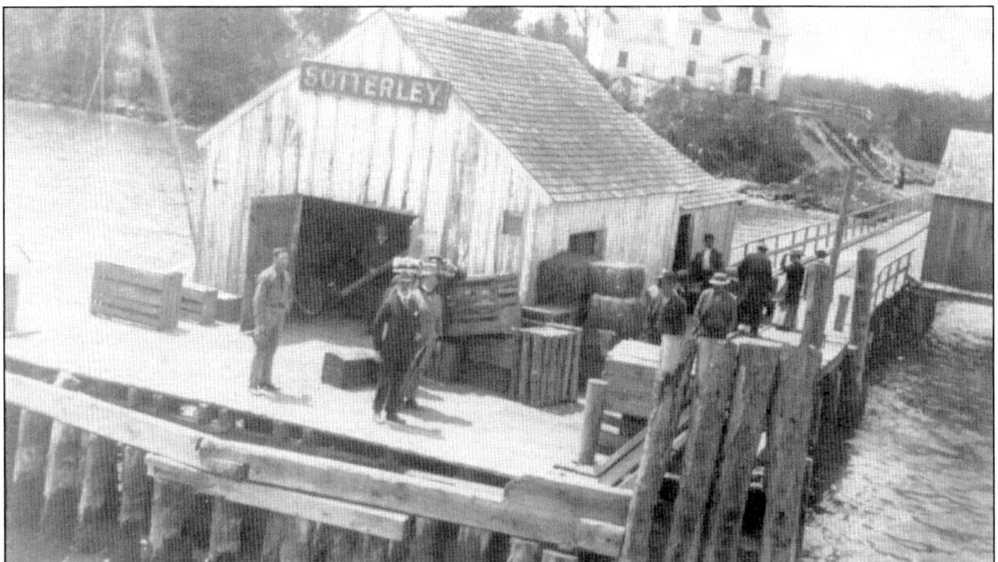

This view shows Sotterley Wharf from an incoming ship in the 1930s, with the wharf house in the background. The wharf was a busy travel center, and cargo is seen here waiting to be loaded and unloaded as people wait for arrivals and departures.

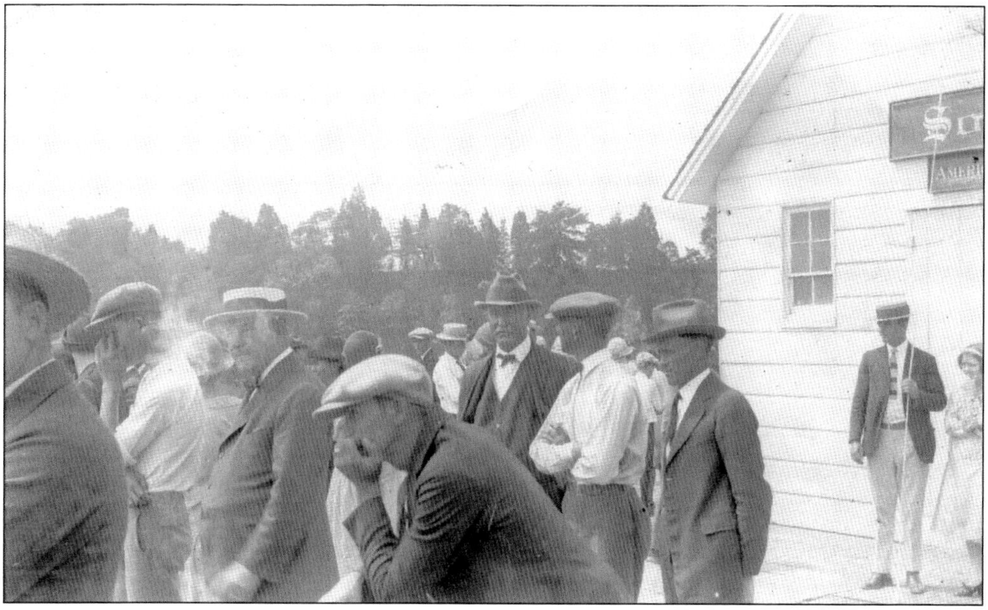

This c. 1920 photograph shows Sotterley Wharf crowded with people waiting to board. One could travel by steamship from Sotterley and go on to Baltimore or New York City. Thus, Sotterley was a busy community gathering place.

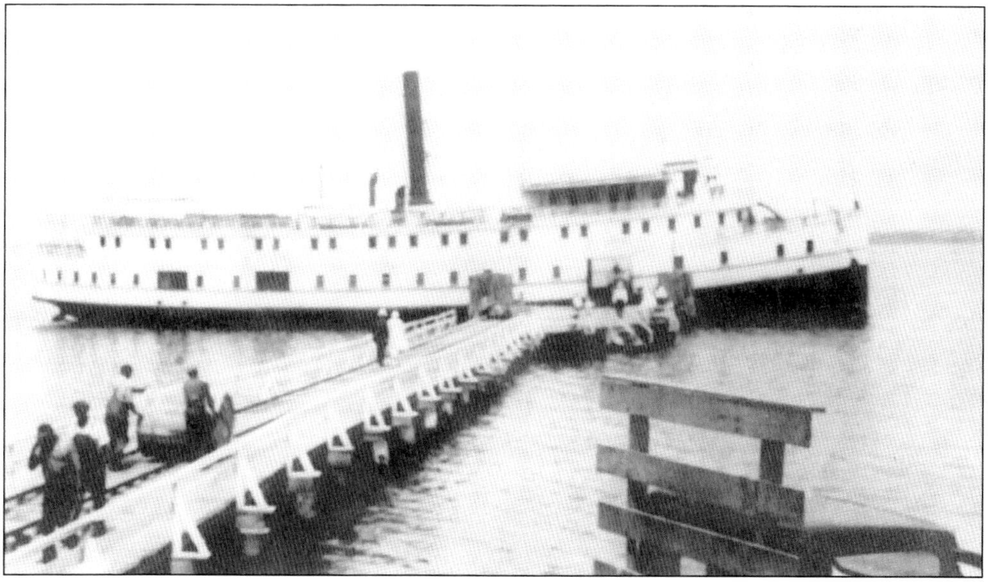

The steamship *Anne Arundel* arrives at Sotterley in 1933. Railcars helped move heavy cargo down the pier to the ship. A category 2 hurricane hit the eastern seaboard in August of that year, damaging many docks and piers along the Chesapeake Bay and its tributaries.

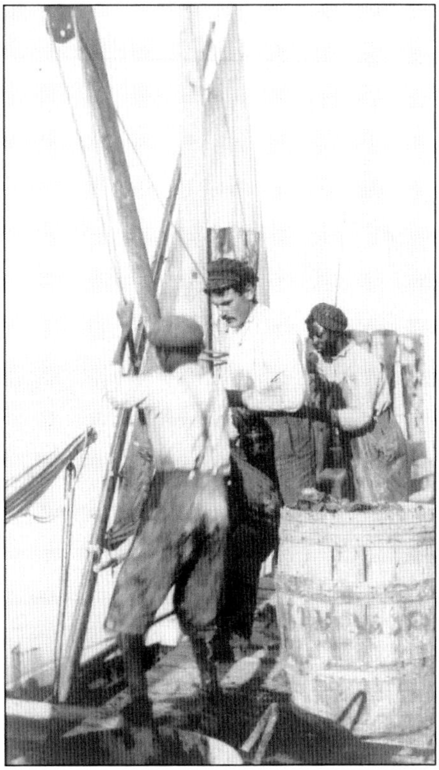

Young dockworkers use deck cranes and booms to lift the heavy crates, barrels, and bags of cargo on and off a ship. This technology had not changed since the tall ships once dropped anchor on Sotterley's shores in the 1700s, still moving barrels, or "hogsheads," of tobacco to market.

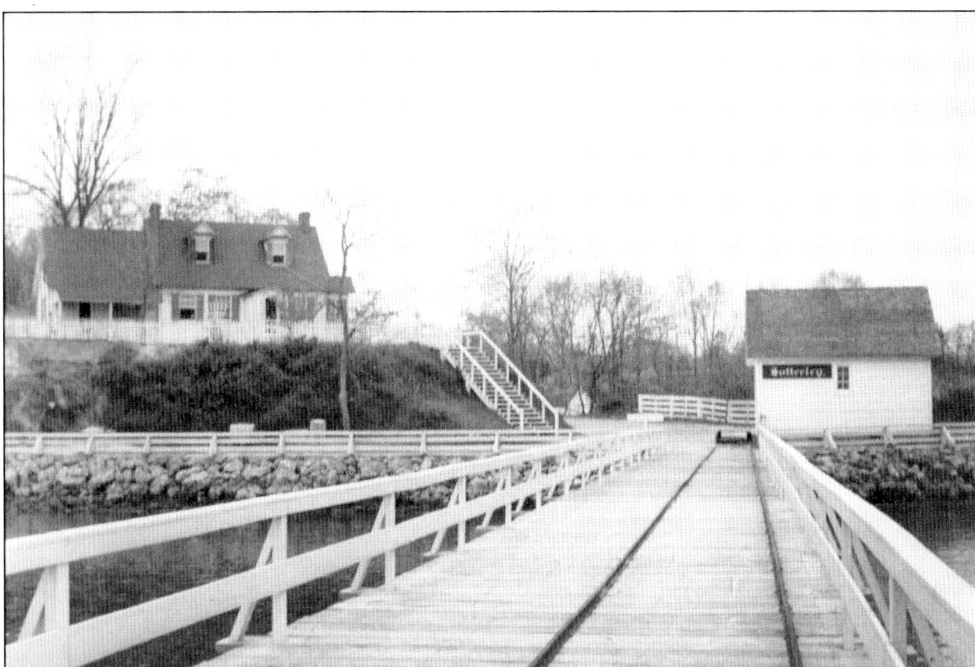

The long wharf rail track that moved cargo from the farms to be loaded on the steamships to the markets in Baltimore is seen here in the 1920s. The pilings from this pier are still visible today. The wharf house (left), built by Jim Mattingly in 1912, is where the dockmaster and his family lived.

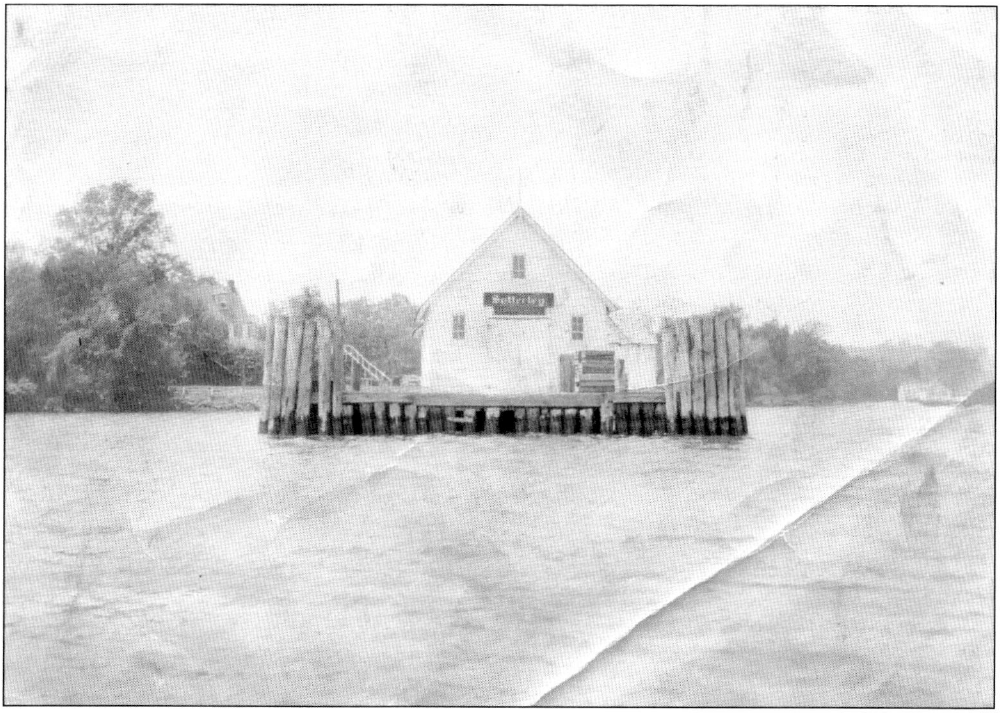

This photograph of Sotterley Wharf in the 1920s also shows Captain Gatton's Oyster House at Sotterley Creek in the right background. Capt. Arthur Gatton, born in 1866, was a waterman and is attributed with building many wharves on the Patuxent River, including Sotterley Wharf. He died in 1953.

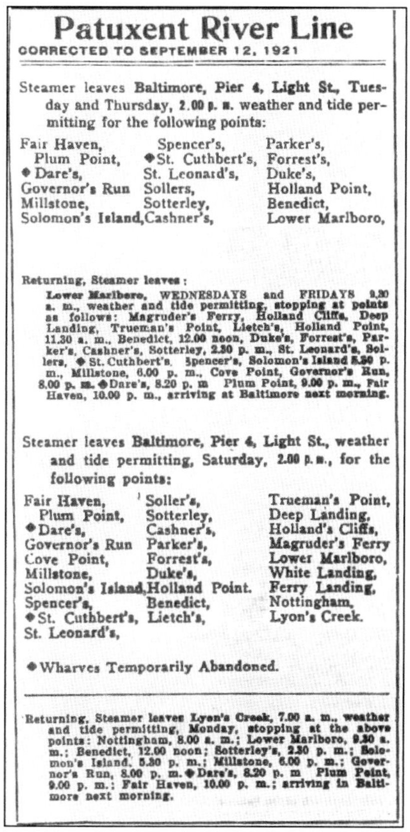

Patuxent River Line

CORRECTED TO SEPTEMBER 12, 1921

Steamer leaves **Baltimore, Pier 4, Light St.,** Tuesday and Thursday, 2.00 p. m. weather and tide permitting for the following points:

Fair Haven,	Spencer's,	Parker's,
Plum Point,	◆St. Cuthbert's,	Forrest's,
◆Dare's,	St. Leonard's,	Duke's,
Governor's Run	Sollers,	Holland Point,
Millstone,	Sotterley,	Benedict,
Solomon's Island,	Cashner's,	Lower Marlboro,

Returning, Steamer leaves:

Lower Marlboro, WEDNESDAYS and FRIDAYS 9.30 a. m., weather and tide permitting, stopping at points as follows: Magruder's Ferry, Holland Cliffs, Deep Landing, Trueman's Point, Lietch's, Holland Point, 11.30 a. m., Benedict, 12.00 noon, Duke's, Forrest's, Parker's, Cashner's, Sotterley, 2.30 p. m., St. Leonard's, Sollers, ◆St. Cuthbert's, Spencer's, Solomon's Island 5.30 p. m., Millstone, 6.00 p. m., Cove Point, Governor's Run, 8.00 p. m. ◆Dare's, 8.20 p. m Plum Point, 9.00 p. m., Fair Haven, 10.00 p. m., arriving at Baltimore next morning.

Steamer leaves **Baltimore, Pier 4, Light St.,** weather and tide permitting, Saturday, 2.00 p. m., for the following points:

Fair Haven,	Soller's,	Trueman's Point,
Plum Point,	Sotterley,	Deep Landing,
◆Dare's,	Cashner's,	Holland's Cliffs,
Governor's Run	Parker's,	Magruder's Ferry
Cove Point,	Forrest's,	Lower Marlboro,
Millstone,	Duke's,	White Landing,
Solomon's Island,	Holland Point.	Ferry Landing,
Spencer's,	Benedict,	Nottingham,
◆St. Cuthbert's,	Lietch's,	Lyon's Creek.
St. Leonard's,		

◆Wharves Temporarily Abandoned.

Returning, Steamer leaves Lyon's Creek, 7.00 a. m., weather and tide permitting, Monday, stopping at the above points: Nottingham, 8.00 a. m.; Lower Marlboro, 9.30 a. m.; Benedict, 12.00 noon; Sotterley's, 2.30 p. m.; Solomon's Island, 5.30 p. m.; Millstone, 6.00 p. m.; Governor's Run, 8.00 p. m. ◆Dare's, 8.20 p. m Plum Point, 9.00 p. m.; Fair Haven, 10.00 p. m.; arriving in Baltimore next morning.

This Patuxent River Line steamboat schedule from 1921 lists the stops on the Patuxent River to Baltimore and back. Travel plans were dependent on weather and wharf conditions. Sotterley Wharf was also serviced by the Rappahannock Line and the Weems Line.

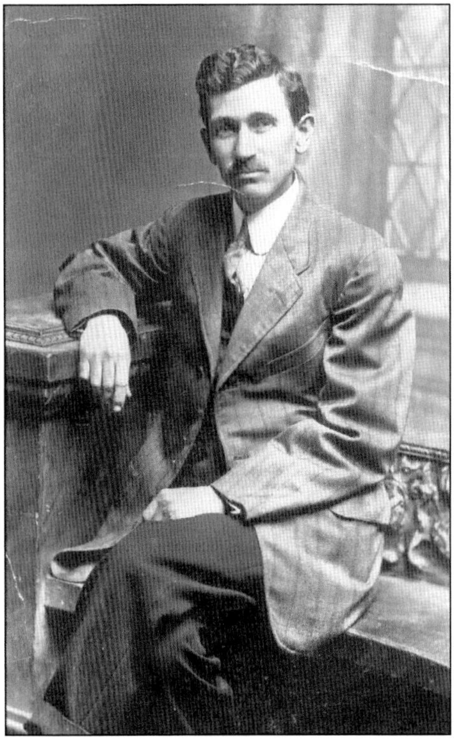

Julius Clifton Callis was born in 1882. He was the dockmaster for Sotterley Wharf. He and his wife, Laura M. Dean, raised their children at Sotterley. Several of his brothers and sons also worked on and off at Sotterley Wharf. After his death in 1938, Julius's younger brother Noah moved into the wharf house with his family as caretakers.

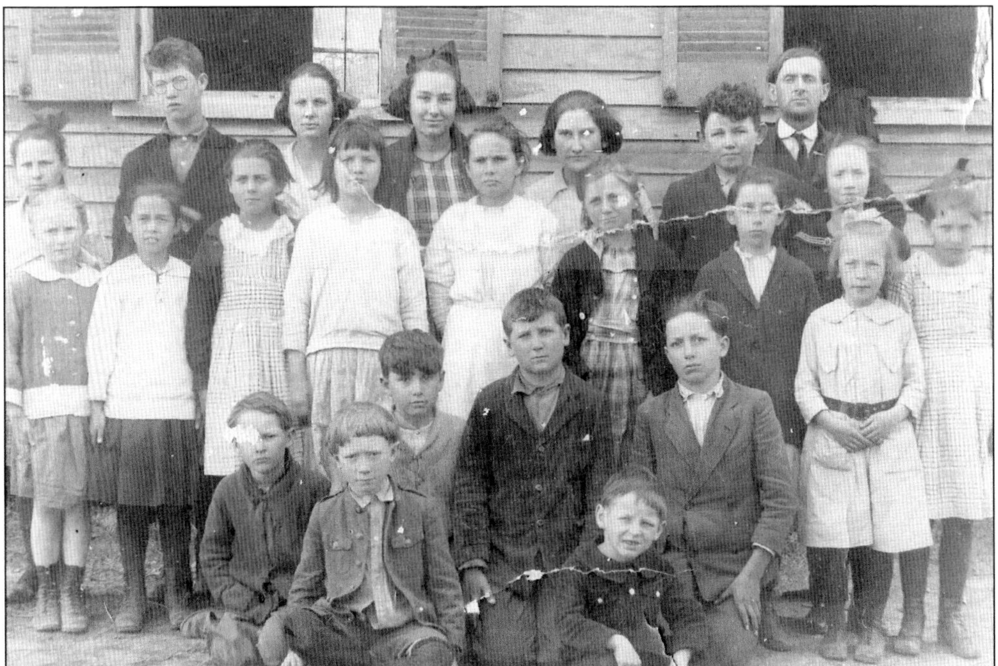

The Cashners donated a parcel of land to the public school system to create a school for white children at Sotterley. It was called the Sotterley School, and this class picture was taken there about 1918. Laura Virginia Callis stands second from the left in the second row. She was the daughter of Julius Clifton Callis and Laura Callis. The school closed by 1922.

Betty Eckart, the granddaughter of Julius Clifton Callis and the daughter of Laura Virginia Callis-Eckart, was born in Sotterley's wharf house. She is seen here as an infant at Sotterley. She is one of hundreds of children born to owners, workers, servants, and slaves through the centuries at Sotterley Plantation. Steamboat travel ended at Sotterley after hurricane damage to the wharf in 1933. Within a few years, steamboat travel had ended completely on the Patuxent River, as widespread storm damage and competition from other modes of transportation forced steamboat companies out of business.

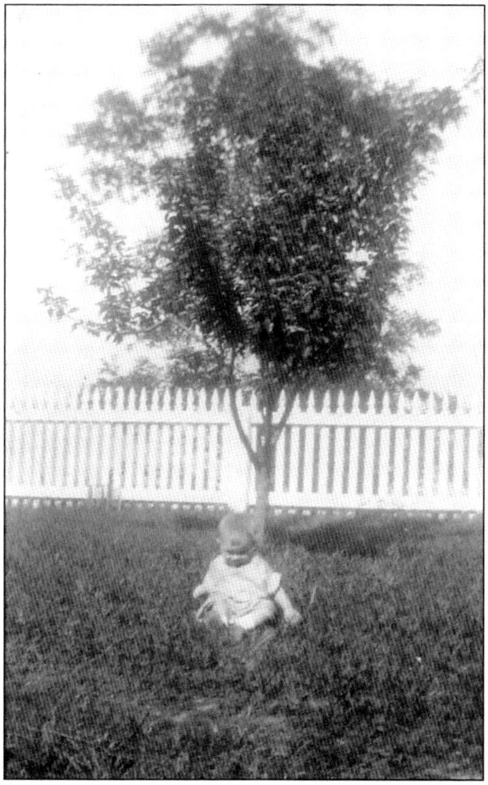

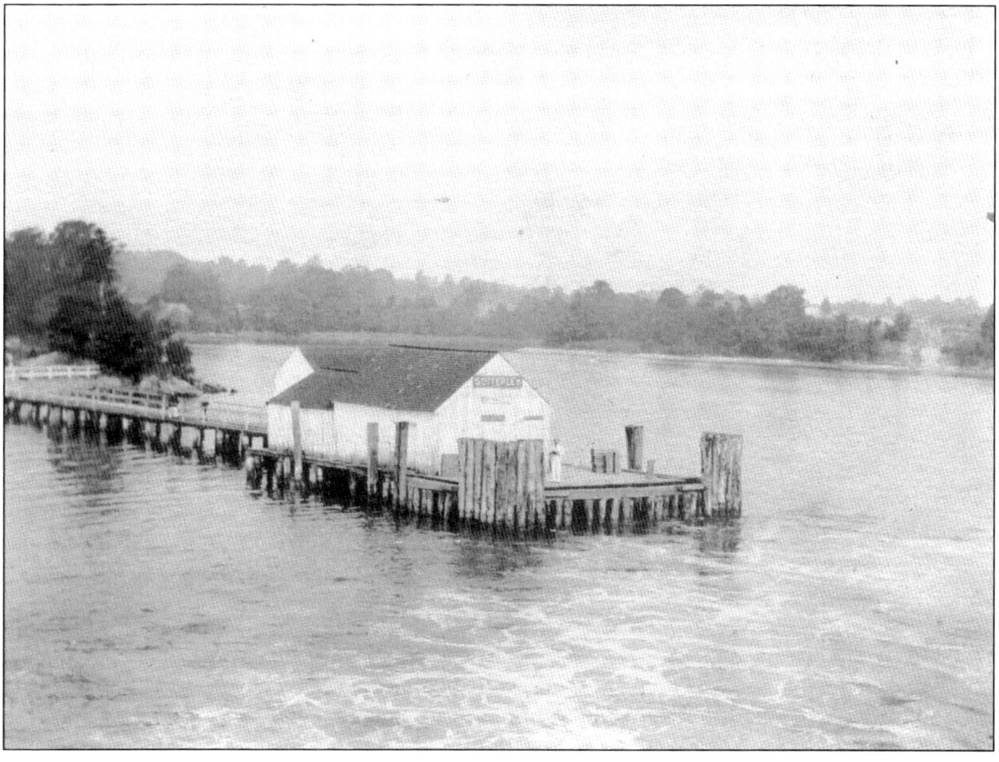

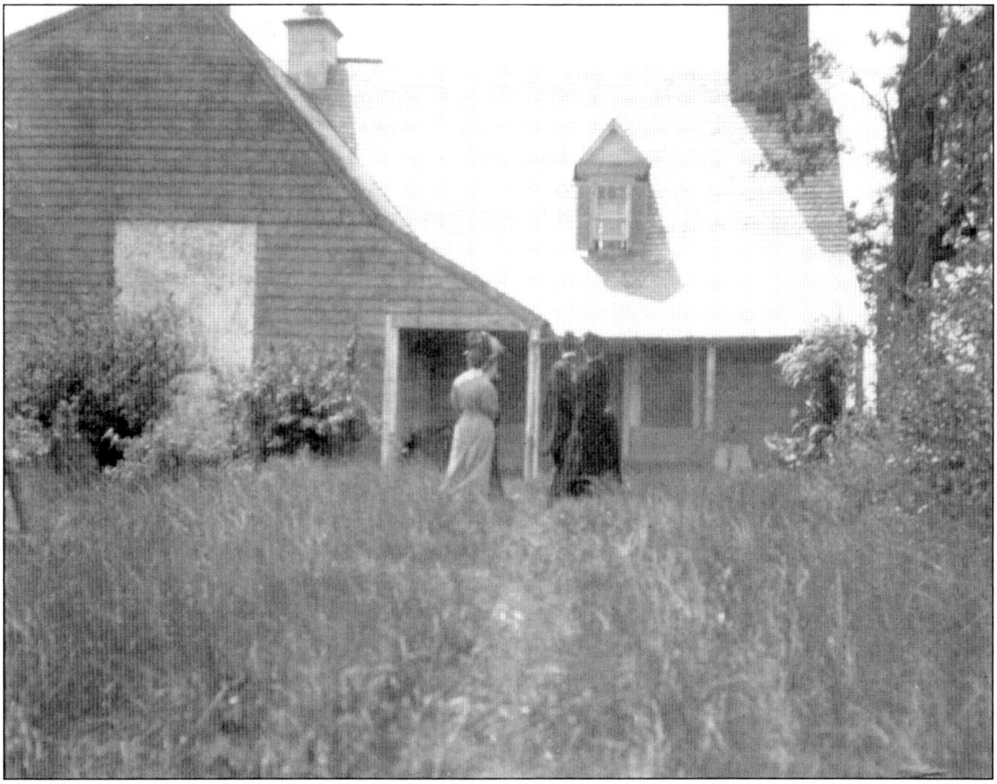

When Herbert and Louisa Satterlee first visited Sotterley Plantation in 1906, they saw a deteriorated house, overgrown grounds, and a farm in serious decline, but Herbert Satterlee had a vision of what Sotterley could become. Louisa Satterlee saw it as "an enchanting old place."

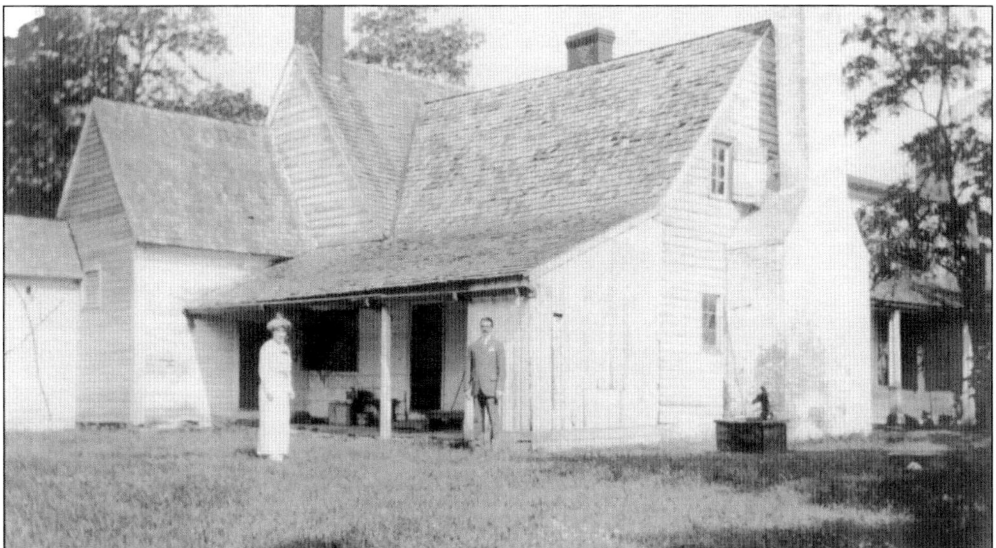

This was the 1910 river-side view of the 19th-century Briscoe kitchen, with the end of the back porch attached to the larder. The Fowlers are seen in front of the porch. To support Sotterley, the Cashners had to rent out portions of the house.

Herbert Satterlee stands in front of the whitewashed outhouse, referred to as the necessary, in an overgrown Sotterley garden.

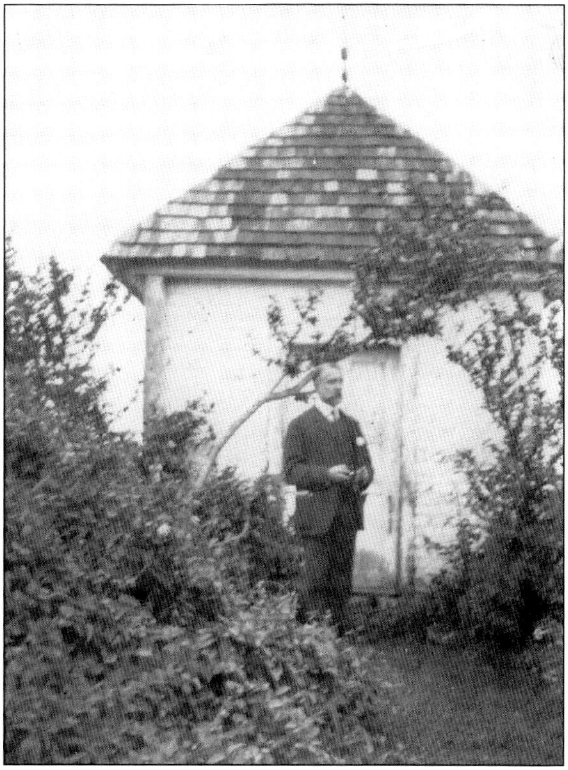

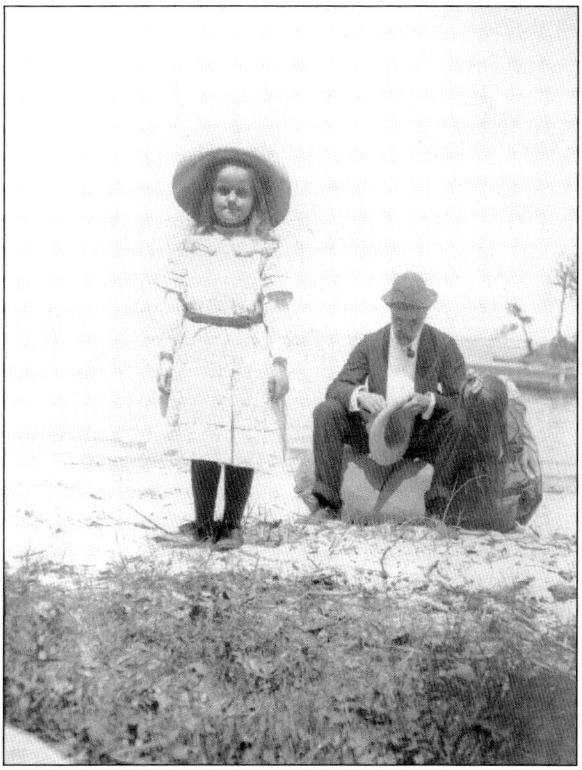

Eleanor Satterlee is seen here in her travel frock while her father, Herbert, sits with Mabel's hat in his hand as she lies on her father's lap.

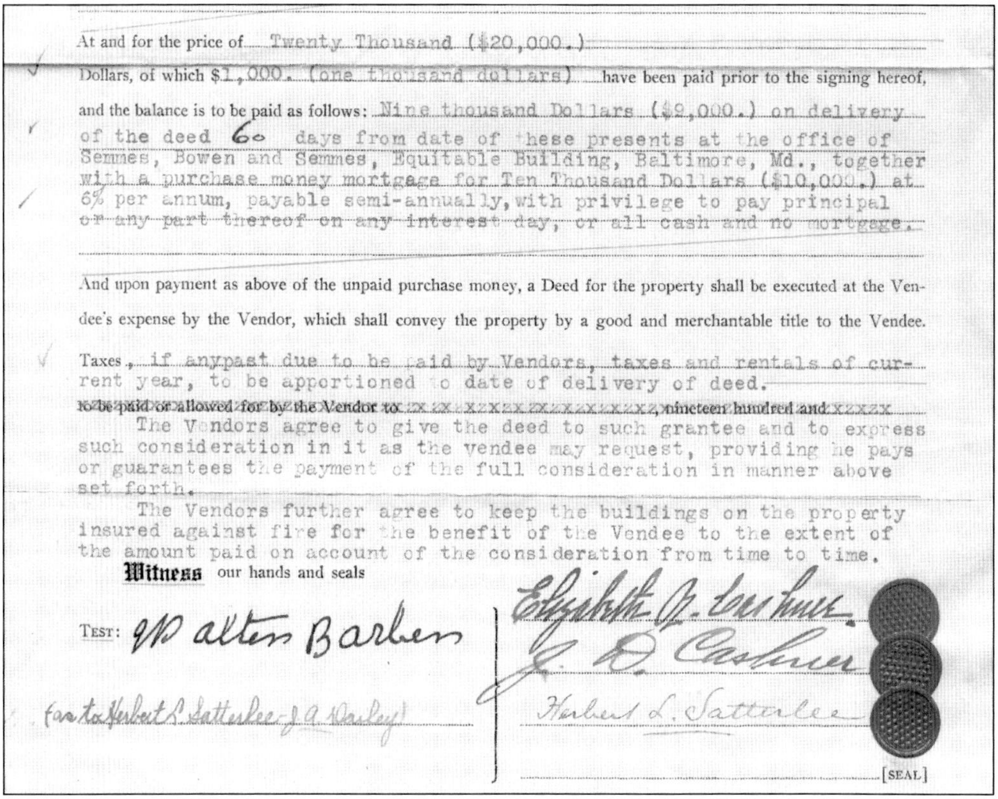
At and for the price of Twenty Thousand ($20,000.)
Dollars, of which $1,000. (one thousand dollars) have been paid prior to the signing hereof,
and the balance is to be paid as follows: Nine thousand Dollars ($9,000.) on delivery of the deed 60 days from date of these presents at the office of Semmes, Bowen and Semmes, Equitable Building, Baltimore, Md., together with a purchase money mortgage for Ten Thousand Dollars ($10,000.) at 6% per annum, payable semi-annually, with privilege to pay principal or any part thereof on any interest day, or all cash and no mortgage.

And upon payment as above of the unpaid purchase money, a Deed for the property shall be executed at the Vendee's expense by the Vendor, which shall convey the property by a good and merchantable title to the Vendee.

Taxes, if any past due to be paid by Vendors, taxes and rentals of current year, to be apportioned to date of delivery of deed.
to be paid or allowed for by the Vendor to xxxx xxxxxxxxxxxxxxxxx, nineteen hundred and xxxxx

The Vendors agree to give the deed to such grantee and to express such consideration in it as the vendee may request, providing he pays or guarantees the payment of the full consideration in manner above set forth.

The Vendors further agree to keep the buildings on the property insured against fire for the benefit of the Vendee to the extent of the amount paid on account of the consideration from time to time.

Witness our hands and seals

TEST: Walter Barber

(as to Herbert L. Satterlee - J. A. Dailey)

Elizabeth R. Cashner
J. D. Cashner
Herbert L. Satterlee
[SEAL]

The Cashners sold Sotterley Plantation to Herbert Satterlee for $20,000 in 1910. This contract was witnessed by Walter Barber. Herbert Satterlee wrote out a three-year promissory note for half of the purchase price. It was paid off on August 9, 1913. J.P. Morgan, Satterlee's father-in-law, had died that March.

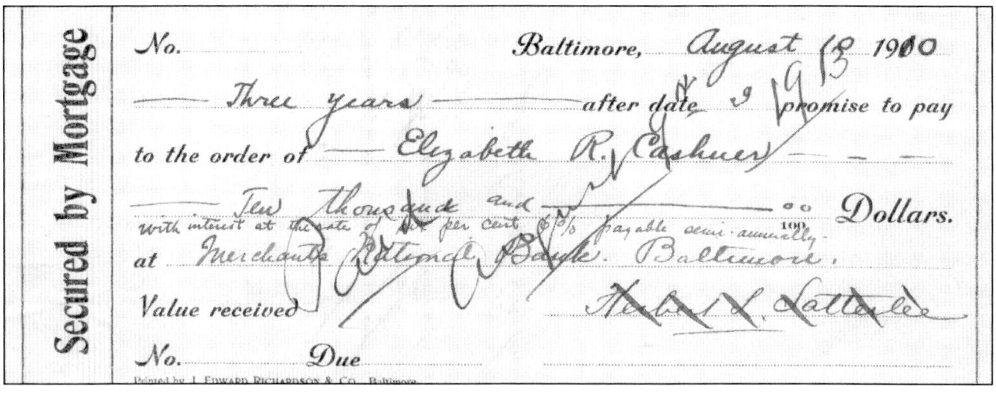
Secured by Mortgage

No. Baltimore, August 18 1910

Three years after date I promise to pay to the order of Elizabeth R. Cashner

Ten thousand and 00/100 Dollars.

with interest at the rate of six per cent 6% payable semi-annually

at Merchants National Bank. Baltimore.

Value received Herbert L. Satterlee

No. Due

Printed by J. Edward Richardson & Co. Baltimore

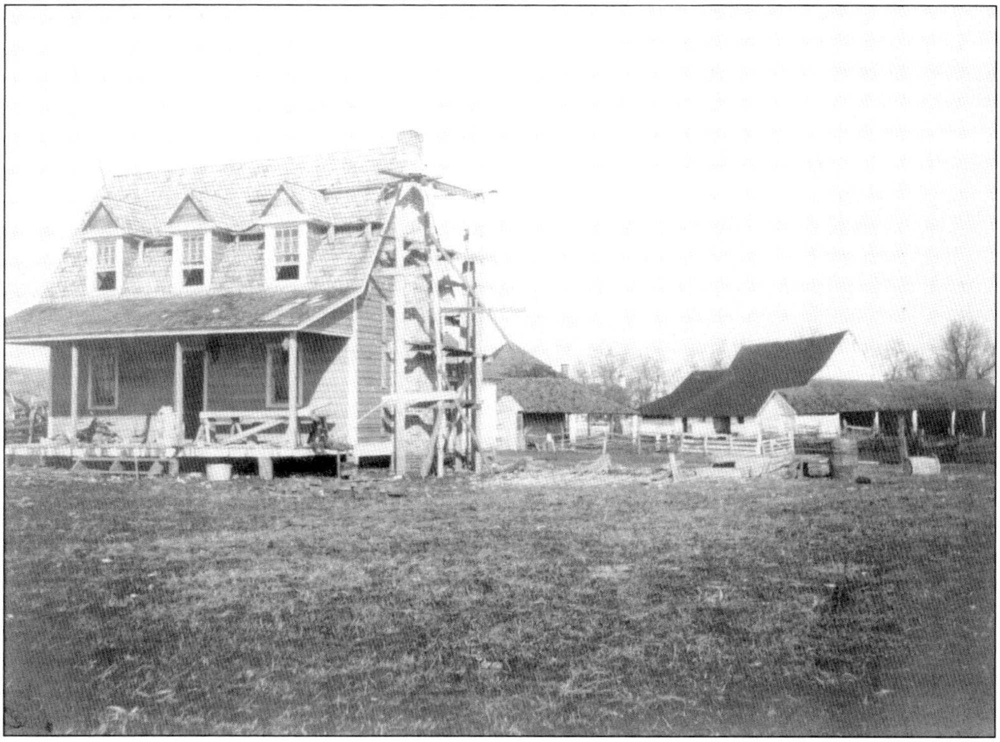

Charles Knott was hired by the Cashners at Herbert Satterlee's request to be Sotterley's new farm manager. Knott was to look the part, wearing a suit and tie. He carried out the wishes of Herbert Satterlee, hiring workers and organizing tasks while raising his own family at Sotterley. Satterlee built Charles Knott this house, which can be seen today facing Sotterley Wharf Road.

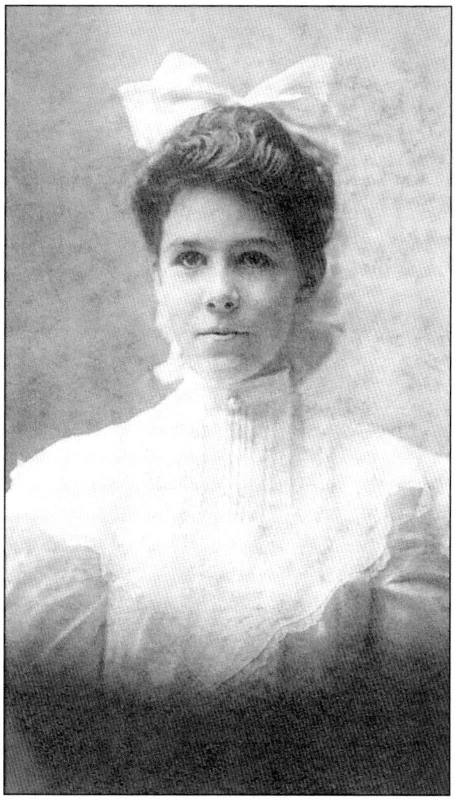

Charles Knott married India Leola Bond, who was also from St. Mary's County, in 1913. Charles and India raised four children: Herbert, Margaret, Edward, and Richard. One son, John, died at birth. India canned vegetables, made preserves, raised turkeys, and helped write her husband's weekly reports to Herbert Satterlee about Sotterley. She also rang the farm bell, signaling the beginning and end of each workday, all while raising her family. Richard Knott says of his mother, "She was a saint." India did not work as a domestic for the plantation house, but the Satterlees loved all the canned goods and preserves she made and had them shipped to New York so they could enjoy them year-round. Richard Knott describes a wonderful and happy childhood growing up at Sotterley.

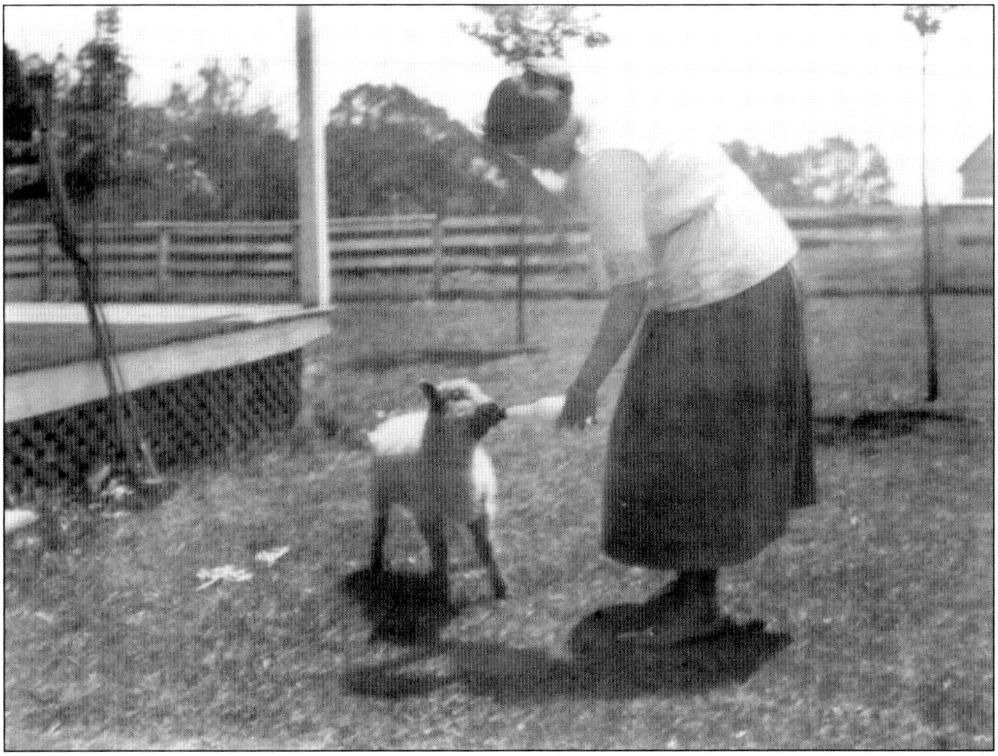

India Knott is seen here feeding her children's pet lamb in front of the Knott home.

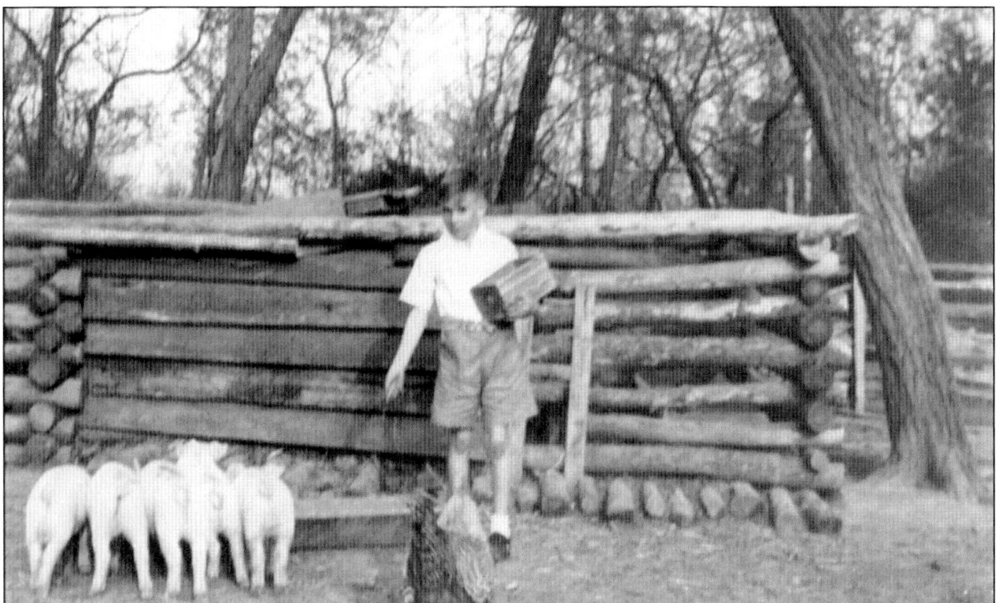

A young Richard Knott feeds the animals at Sotterley. Richard Knott worked for Herbert Satterlee and later for his daughter Mabel. Along with his grandson Shawn Knott, Richard helps to preserve Sotterley's 20th-century family and farming history.

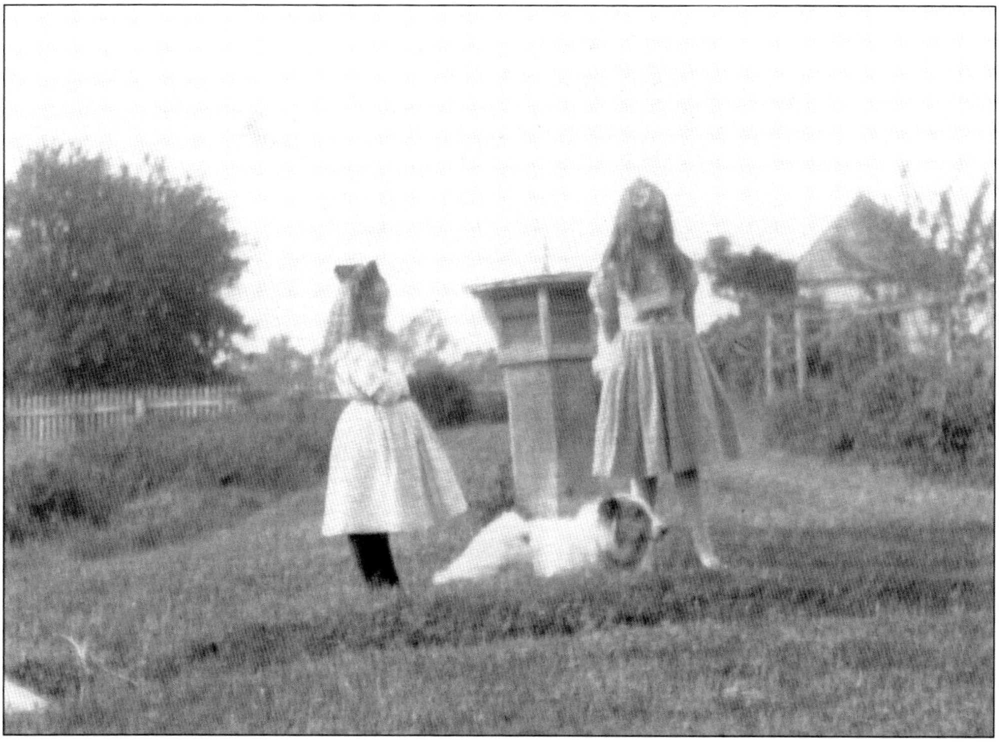

Eleanor and Mabel Satterlee play with the family dog, Shep, near Sotterley's old sundial. This photograph, taken around 1910, shows the garden before its revival transformation, as it still has white wooden fencing, a whitewashed necessary, and overgrowth.

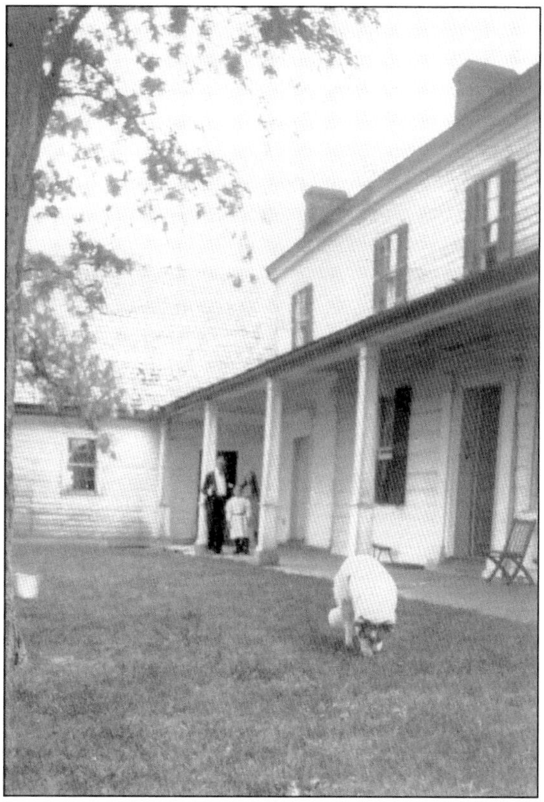

Herbert Satterlee and his daughters Eleanor and Mabel watch Shep from the Briscoe kitchen. Sotterley was a quiet and rustic departure from their lives in New York.

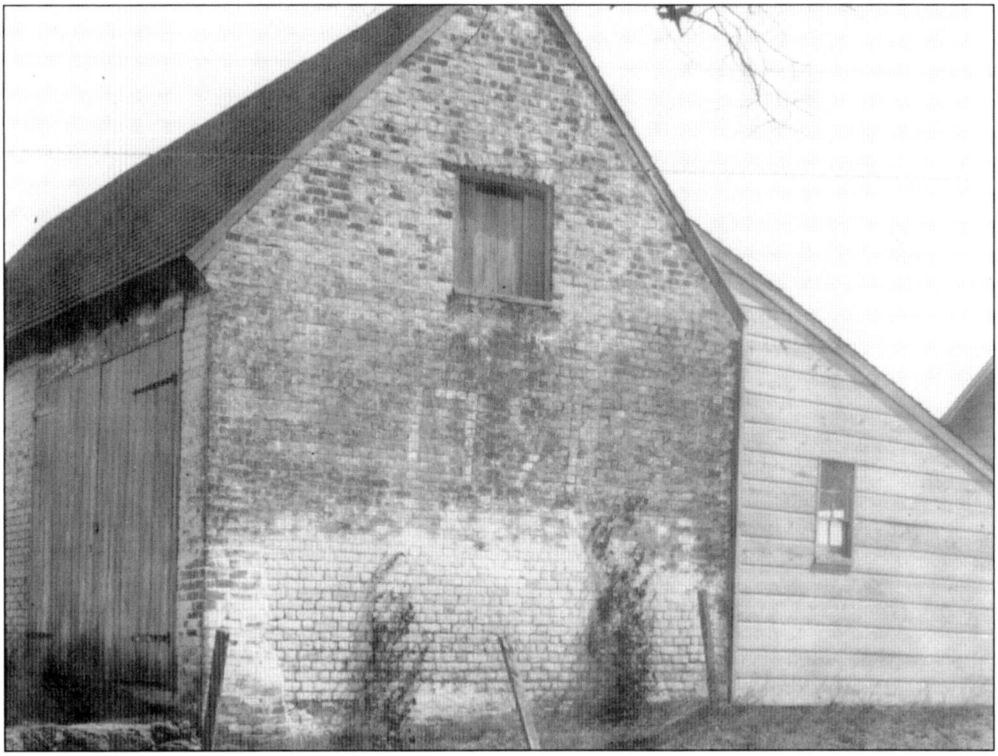

This brick stable, known as the warehouse, is distinguished by the 1757 date on the side of the building. It is one of Sotterley's remaining 18th-century structures. The double wooden doors are seen on the left.

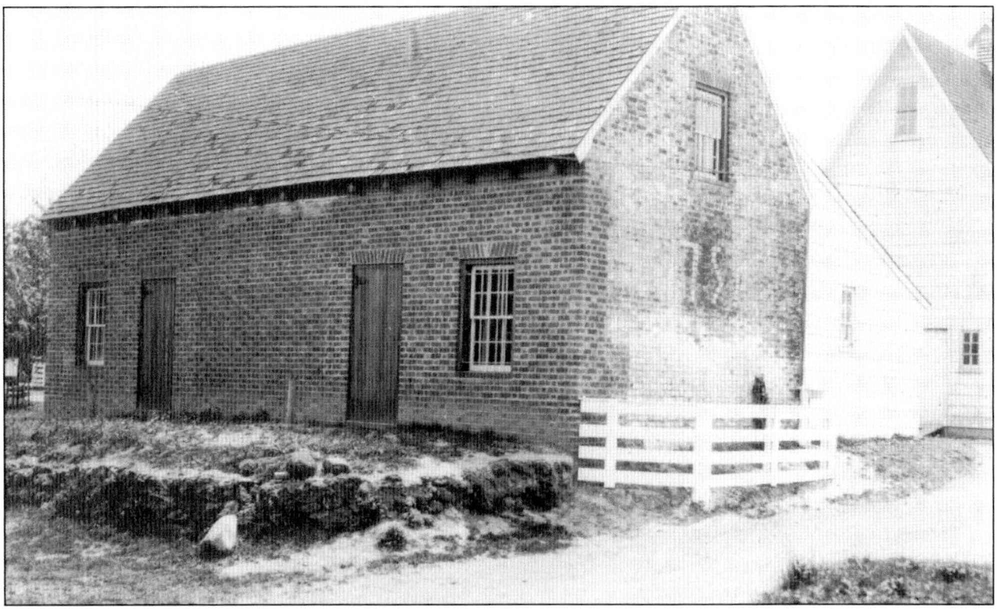

Herbert Satterlee changed the slope of the ground near the stable and installed two doors instead of a wide barn door. The fencing was replaced to keep animals from rubbing the brick. The horse barn on the right was torn down in the 1950s.

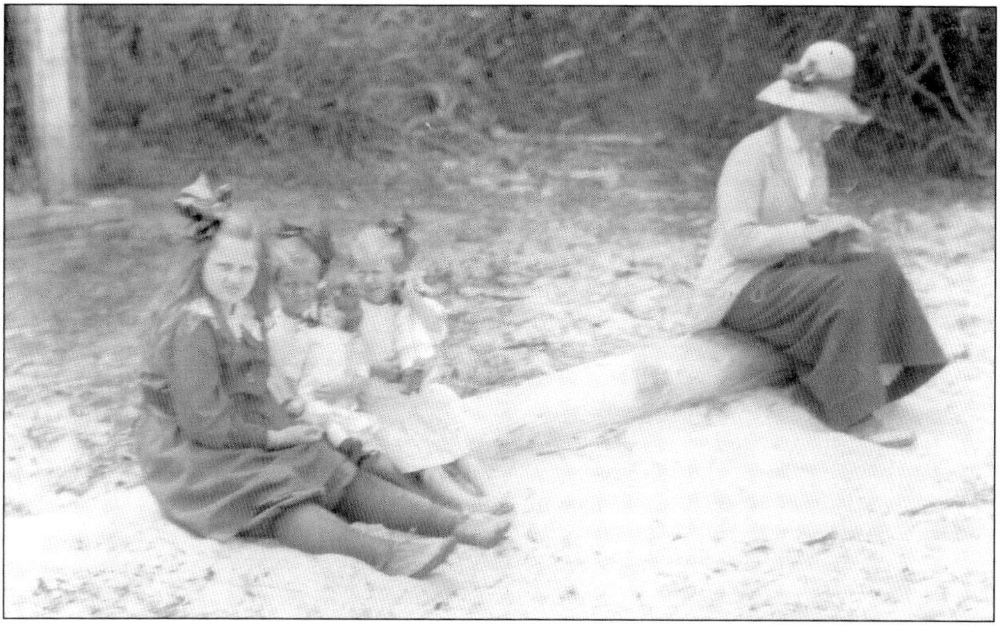

Eleanor Satterlee is seen here with some Sotterley playmates. The woman on the right is Adelaide M. Orr, Eleanor's nurse, who emigrated from Ireland in 1890. She is one of eight Irish immigrant servants listed on Herbert Satterlee's 1910 census. She was 45 years old at the time. When the Satterlee's visited Sotterley Plantation, they would bring with them an entourage of nurses, maids, servants, and a chauffeur.

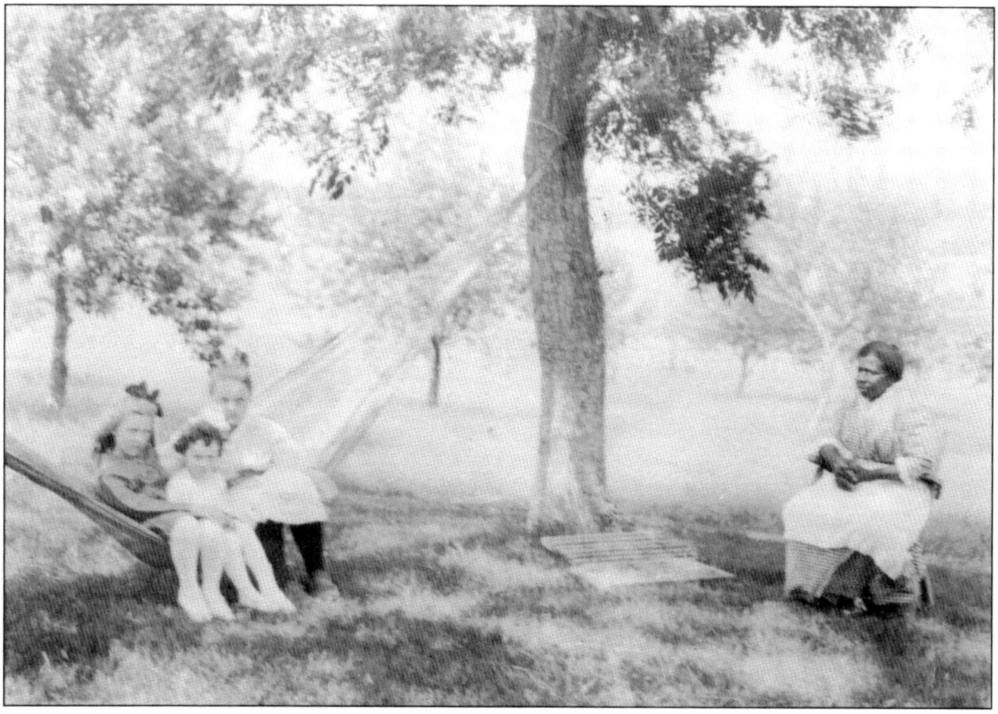

Eleanor and Mabel Satterlee rest with a playmate between them on a hammock. Harriet Barber watches them from nearby.

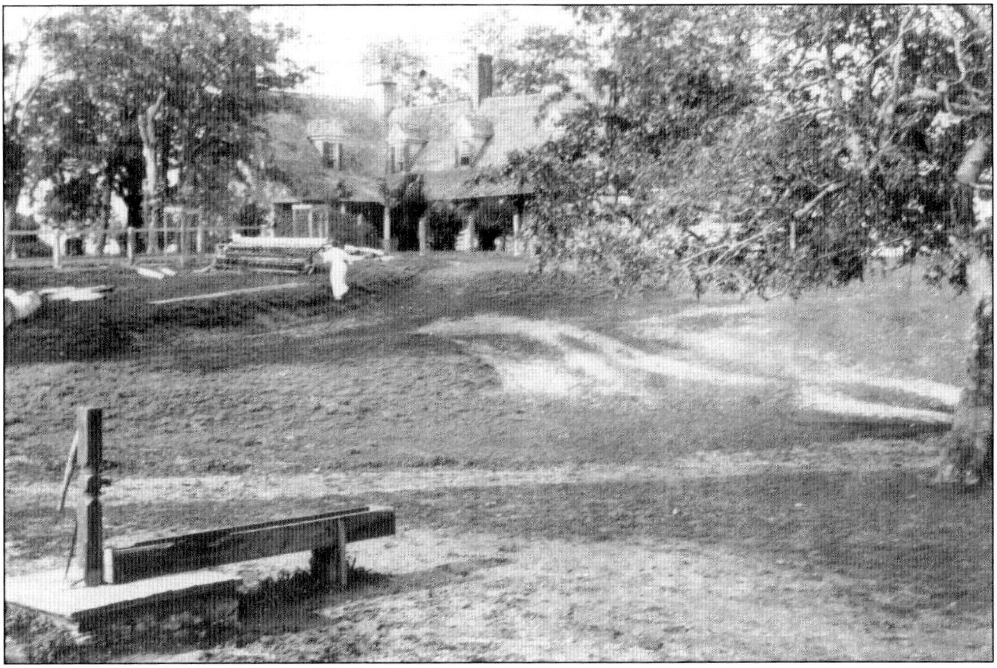

A woman walks up the hill to the house yard, where new plantings and fencing are being installed, separating the house yard from the farming operations. A water trough is in the foreground.

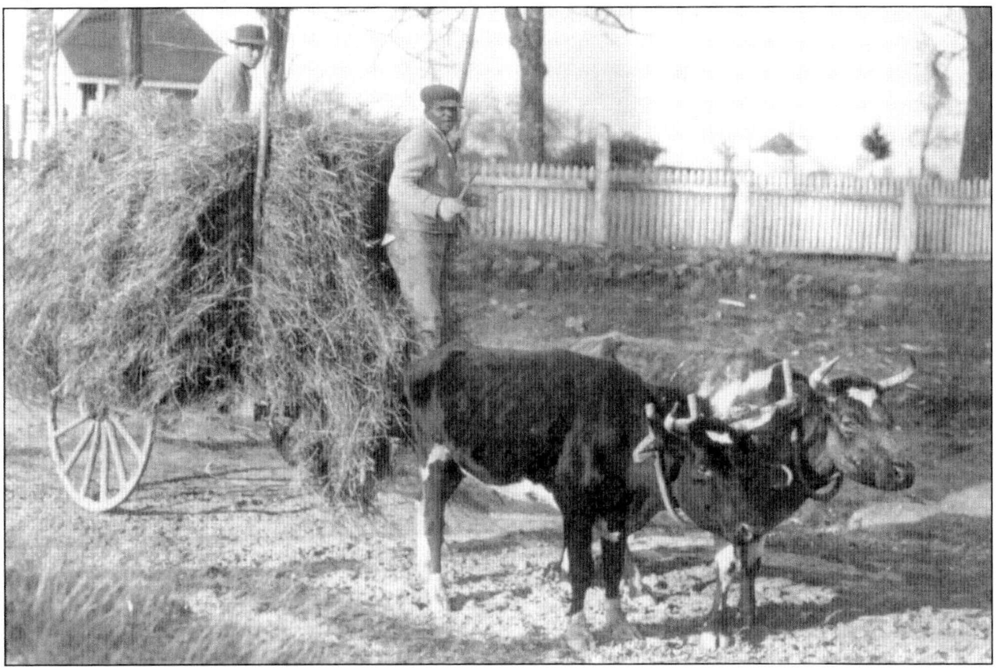

Earnest Knott and Walter Barber transport wheat on an ox cart in the 1910s. Wooden fencing now encloses the plantation house yard. The north gatehouse, where the Briscoe School likely held classes in the 1800s, is visible, but the south gatehouse had not yet been built. Ernest Knott, Charles Knott's brother, lived in a house near Sotterley's front gate. The house was later moved near the wharf house and is now called Brink Cottage.

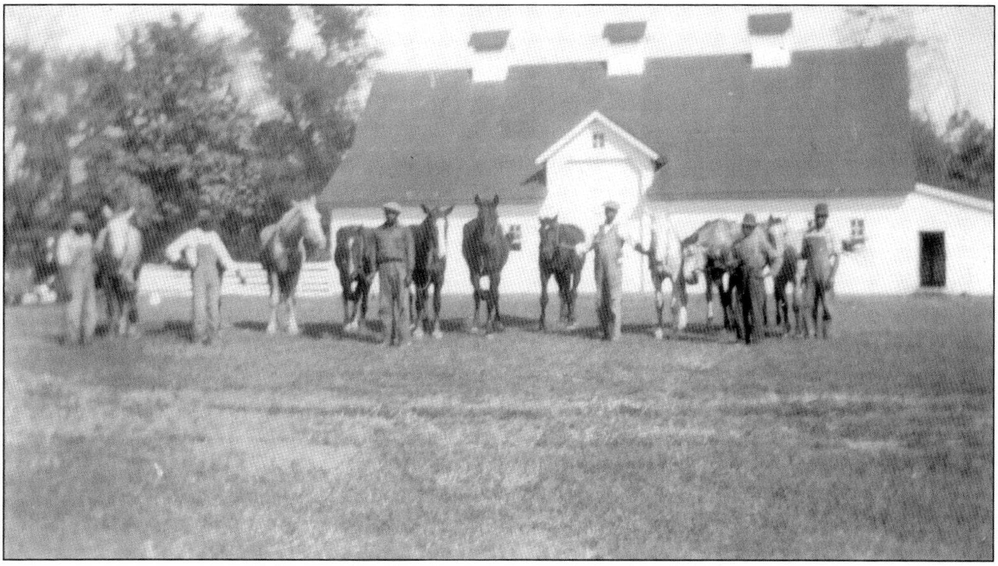

African American farm laborers display their horses in front of the 1920s cow barn, which still stands today. The barn is now used for hosting events and receptions.

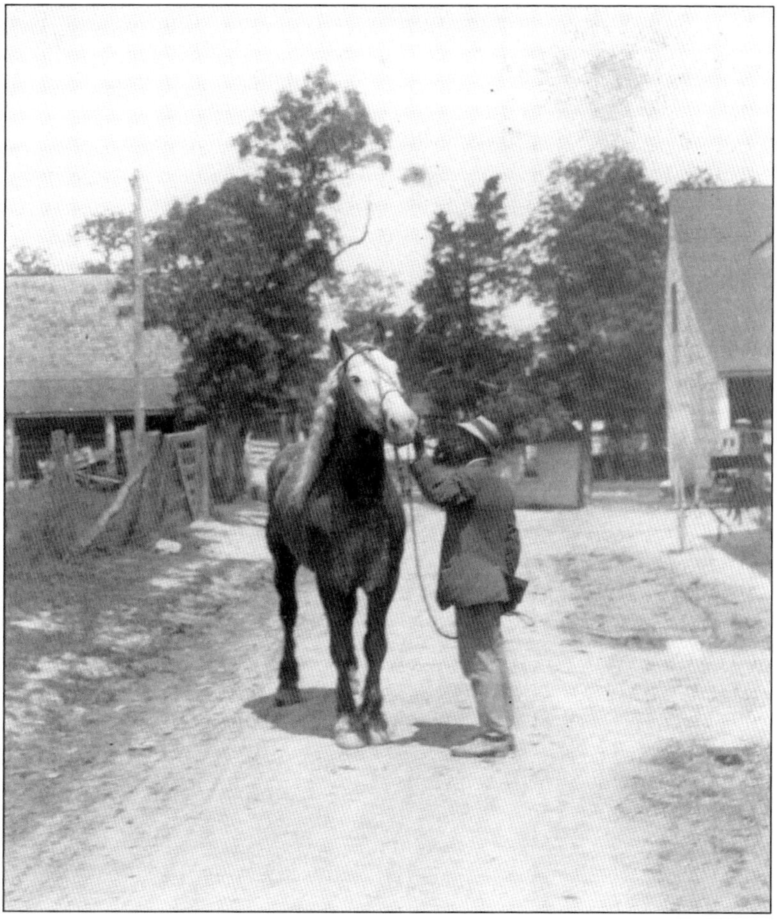

A farm laborer handles a horse. The corncrib is on the left, and the brick stable is on the right. The small building in the middle was used to store bridles and saddles. It was later called the customs house.

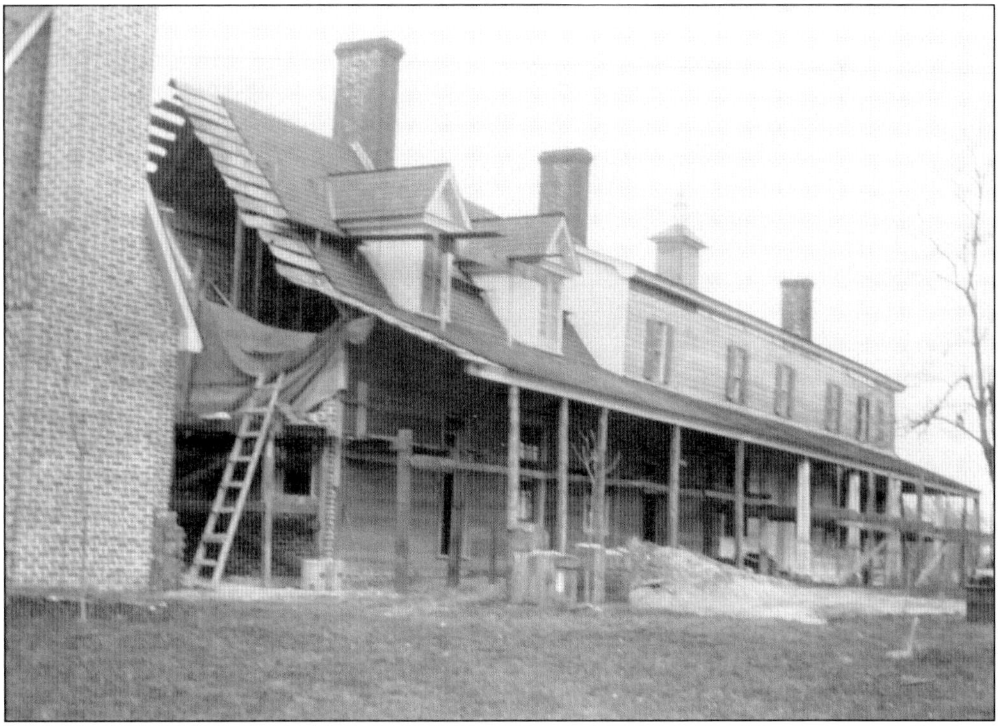

In 1916, Herbert Satterlee had major restoration and renovations done on the plantation house, including the removal of the entire Briscoe kitchen. A new Colonial-style kitchen was built on the south end of the house; the roofline was extended to completely cover the larder, roof, and all; the portico on the river-side porch was extended the whole length of the house; and new siding was placed on the scar from the kitchen. Below, the pump that was at the end of the Briscoe kitchen by the chimney can still be seen.

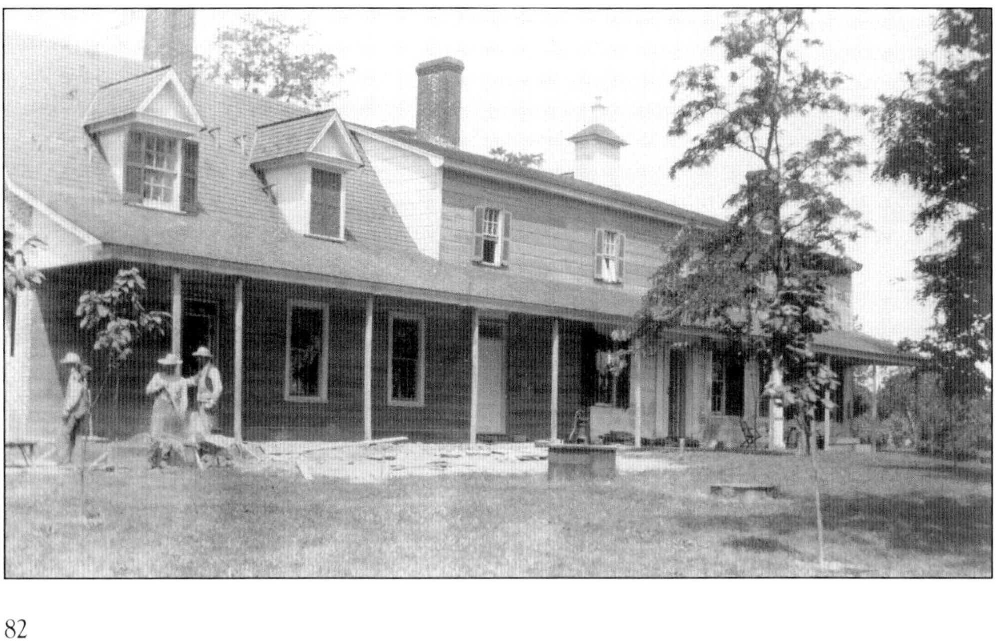

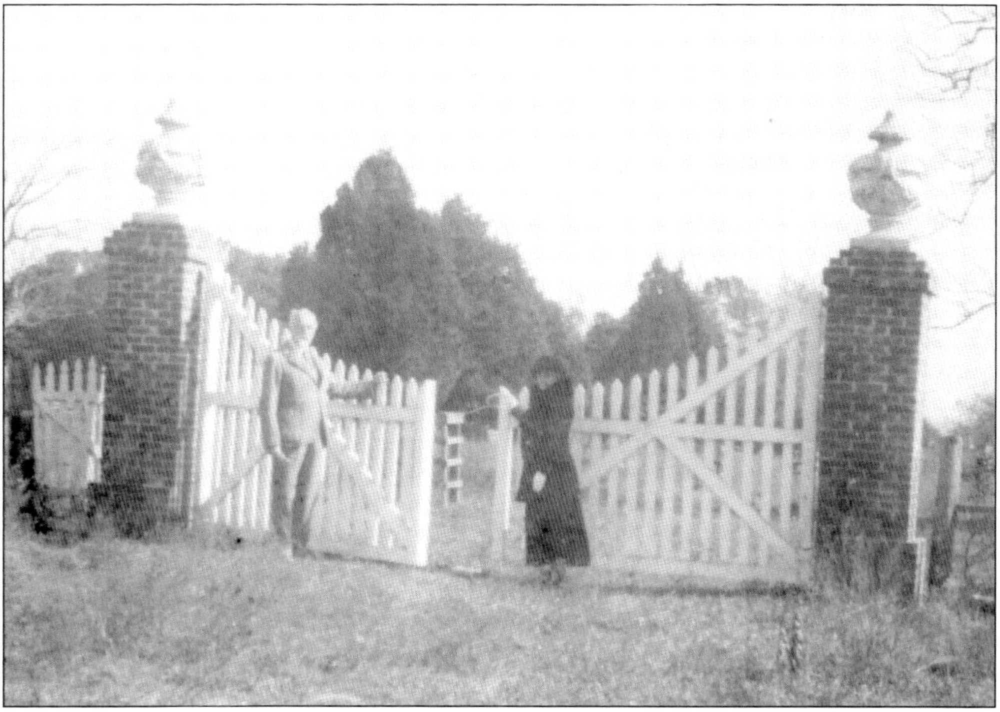

Herbert Satterlee created this grand brick columned gateway with a white picket gate to the tree allee that leads to the front of the plantation house in the 1930s.

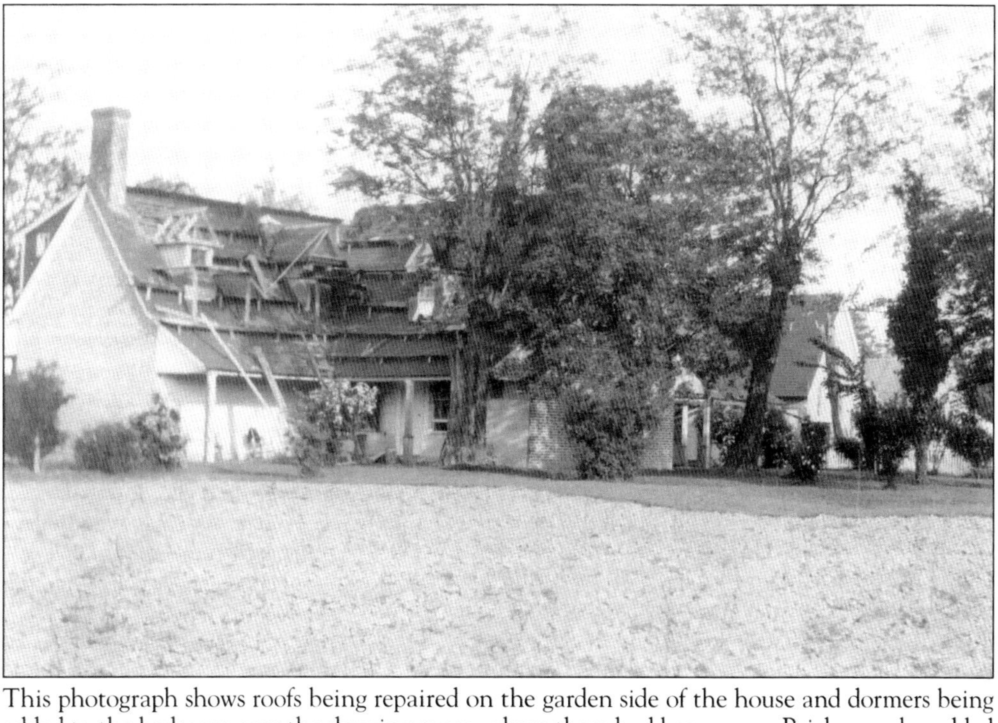

This photograph shows roofs being repaired on the garden side of the house and dormers being added to the bedroom over the drawing room, where there had been none. Brick was also added to the north and west ends of the house.

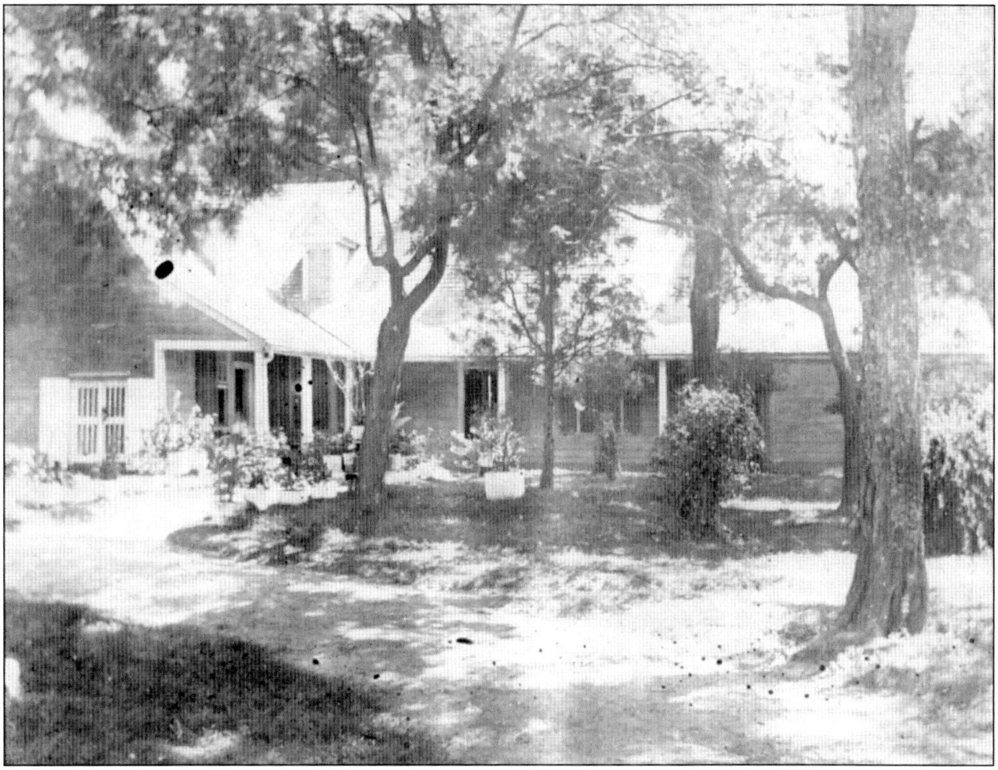

Brush was cleared and a circle drive was built on the road side of the house. Potted plants lined the porch for landscaping.

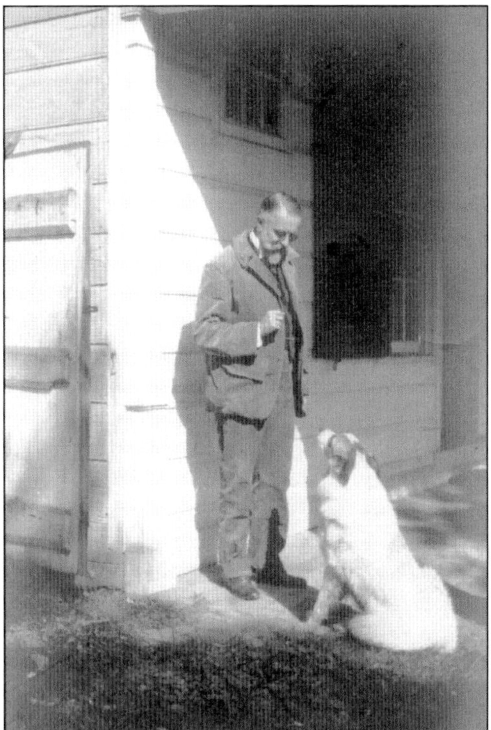

Herbert Satterlee is seen here playing with Shep on the New Room porch. Note that white beaded clapboard siding has been installed, replacing the narrower German siding.

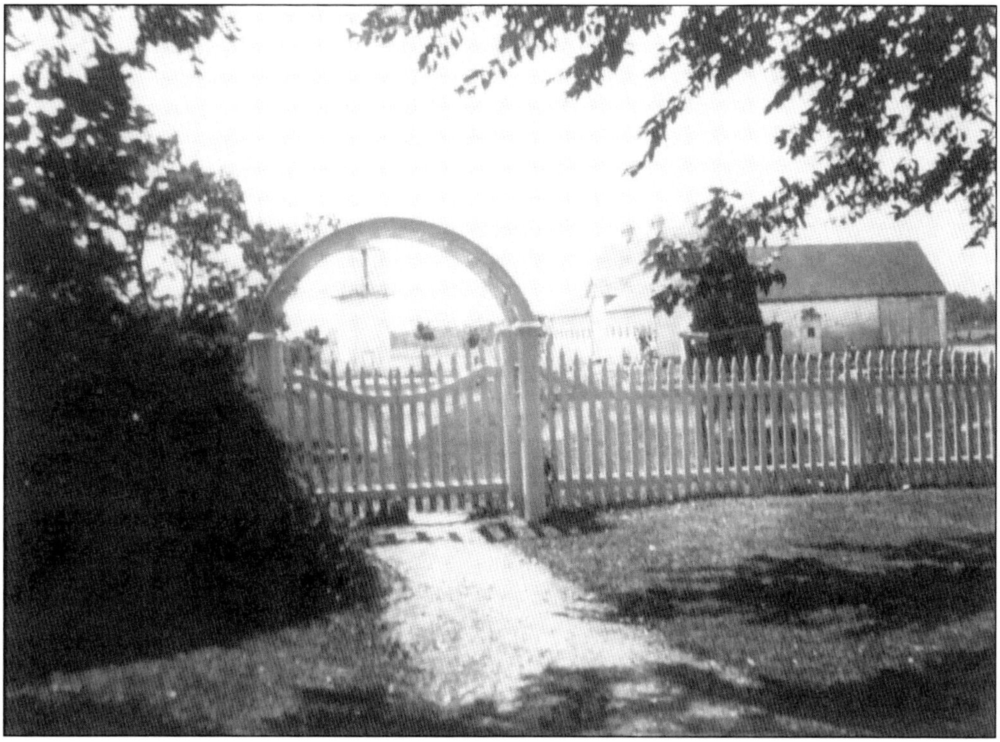

This view from the house lawn looks through the rose arbor at the farm in the 1910s, showing the horse barn and the water tower, which were torn down in the 1950s, and the brick stable, which is now called the warehouse.

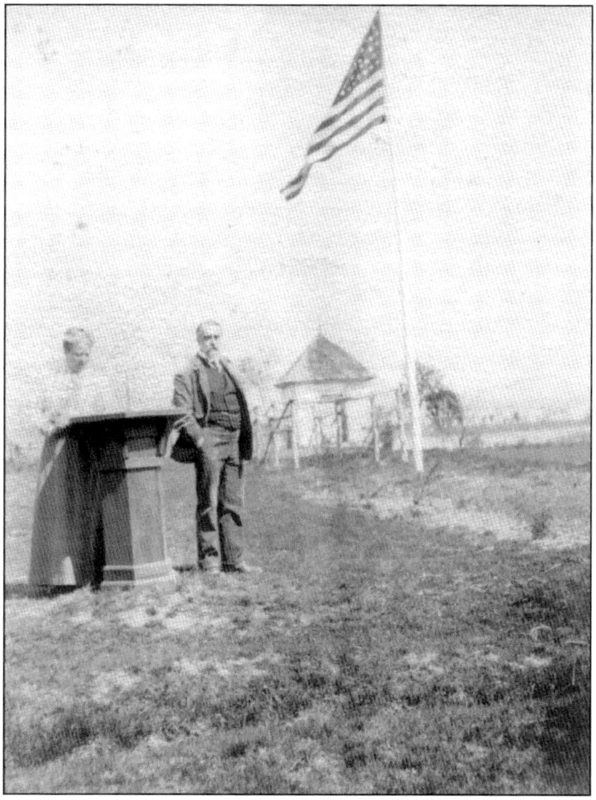

Herbert and Louisa Satterlee are seen here in the garden at the sundial in the 1910s. Herbert Satterlee installed the flagpole, and the flag was raised and lowered every day. In 1910, there were 46 stars on the flag. In this photograph, the overgrowth has been cleared in the garden and new plantings have been started, but the necessary is still whitewashed.

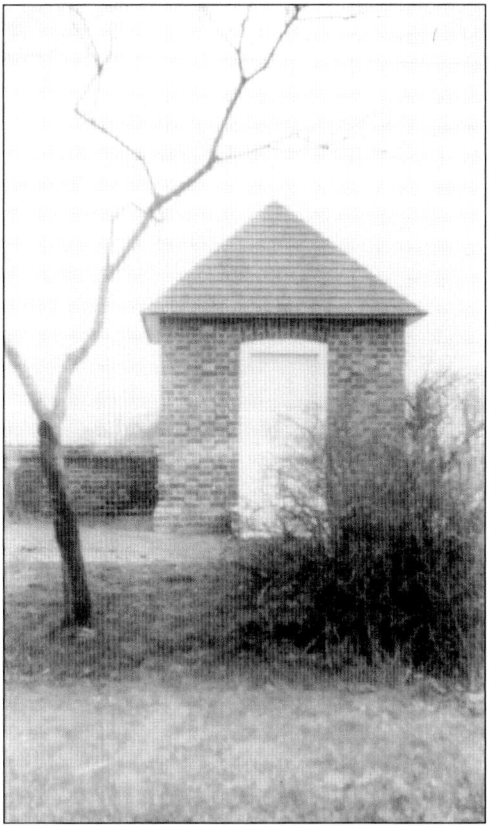

Herbert Satterlee had the whitewash taken off the brick of the necessary. Another structure identical to the necessary was built on the opposite side of the garden. It is now called the toolshed and has been used for various purposes over the years.

This brick wall was installed at the back of the garden. Sotterley's Colonial Revival garden resembles an English manor garden instead of the Colonial kitchen garden that existed in the Bowles and Plater periods of the 1700s. Sotterley's new garden exhibits the desired symmetry required of a formal garden and includes an herb garden, a cutting garden, a vegetable garden, trees, manicured shrubs, and spectacular views of the Patuxent River.

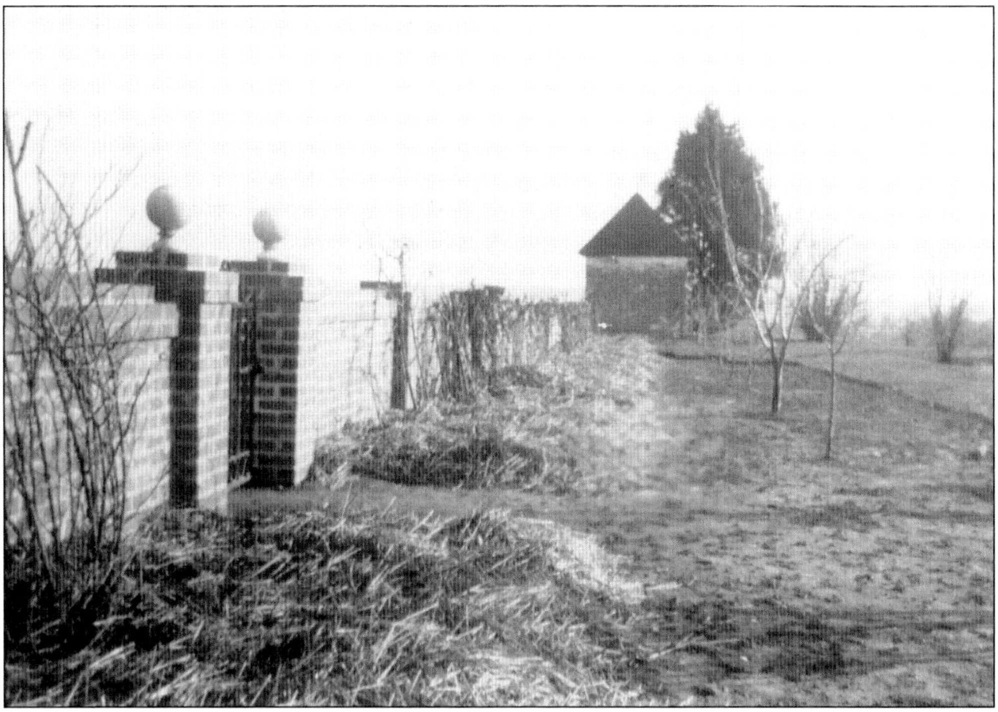

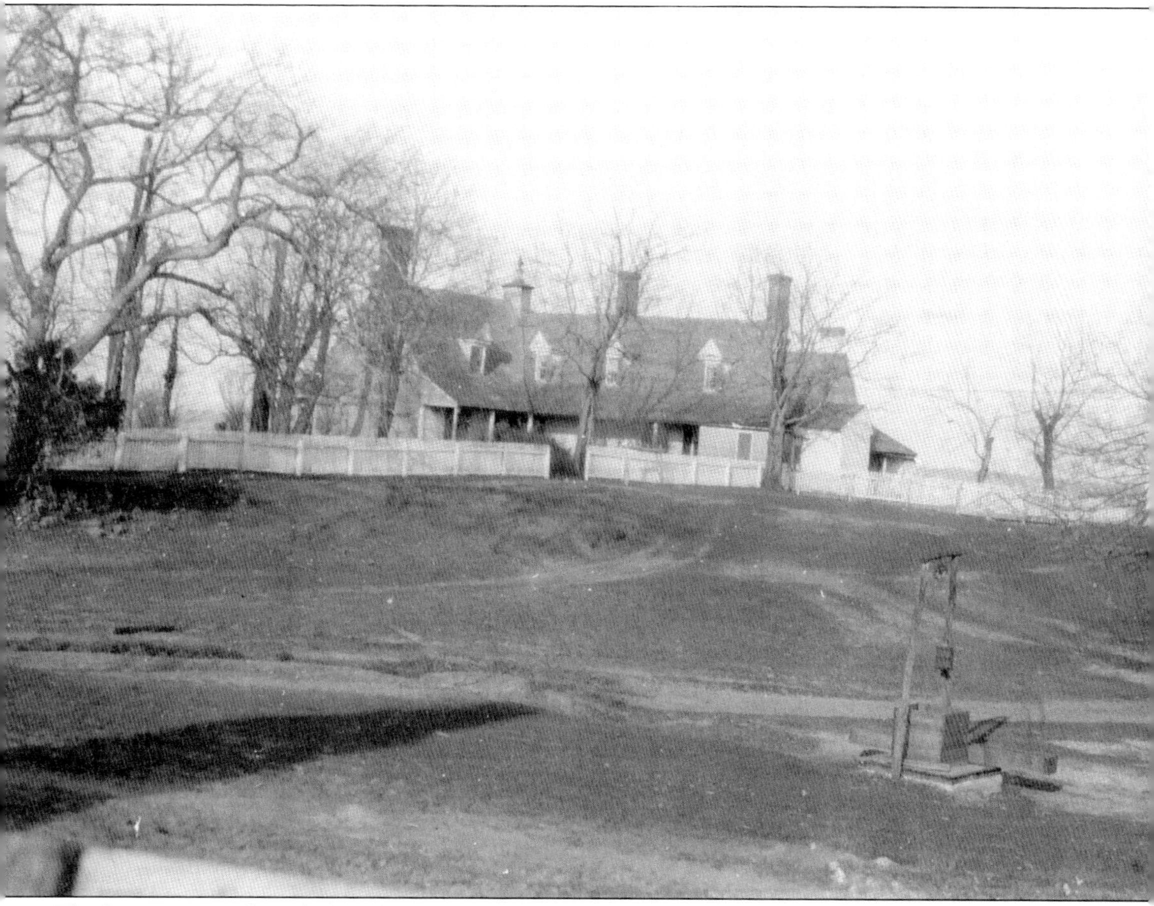

The house is seen here before the new Colonial-style kitchen was added. Note the space left in the fence for the future rose arbor and the water well in the foreground. The slave quarter that existed between the south end of the house and the smokehouse has been removed. Brush and overgrowth were also removed, and the beginnings of another circle drive can be seen.

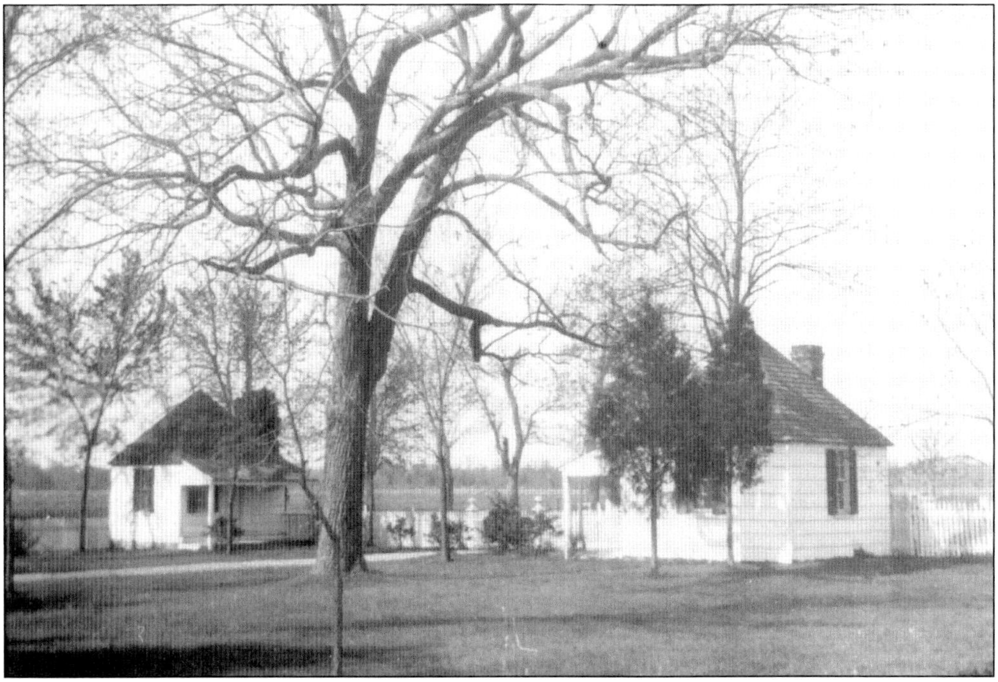

The south gatehouse was built to match the existing north gatehouse in the 1920s. The gatehouses have served many purposes over the years. They also added the symmetry desired by Herbert Satterlee for the house and grounds.

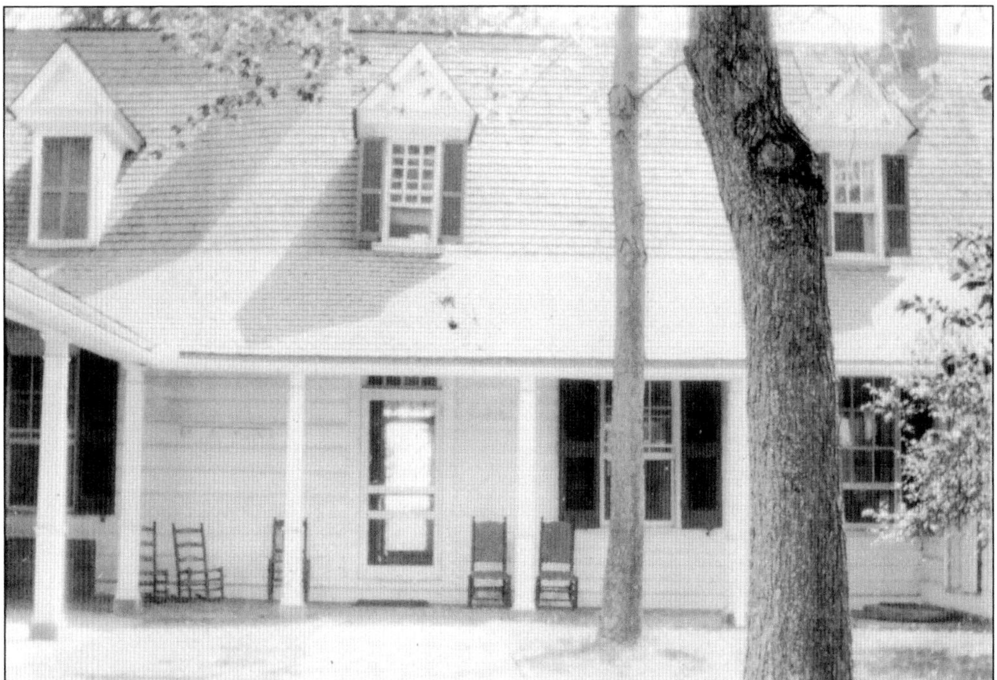

The spruced-up dining room passageway entrance is seen here with a view from the road side to the river side of the house.

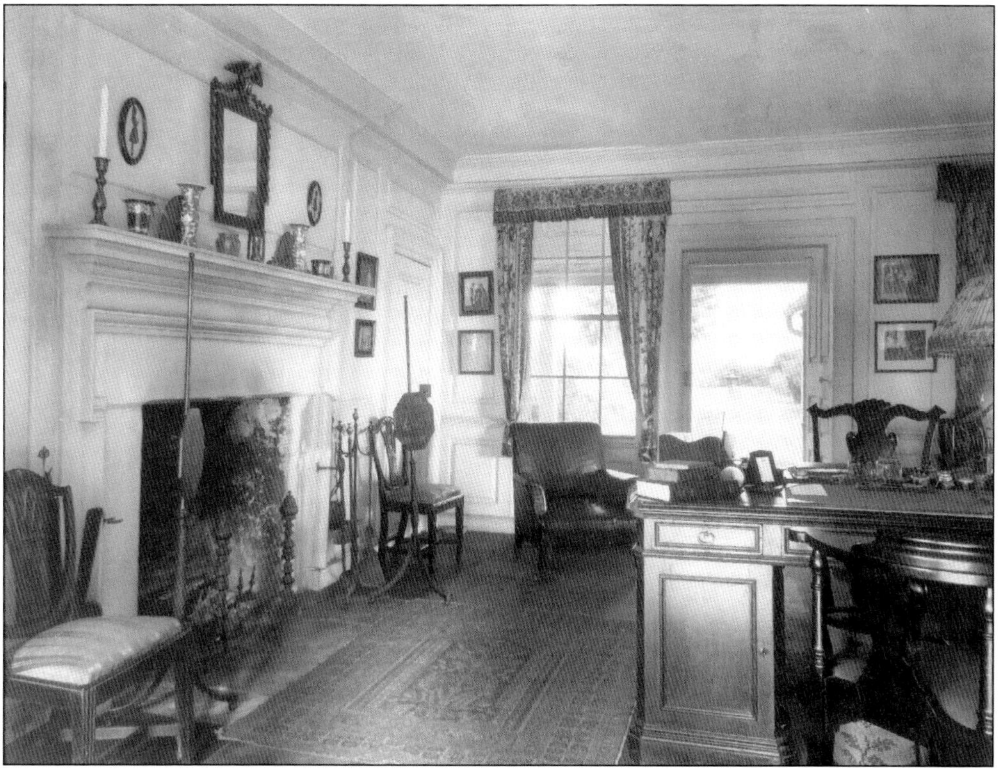

This photograph looks from the New Room to the garden in the 1920s, showing Herbert Satterlee's desk on the right. Note the white marble fireplace and the white paint on the interior walls. Satterlee called this room the library. Silhouettes of Mabel and Eleanor are featured above the mantel.

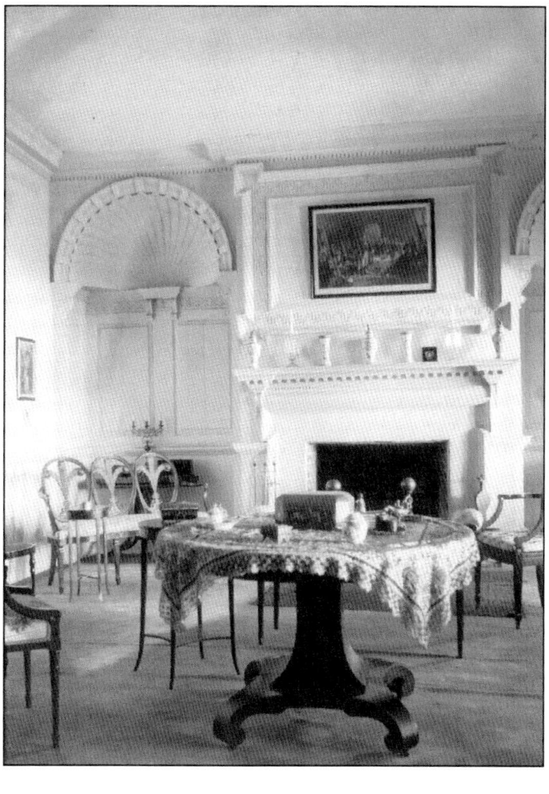

The drawing room is seen here in the 1920s. It is painted Satterlee white with Satterlee furnishings and features an Edwardian settee from J.P Morgan's London townhouse. Above the mantel is one of many George Washington subject prints owned by Herbert Satterlee. The Victorian parlor stoves from the 1800s have been removed from the first-floor hearths.

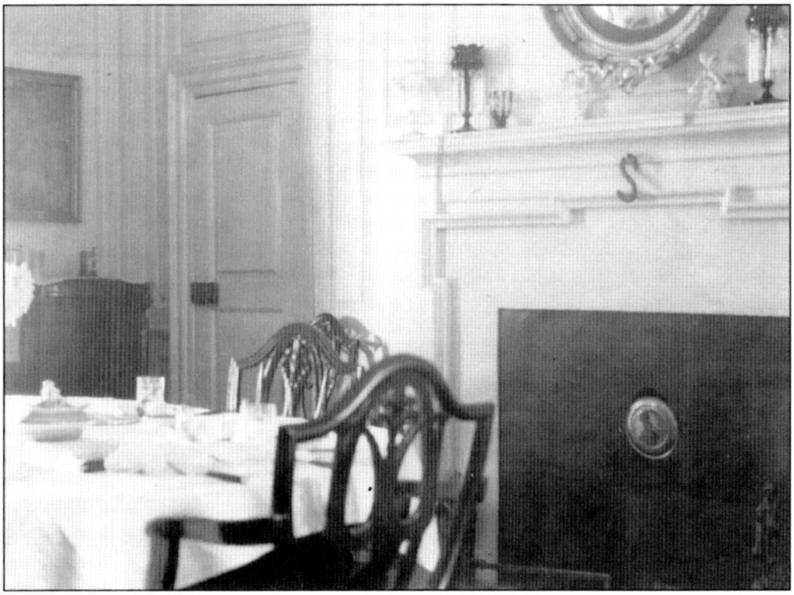

The dining room is seen here in the 1920s painted in the Satterlee white color. The walls were plastered and molded to look like the wood paneling in the rest of the house, and the hearth is covered.

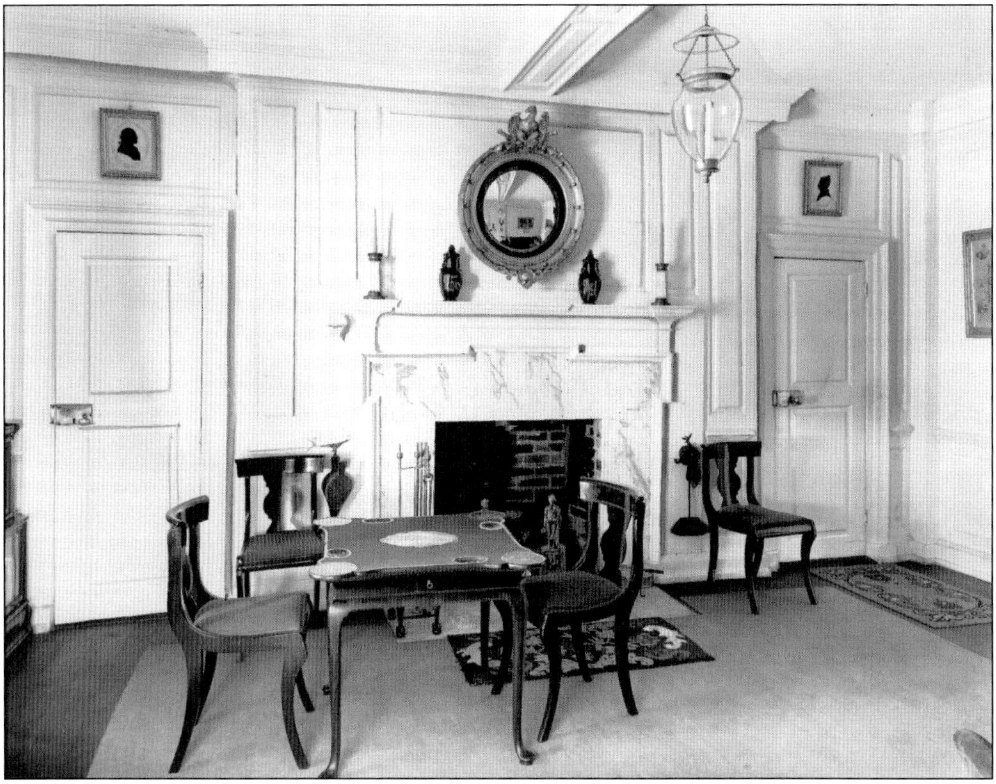

The original Bowles bedchamber is seen here after it was reinterpreted by Herbert and Louisa Satterlee in the 1920s. The room features a game table, a concave mirror, a white marble fireplace, and various George Washington likenesses.

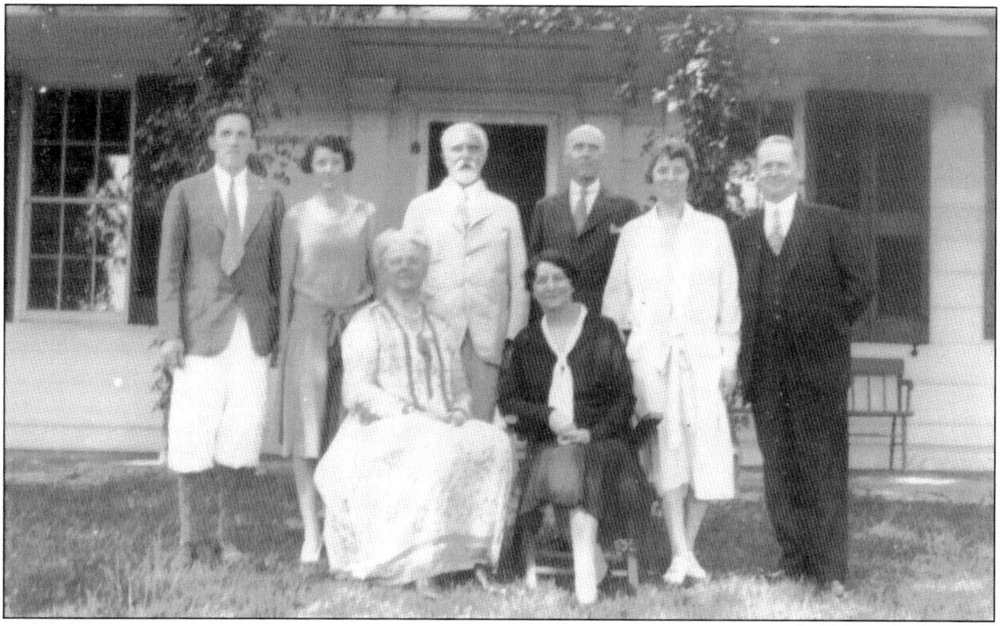

Herbert Satterlee contacted Plater descendants and invited them to come to Sotterley. He had several such Plater reunions over the years. This group photograph, taken during a weeklong reunion in May 1930, shows, from left to right, (first row) Louisa Satterlee and Mrs. Richard C. Plater; (second row) Richard C. Plater Jr., Louise Plater, Herbert Satterlee, Richard C. Plater, Anna Plater Williams, and Myron Clark Williams.

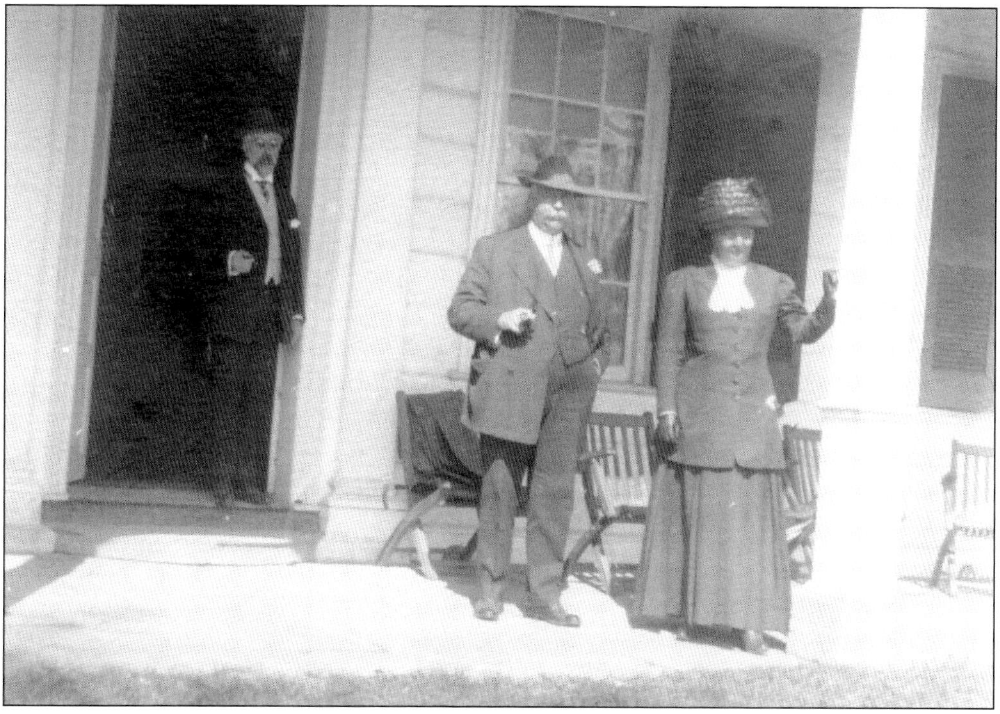

Herbert Satterlee stands in the doorway and entertains guests on the portico in the 1910s, with cigars for him and his gentleman guest.

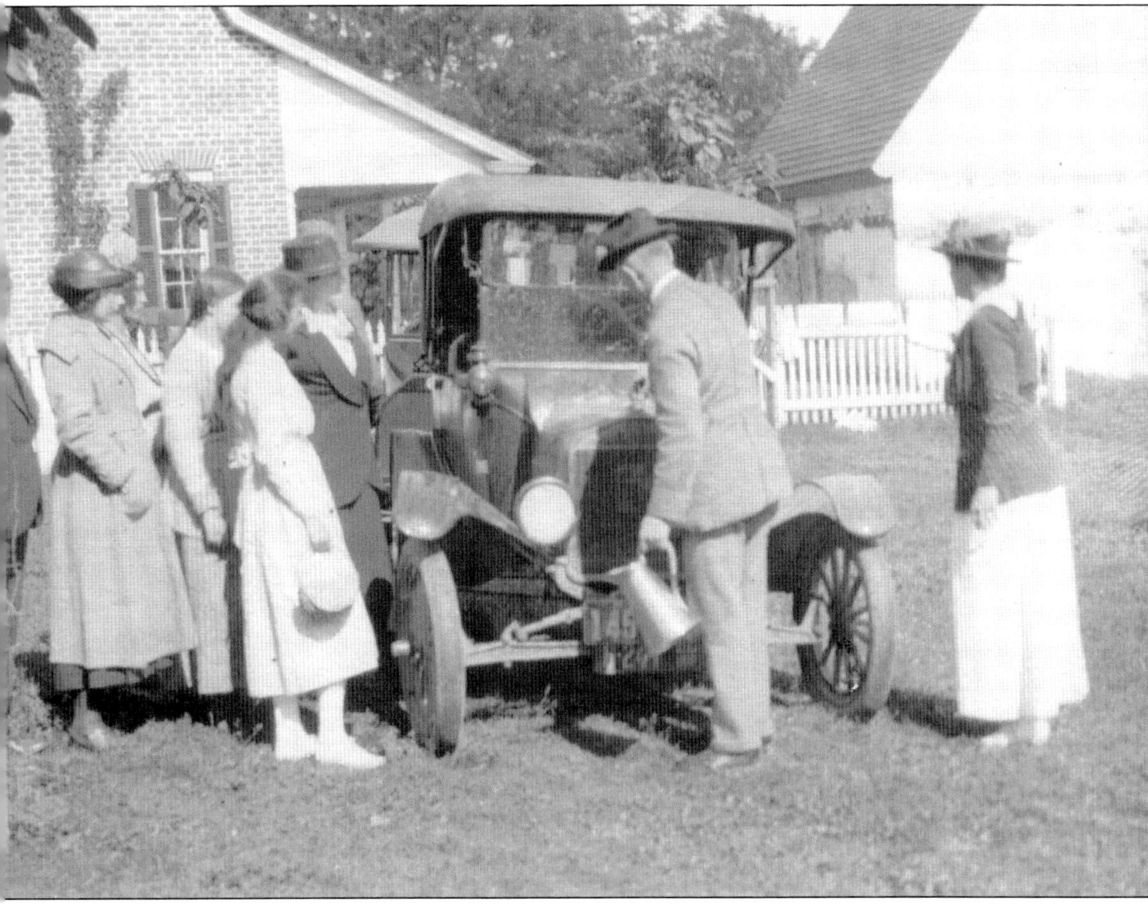

Guests crowd around two cars at Sotterley about 1916. As transportation improved, Herbert Satterlee (extreme left) would travel by chauffeur-driven car. Charles Knott would drive to meet them and transport their baggage. Eleanor and Mabel are the two young girls with long hair in this photograph. The new kitchen porch and the smokehouse are in the background. When they came to Sotterley, Herbert and Louisa Satterlee often went sightseeing with friends or to community events such as the county fair or other historical sites. Herbert Satterlee took the ferry in his chauffeured Rolls-Royce. Louisa Satterlee often served as the family photographer.

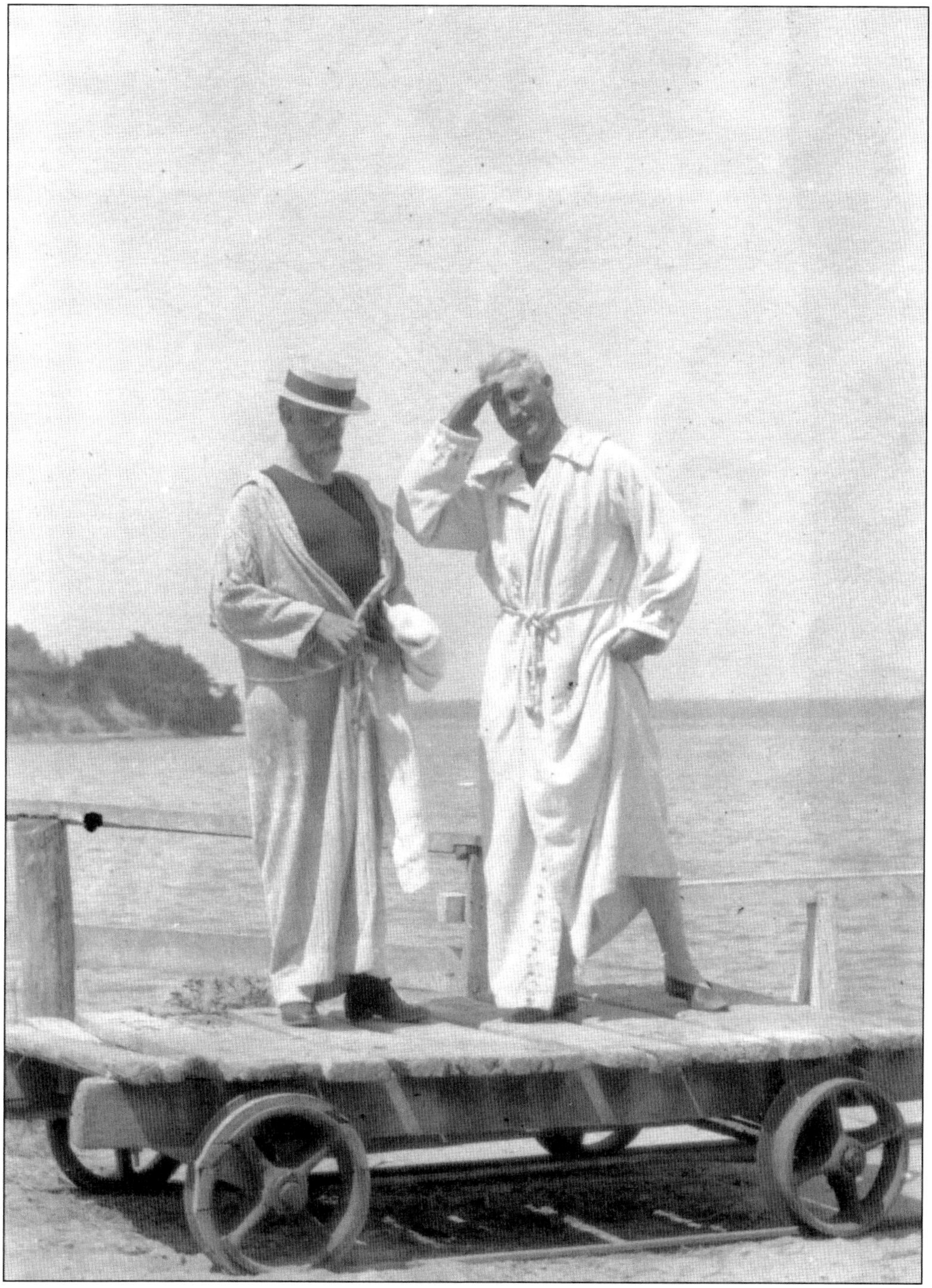

Herbert Satterlee (left) and a friend enjoy the sun as they stand on a rail cart at the wharf in the 1920s. The Satterlee family often enjoyed swimming, fishing, walking, and hunting at Sotterley. Herbert would often invite naval officers and cadets from Annapolis to enjoy some summer fun.

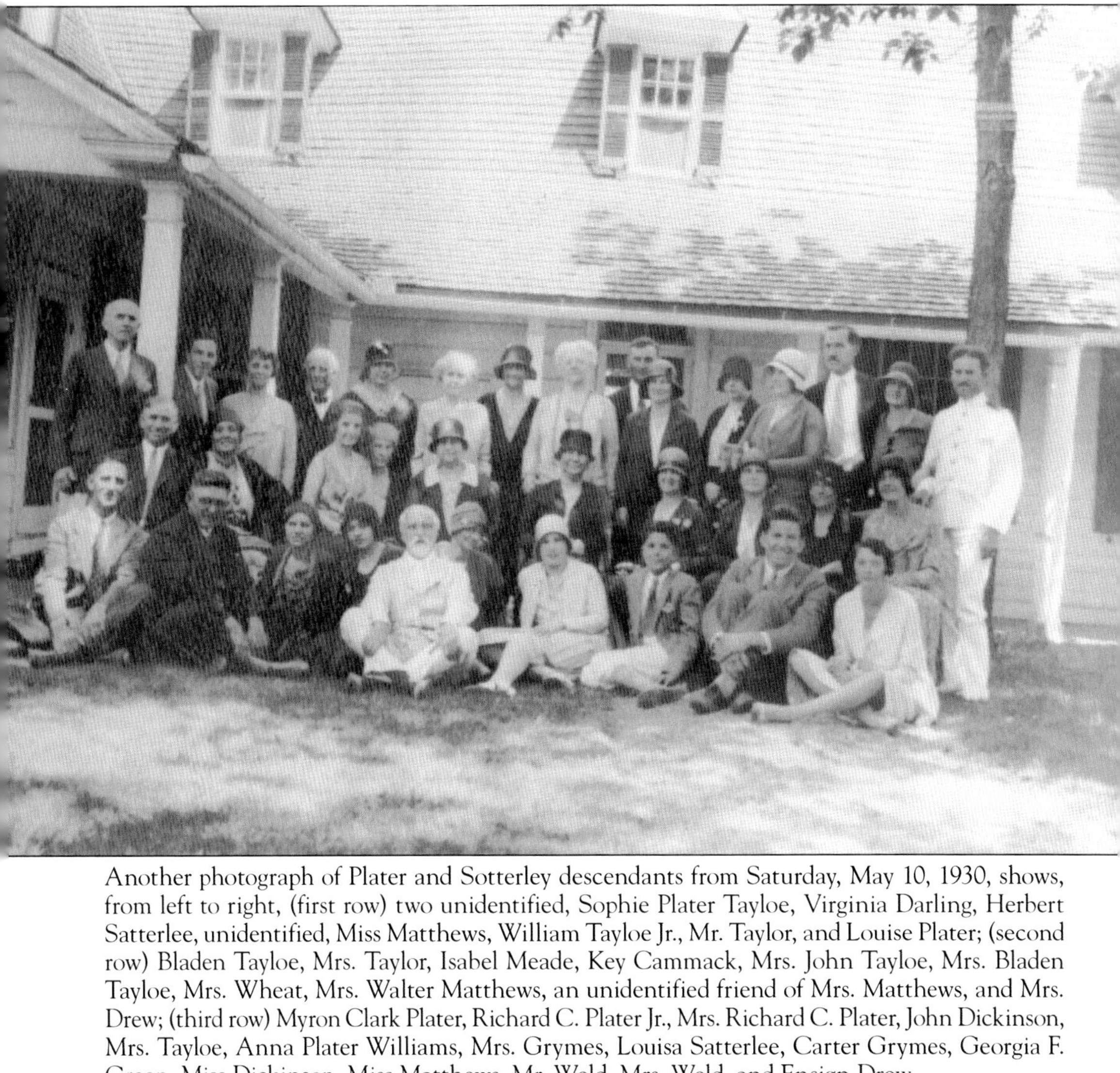

Another photograph of Plater and Sotterley descendants from Saturday, May 10, 1930, shows, from left to right, (first row) two unidentified, Sophie Plater Tayloe, Virginia Darling, Herbert Satterlee, unidentified, Miss Matthews, William Tayloe Jr., Mr. Taylor, and Louise Plater; (second row) Bladen Tayloe, Mrs. Taylor, Isabel Meade, Key Cammack, Mrs. John Tayloe, Mrs. Bladen Tayloe, Mrs. Wheat, Mrs. Walter Matthews, an unidentified friend of Mrs. Matthews, and Mrs. Drew; (third row) Myron Clark Plater, Richard C. Plater Jr., Mrs. Richard C. Plater, John Dickinson, Mrs. Tayloe, Anna Plater Williams, Mrs. Grymes, Louisa Satterlee, Carter Grymes, Georgia F. Green, Miss Dickinson, Miss Matthews, Mr. Weld, Mrs. Weld, and Ensign Drew.

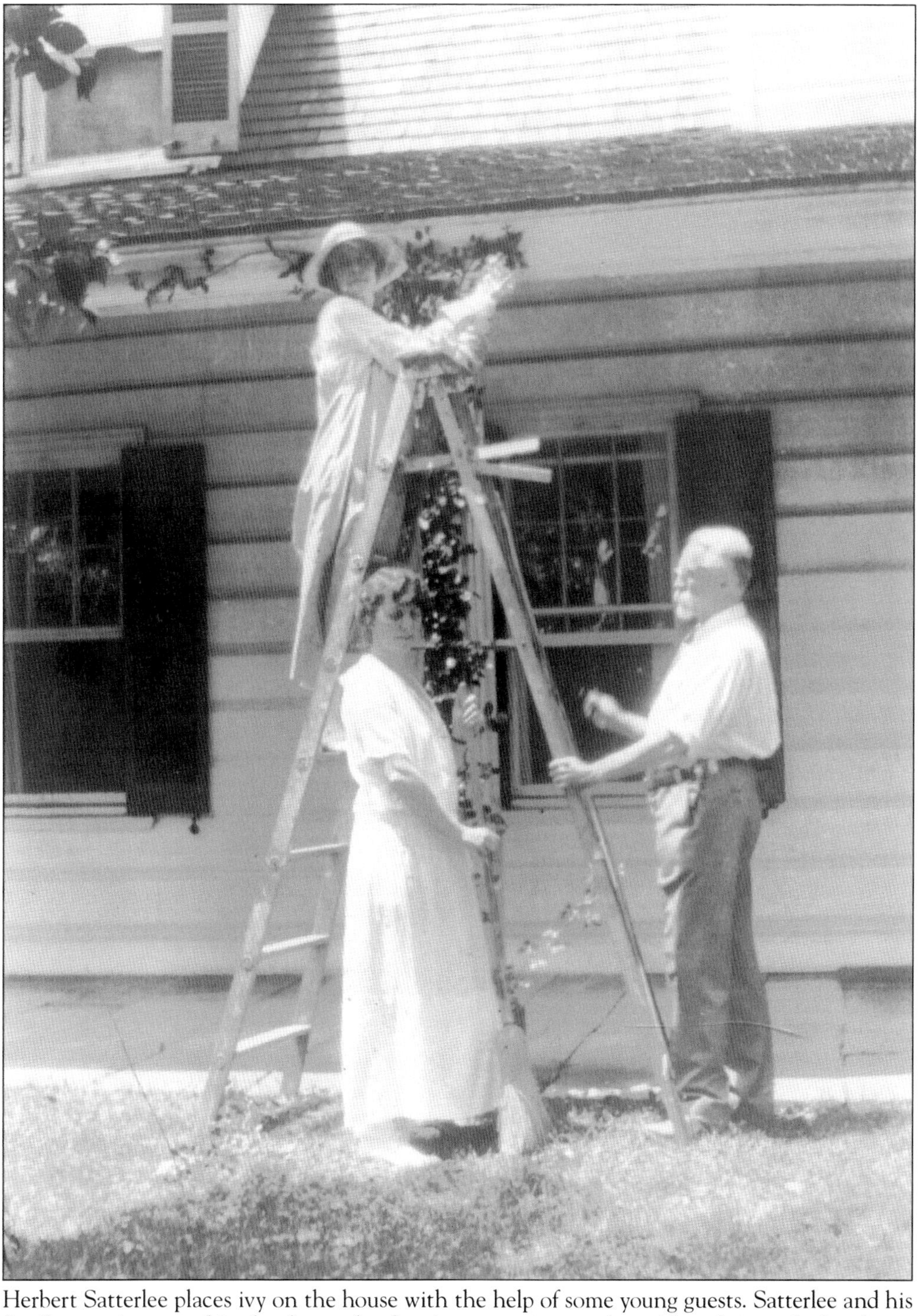

Herbert Satterlee places ivy on the house with the help of some young guests. Satterlee and his family were interested in the day-to-day farming operations and would pitch in with the chores now and then. Farming was seen as an idyllic and iconic American way of life, and Herbert Satterlee's vision included restoring Sotterley's farming community on its 1,000 acres.

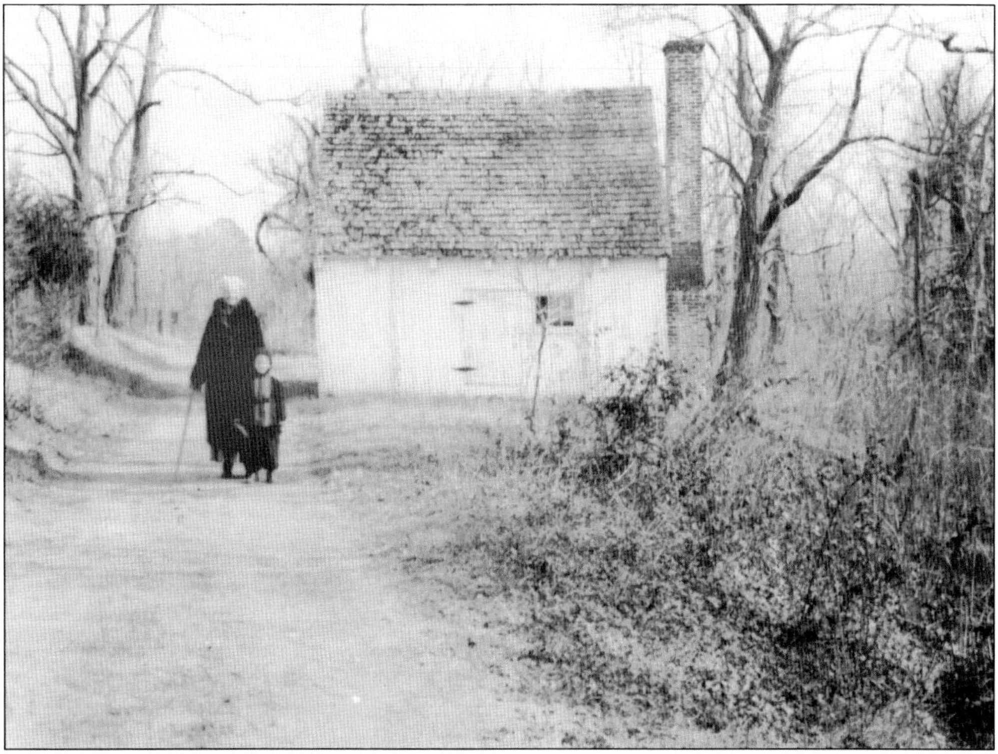

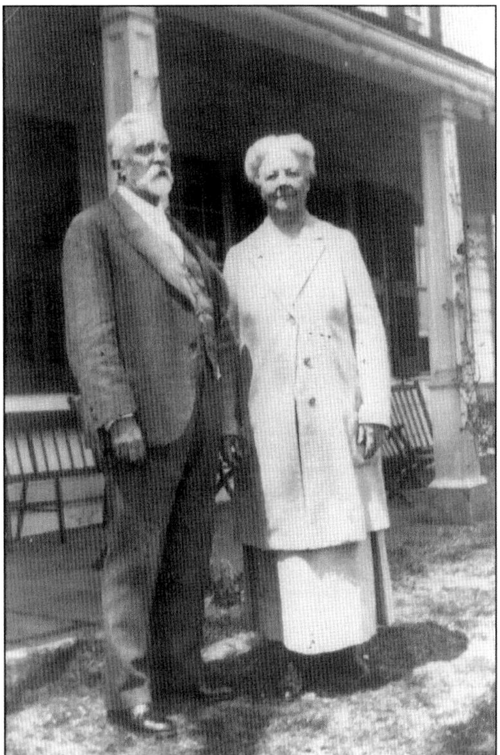

Louisa Satterlee and her granddaughter Sandra Ingalls walk on Rolling Road near the slave cabin in November 1938. The Satterlees spent several Thanksgiving weekends at Sotterley Plantation over the years.

Herbert and Louisa Satterlee enjoyed time together at Sotterley in their later years.

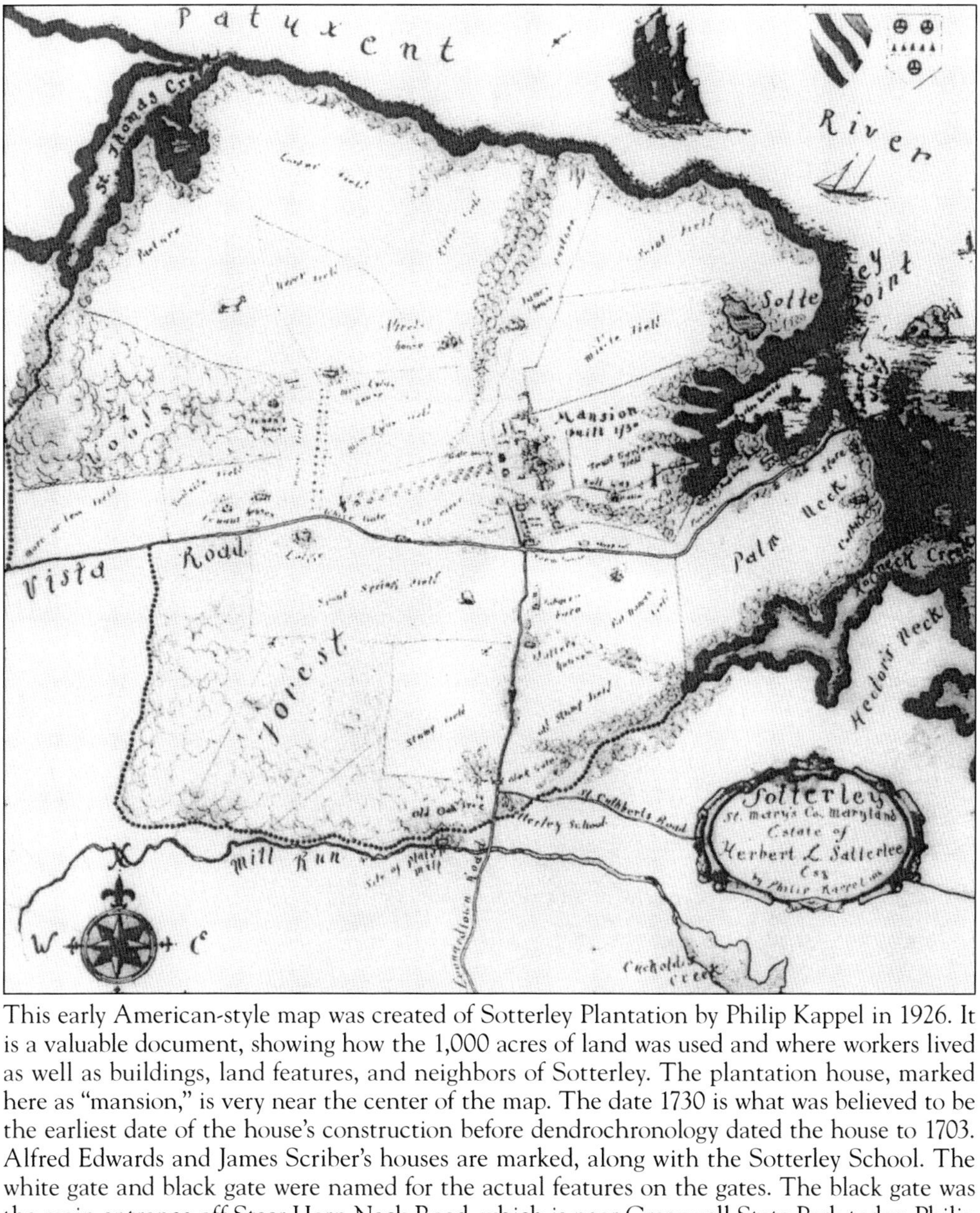

This early American-style map was created of Sotterley Plantation by Philip Kappel in 1926. It is a valuable document, showing how the 1,000 acres of land was used and where workers lived as well as buildings, land features, and neighbors of Sotterley. The plantation house, marked here as "mansion," is very near the center of the map. The date 1730 is what was believed to be the earliest date of the house's construction before dendrochronology dated the house to 1703. Alfred Edwards and James Scriber's houses are marked, along with the Sotterley School. The white gate and black gate were named for the actual features on the gates. The black gate was the main entrance off Steer Horn Neck Road, which is near Greenwell State Park today. Philip Kappel was best known for his marine and architectural etchings. Born in Connecticut in 1901, he was the same age as Mabel Satterlee, and Mabel had Kappel created this map as a gift for her father the year she was married, in 1926.

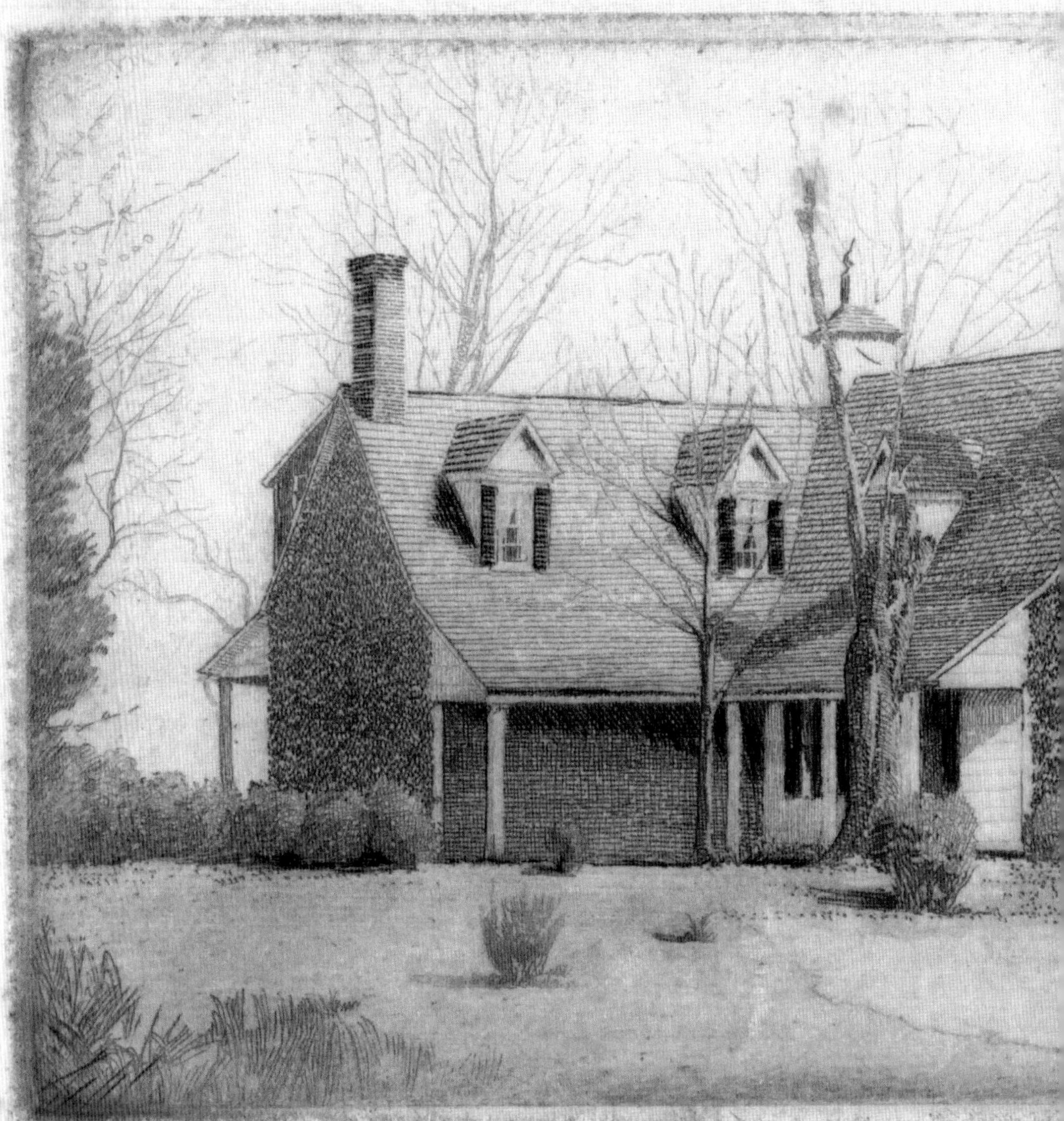

This detailed pencil drawing of the road-side view of the house was done for Herbert and Louisa Satterlee's Christmas cards in 1938. The note inside read, "For Richard and Nan Plater who belong to Sotterley, from Herbert and Louisa Satterlee, with loves' best wishes for a Merry Christmas and Happy New Year." The Satterlees made several booklets, cards, and mementos about Sotterley to send to friends over the years. Sotterley Plantation was just one of their homes, but the Satterlees put their hearts—and their money—into the home, the property, and the farm. Their two daughters,

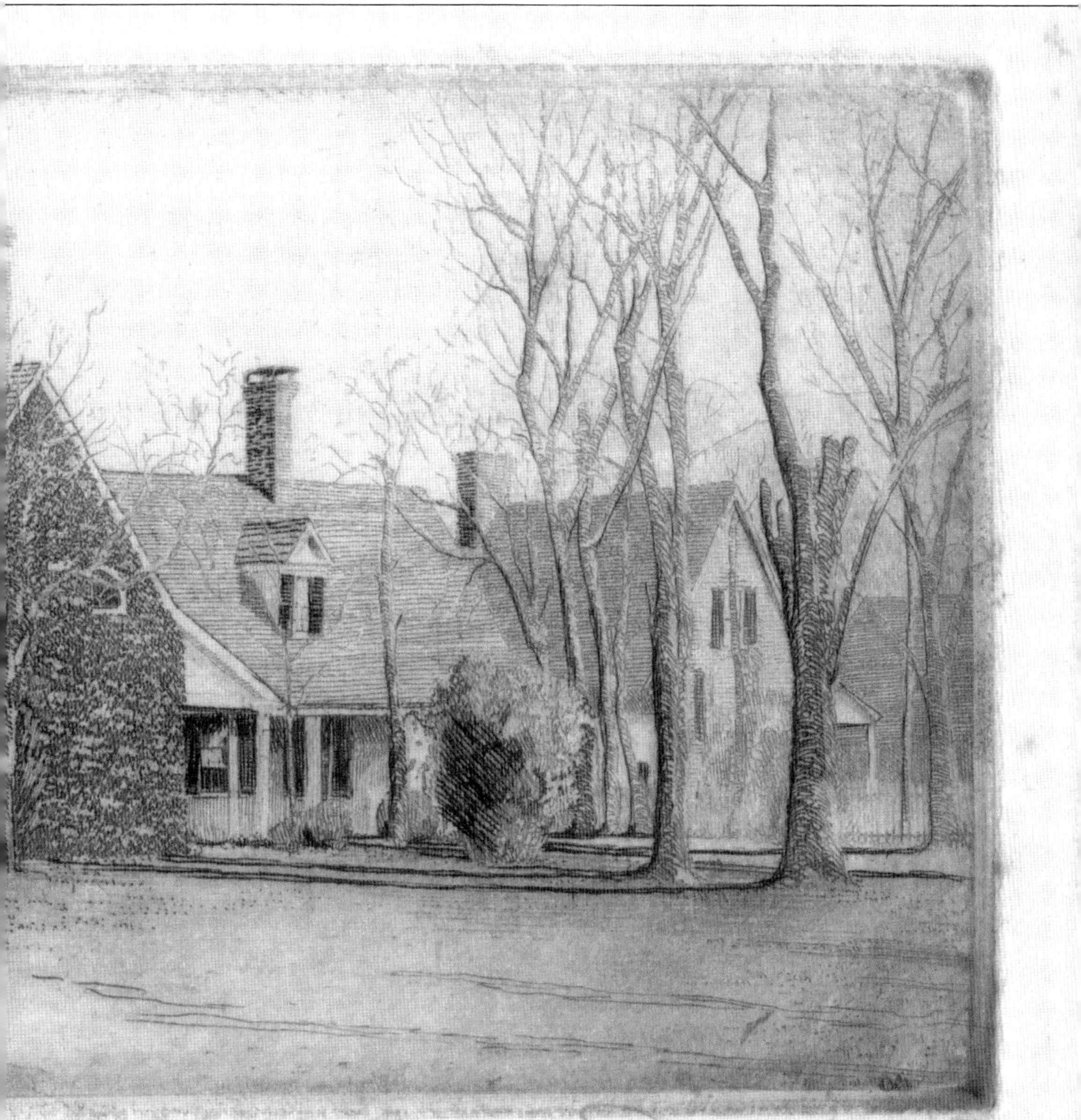

Mabel and Eleanor, grew up with fond memories of their childhood days as Sotterley, relaxing and having fun. Several families' livelihoods depended on Herbert Satterlee, and the farm was the childhood home of many. Descendants of owners and workers can still find their way back to visit and share their history with future generations. Without Satterlee's ownership, Sotterley Plantation would have ended up in ruin or been destroyed, as nearby Resurrection Manor was. Thankfully, Sotterley was saved for all to learn from and enjoy today.

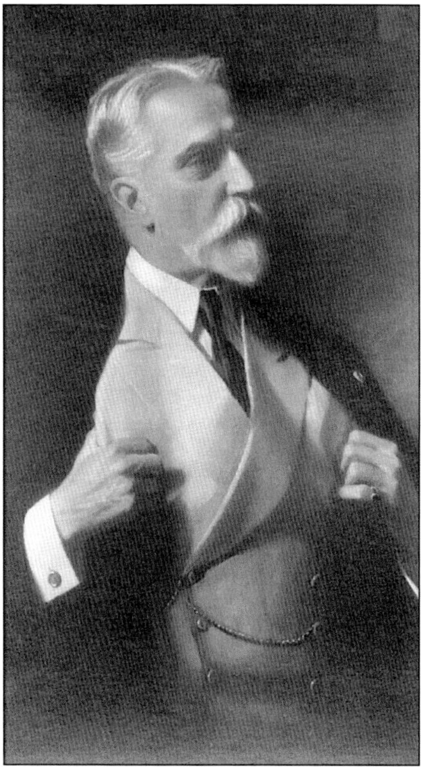

Herbert and Louisa Satterlee were a very traditional couple in rapidly changing times. Herbert wrote and spoke against women's suffrage before women were finally given the right to vote in 1920. As large corporations were broken up and more regulation and taxes were imposed by the government, it became increasingly difficult to maintain the extravagant lifestyles lived by some in the early 1900s. Herbert Satterlee was deeply patriotic, nostalgic, and sentimental, and the Satterlees, as well as most of the past owners of Sotterley Plantation, were part of a clear and strict class system, where money bought privilege, comfort, responsibility, and power. That world changed around them by the time they had seen two world wars come and go. Herbert and Louisa had a close family relationship that was evident in their letters and actions. They were loving parents, and those feelings were reciprocated by their children. Sotterley was a pleasant and happy place for Herbert and Louisa, and they spent almost 40 years and most of their married life visiting Sotterley as much as they could. In October 1946, Louisa Pierpont Morgan Satterlee passed away. In July 1947, in ill health and bereaved from the loss of his wife of many years, Herbert Satterlee died by his own hand at his home in New York. He was 83 years old.

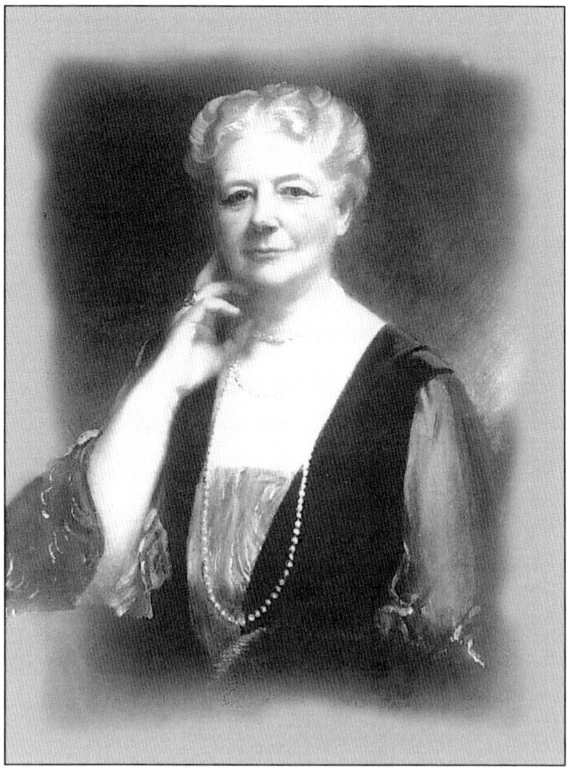

Four

Past and Promise 1948–2012

In 1947, the year after her mother died, Mabel Satterlee Ingalls went through a divorce and suffered the loss of her father. Disappointed that her father's beloved Sotterley Plantation was not left to her, she decided to purchase Sotterley from her father's estate for $120,000, with the intention of selling some of the farm acreage. Members of the Sotterley community were also deeply saddened by Herbert Satterlee's passing, as he had employed them for almost 40 years, through the Great Depression and two world wars. As was the case for workers at Sotterley in previous centuries, the death of an owner always meant change. However, some members of the Barber, Knott, and Scriber families who had worked for Herbert Satterlee stayed on to work for Mabel Ingalls for another 30 years.

Mabel was close to her father. He had encouraged her great love of science and nature. As a child, Mabel spent time with her family at Sotterley and at the Satterlees' other homes, enjoying hunting, fishing, boating, and horseback riding. She married Abbott Ingalls in 1926, and their daughter Sandra was born in 1932. Mabel Satterlee Ingalls had more formal education than anyone else who ever lived at Sotterley, with a degree from Radcliffe, a master's degree from Barnard, and a master's and a doctorate from Columbia University. She worked and served in public health and community development fields her entire adult life.

During her visits to Sotterley, she loved to entertain friends from New York and Washington, DC. She redecorated the plantation house to reflect the times and her tastes, making few structural changes aside from the installation of electricity and modern plumbing. She converted some rooms and outbuildings to guest housing and began to sell parcels of land to friends, leaving the nearly 100 acres that remain today. By the early 1960s, Sotterley had become a financial burden to maintain, as it had been for owners throughout its history. High taxation on the very wealthy was the order of the day, and Mabel Ingalls searched for a way to maintain and preserve Sotterley in order to benefit the community.

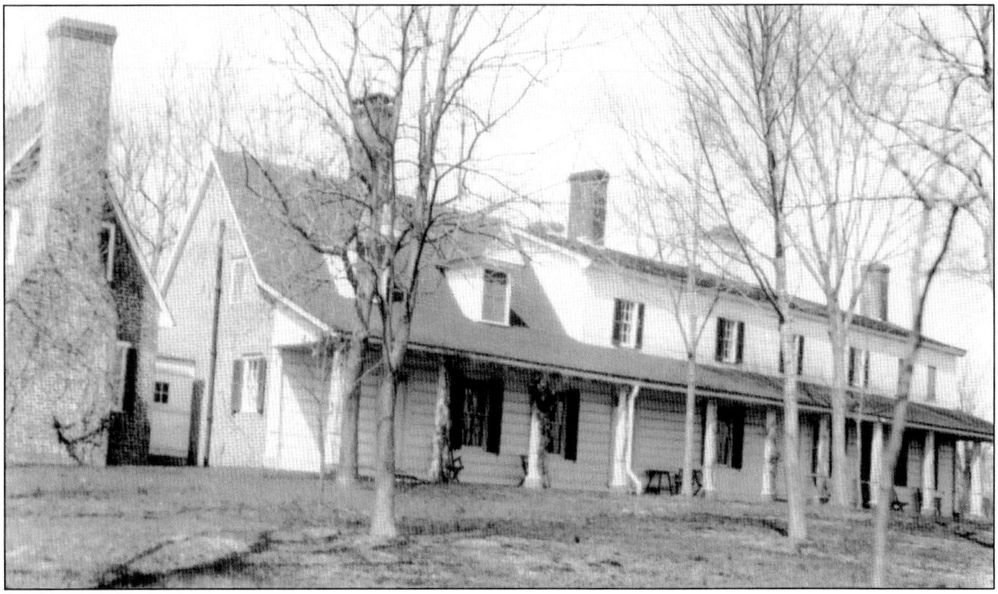

Mabel Satterlee Ingalls set about making Sotterley her own. She had played along with many of the children of the Sotterley community as a child, but as an adult, she had led a different life, far removed from the people living and working at Sotterley. She was well traveled, and she brought friends and influences from those travels to Sotterley, with some friends even buying land and homes nearby. Sotterley's plantation house is seen here from the river side after her father's major renovation and restoration, and it still looks this way today.

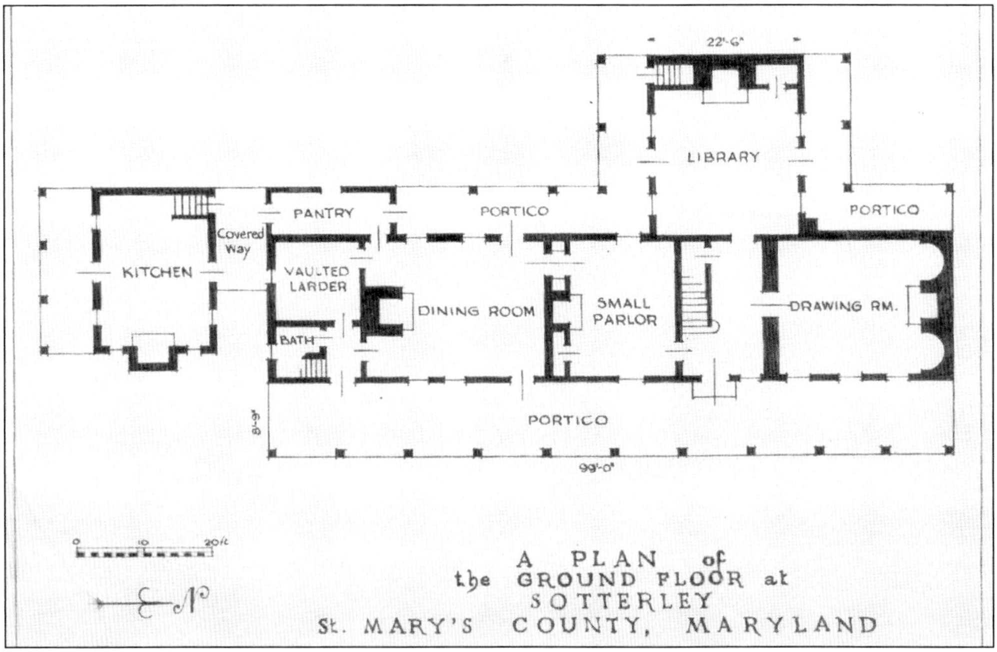

This floor plan of the plantation house shows the rooms named for the Satterlees' use. The New Room was now called the library, and the small parlor was the original Bowles bedchamber. The larder and pantry were leftovers from the 19th-century house, and Herbert Satterlee had added a narrow back staircase.

Mabel Satterlee Ingalls (right) had enjoyed the outdoor life at Sotterley as a child, and she continued to do so as an adult. She was often seen fishing (below), hunting, or gardening. By the time of her ownership, the second generations of the Barber, Scriber, and Knott families were raising their own families on the property, and many stayed on to work at Sotterley. Still suffering the scars of slavery, St. Mary's County was still segregated in the 1950s and 1960s. The African American children who lived on the farm were bused to the Banneker or Phyllis Wheatley schools. They all worked together on the farm, but they could not go to school or to local restaurants or movie theaters together. Schools were not fully desegregated in St. Mary's County until 1967.

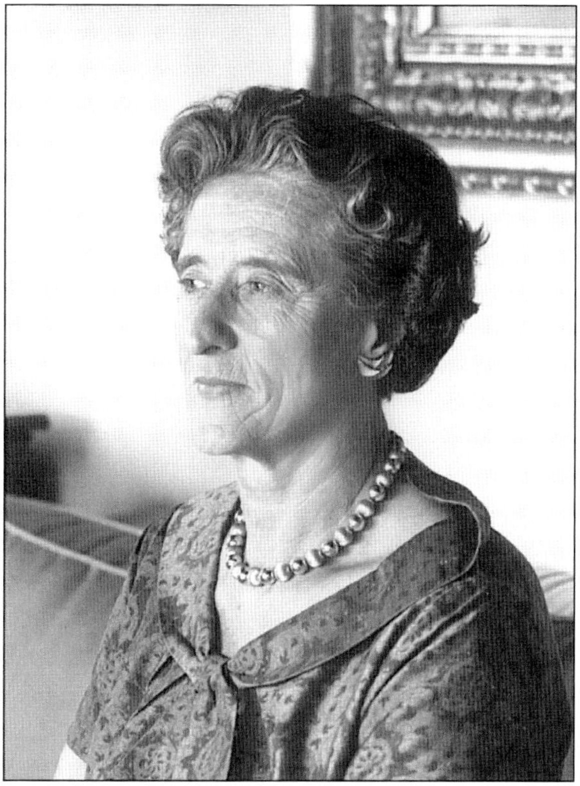

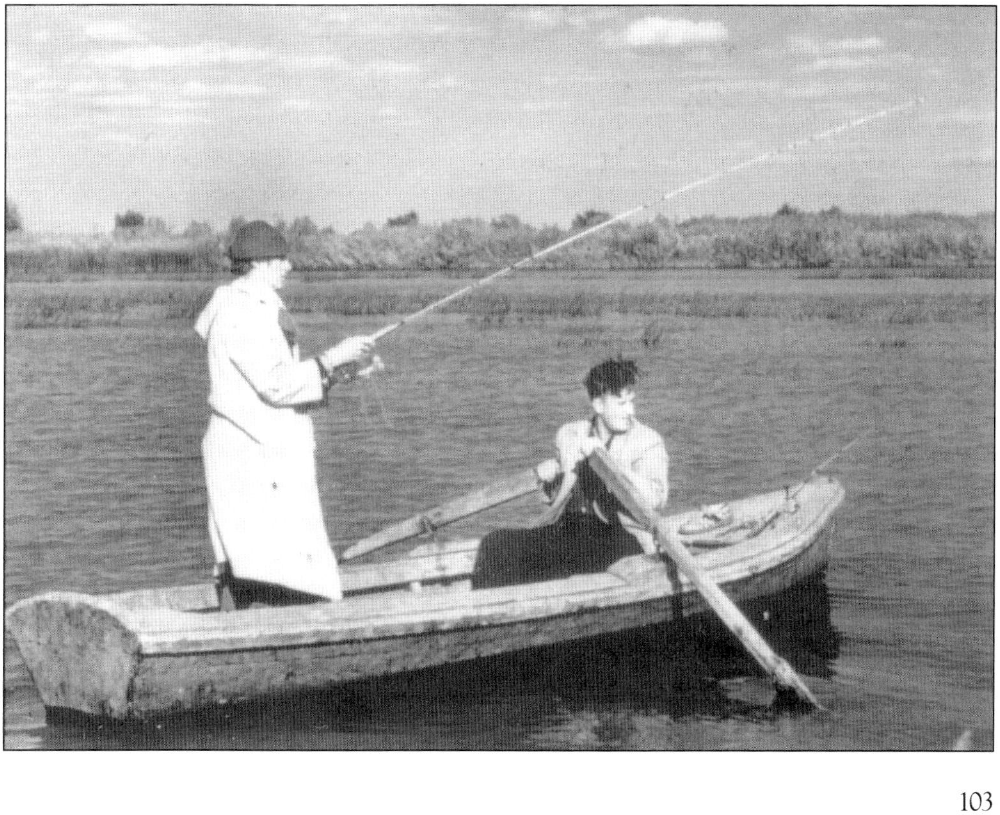

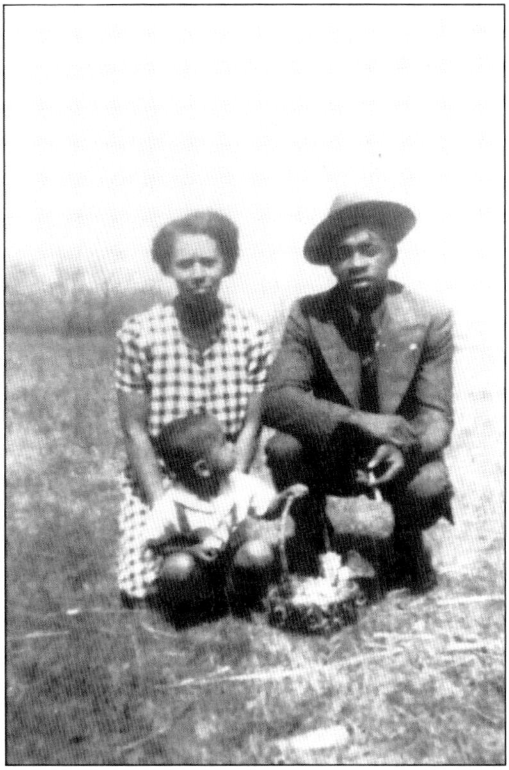

Bernard Barber and his wife, Ruth, are seen at left with their son Bernard Jr. in 1957. They were the second generation of the Barber family to work at Sotterley and had seven children. Bernard Sr. (below) was a farm laborer along with his older brother Ford. Ruth Barber worked in the plantation house and the kitchen, doing cleaning, laundry, and cooking. The Barbers worked at Sotterley all of their lives, but none of their children grew up to make a living at Sotterley. Their son Donald, now a Sotterley trustee, remembers spending many days in the kitchen helping his mother as he was growing up.

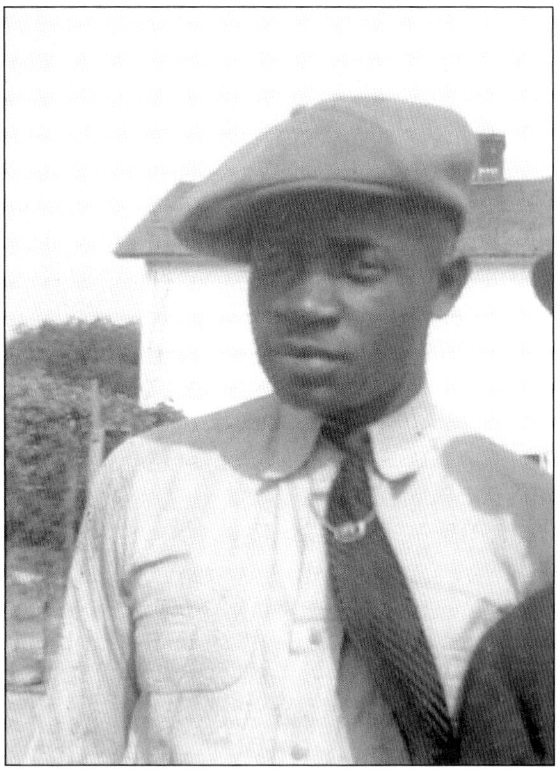

James Scriber (right), his wife, Nettie, and their 16 children worked at Sotterley. Nettie worked in the plantation house while James sharecropped on the farm, helped by their sons from the time they were seven or eight. After Nettie died in 1937, their daughter, also named Nettie, worked at Sotterley and helped take care of her brothers and sisters. As his sons grew up and left Sotterley, James Scriber could not work the farm alone. He married Laura Coats, and, by 1943, he had taken a job at the newly opened Patuxent River Naval Air Station, south of Sotterley. Charles Knott still worked at Sotterley for Mabel Ingalls, and he was joined by his grown sons Edward and Richard to help run the farm. Below, Charles takes a break and stands up as others pick strawberries in the patch that was part of the Sotterley garden.

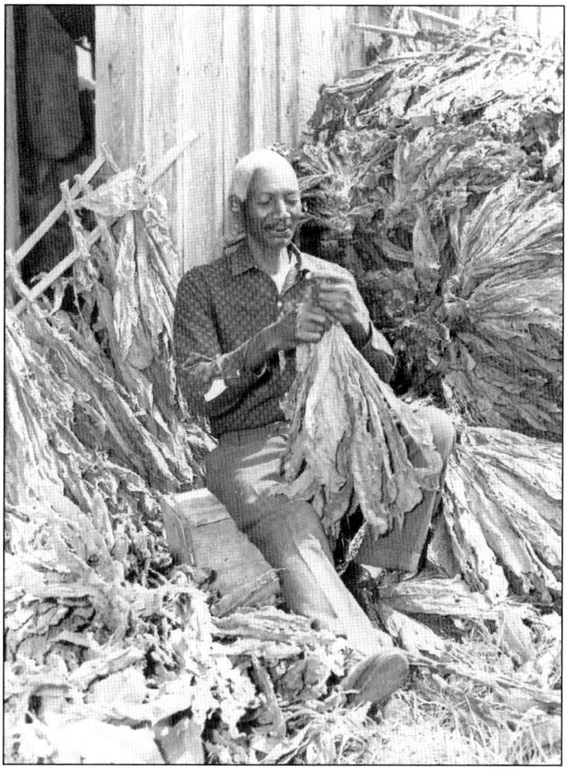

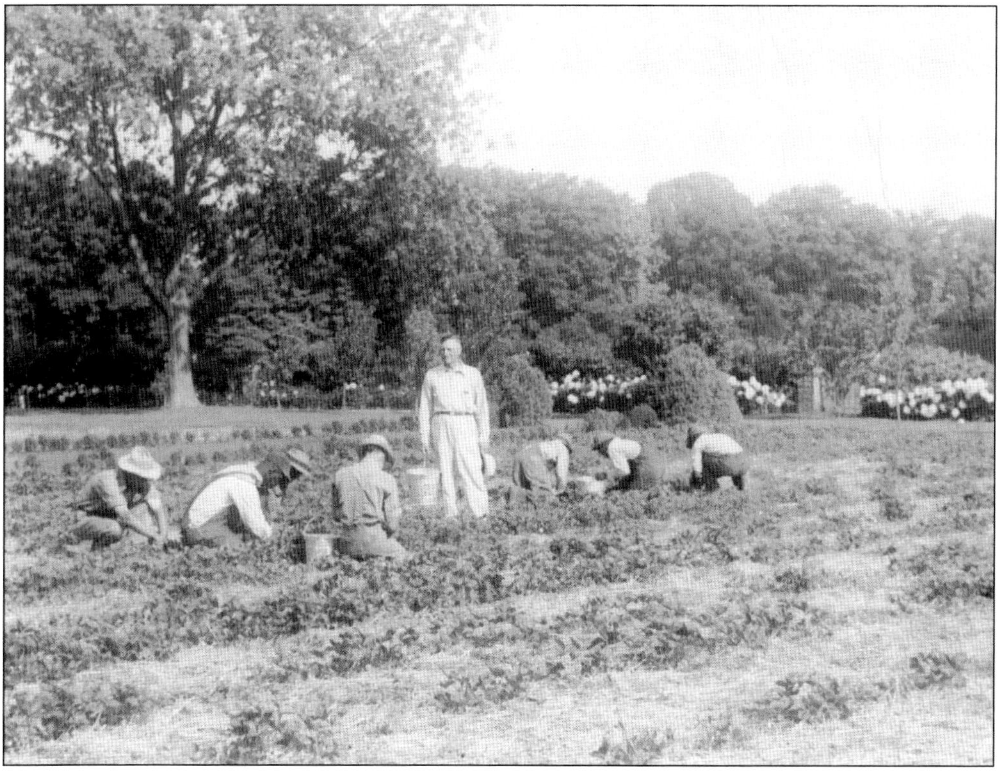

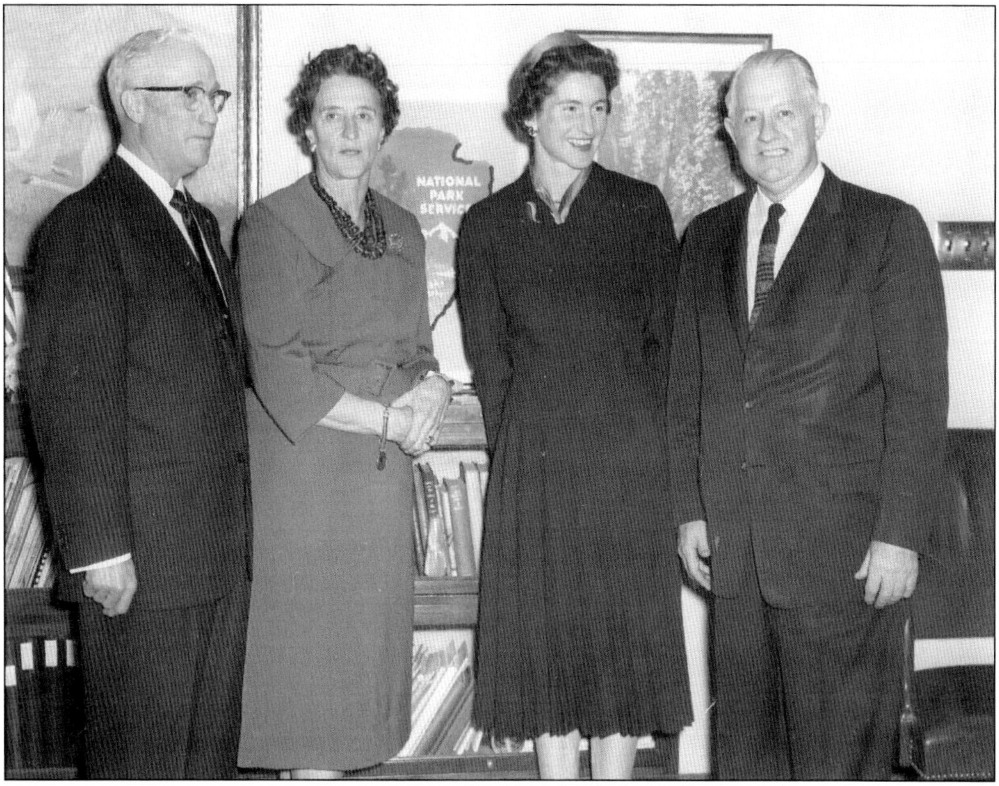

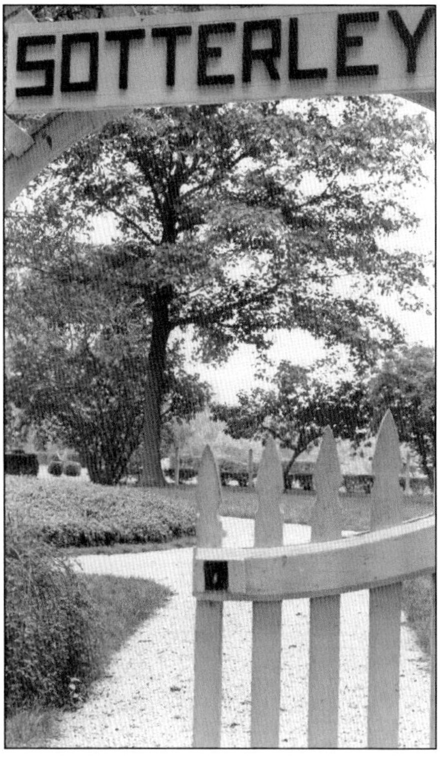

By 1960, Mabel Ingalls found that owning Sotterley was costing her too much money, the last in a long line of owners to experience this. Sotterley had always been an expensive estate to keep together, as war, drought, or a ruined crop heavily influenced profits and losses. Mabel recognized that Sotterley was an important historic property, so her lawyer suggested that she turn Sotterley into a nonprofit foundation and open its doors to the public. One of the first steps was getting a historical designation. Once this was accomplished, Mabel Ingalls created the Sotterley Foundation in 1961. For the early museum, Mable Ingalls hired Edward Knott to work the maintenance side of the property, and Richard Knott was hired to take charge of farming operations. Charles Knott died in 1970, and his wife, India, died in 1975. Above, Sotterley receives its historic property designation from the National Park Service and the National Trust of Historic Preservation in April 1961. From left to right are assistant director Hillory A. Tolson of the National Park Service, Mabel Satterlee Ingalls, Sandra Ingalls Van Heerden, and Robert E. Smith, the chief architect of the National Park Service. At left, Sotterley's rose arbor welcomes visitors in the early days of the museum.

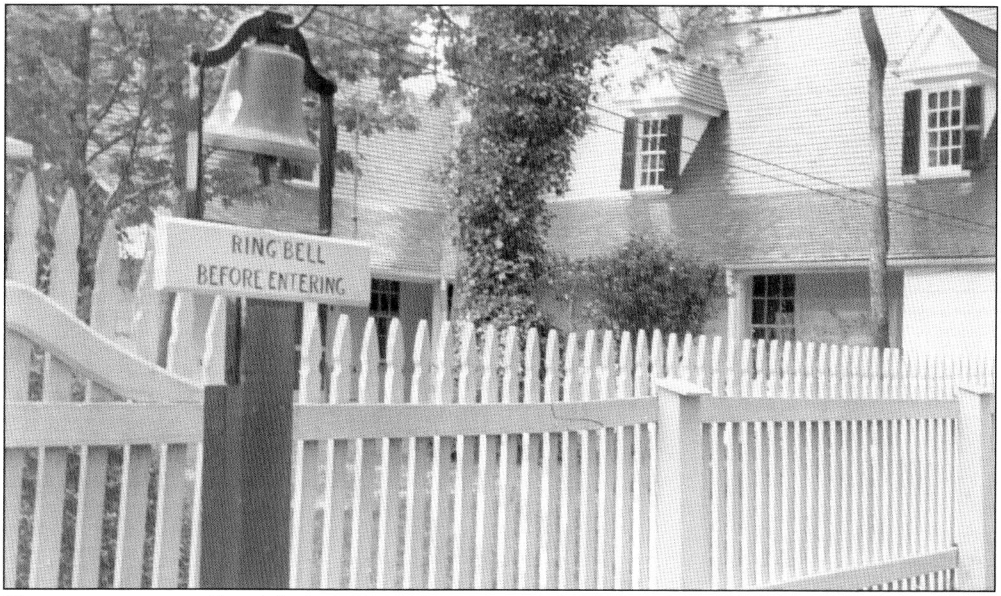

House tours were offered first on an appointment basis and then for a few days a week during the warmer months. In the early decades of the museum, Sotterley only employed two or three people to run the museum operation, and the bell would ring when visitors arrived. Mabel Ingalls still owned the house and would visit and bring friends. Guests could stay in one of the upstairs bedrooms or in one of the other buildings, such as the Spinning Cottage, or in the north and south gatehouses, which were also converted to guest rooms.

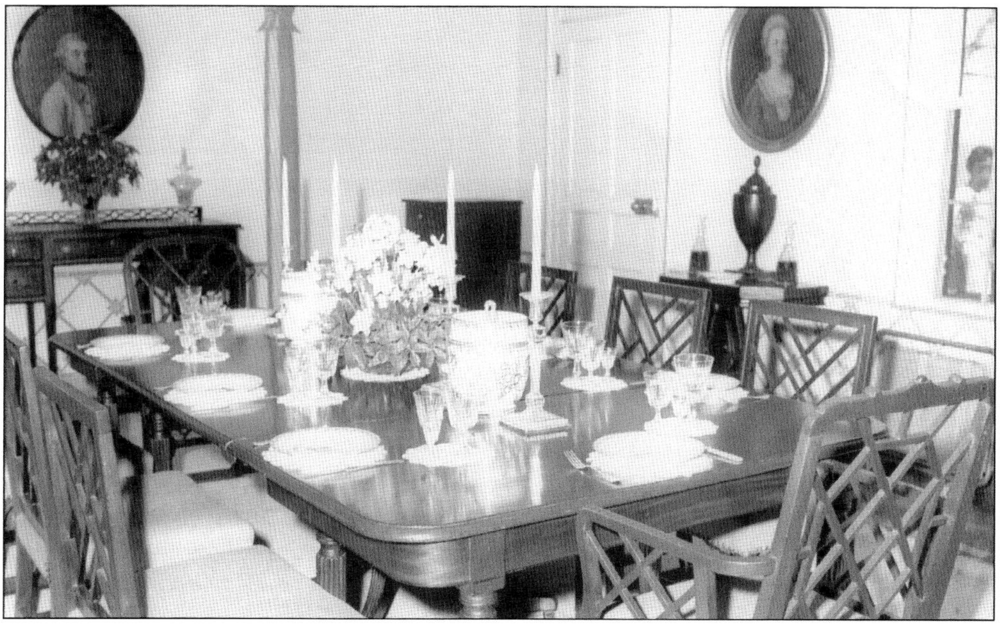

Mabel Ingalls redecorated the dining room and repainted walls between 1955 and 1960. She had the plaster walls removed in the dining room and had a tropical green wallpaper pattern installed, designed after something she had seen at Brighton Pavilion in England. She bought a rug made in Hong Kong to match. This drastically changed the look of this room and modernized its decor to the popular colors of the day.

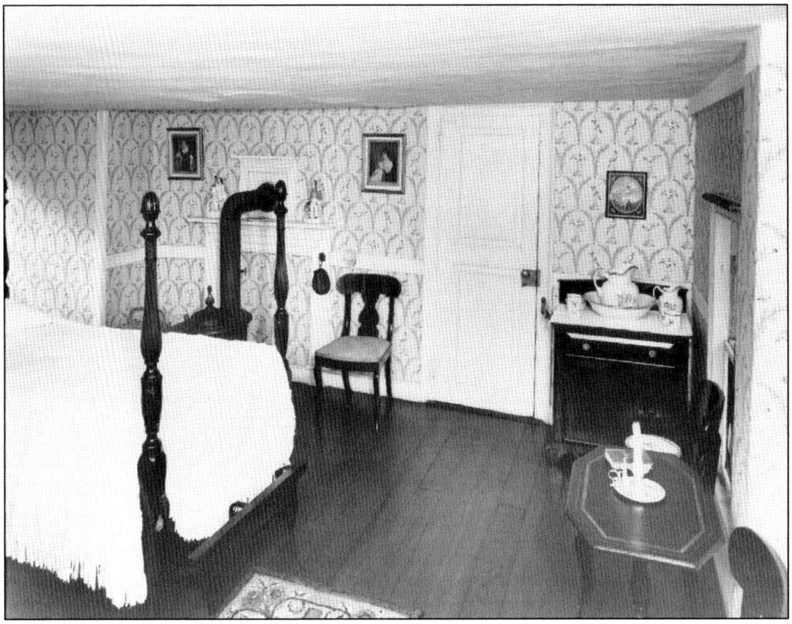

The bedroom above the drawing room, with its very low ceiling, was used in the 1800s by the girls and teachers at the Briscoe boarding school. Mabel Ingalls named it the Briscoe Room.

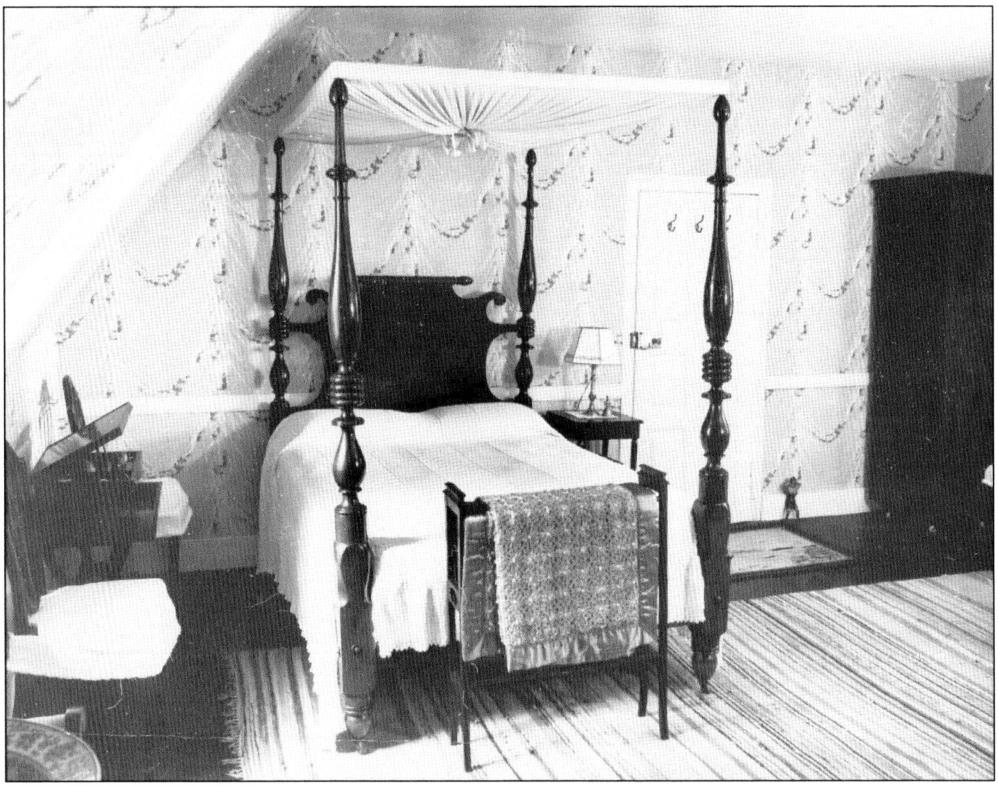

The master bedroom, with its three-quarter bed, was named the Satterlee Room. The upstairs wallpapers were all installed in the 1950s. They were designed and made in New York and chosen by a lifelong friend of Mabel's, Molly Thayer.

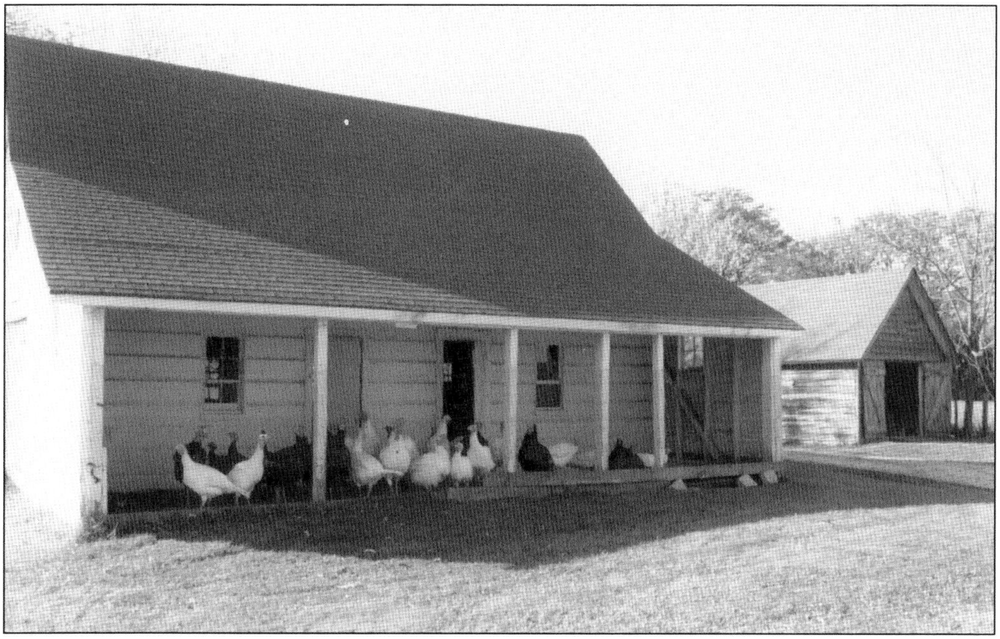

This building was used by India Knott and others to raise turkeys, which were sold in the early gift shop and could be ordered and shipped from Sotterley Farms. The turkey shed was eventually moved to the west side of the garden by the toolshed. It is now used for educational purposes.

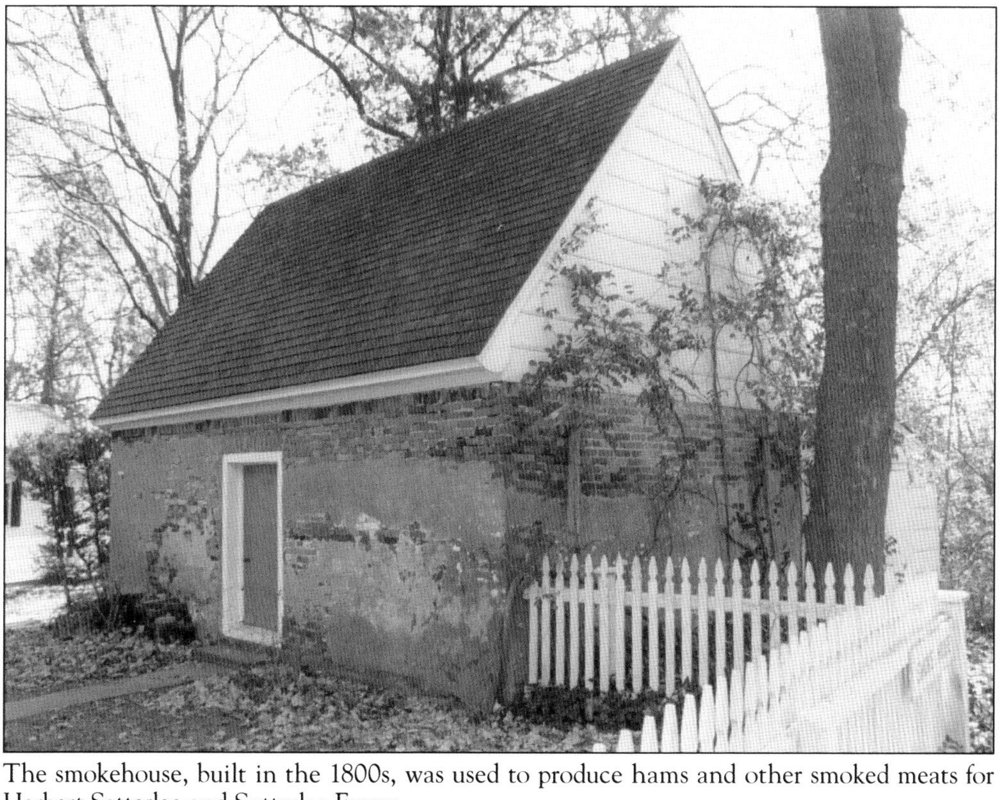

The smokehouse, built in the 1800s, was used to produce hams and other smoked meats for Herbert Satterlee and Sotterley Farms.

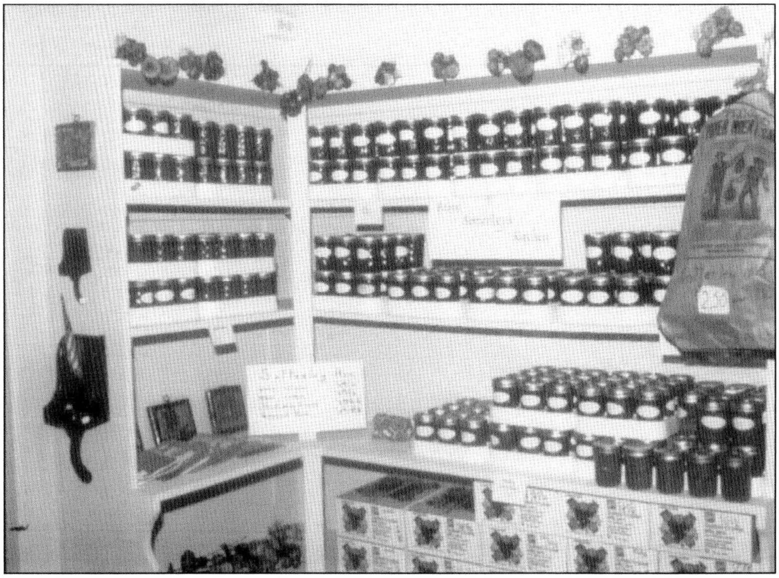

The first gift shop was located in the larder of the house. Preserves, canned goods, hams, turkeys, and postcards could be purchased after house tours.

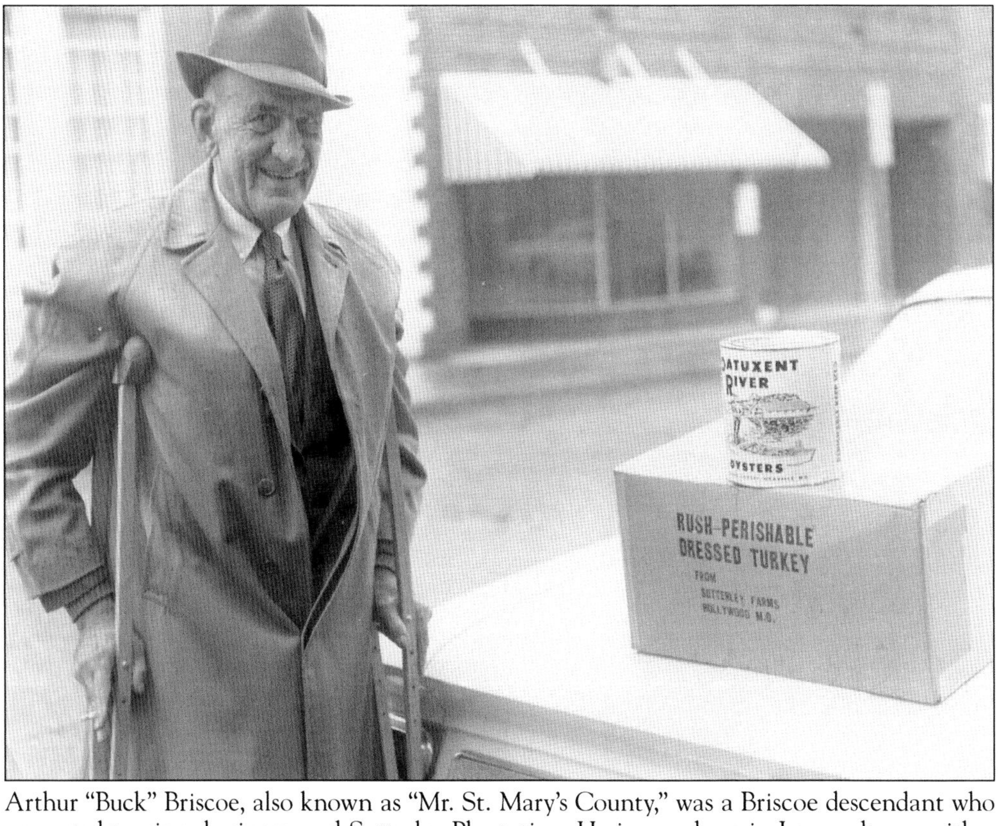

Arthur "Buck" Briscoe, also known as "Mr. St. Mary's County," was a Briscoe descendant who promoted tourism, business, and Sotterley Plantation. He is seen here in Leonardtown with a can of Patuxent oysters and a boxed, dressed turkey from Sotterley Farms ready to be served to Pres. Lyndon B. Johnson at the White House in 1964.

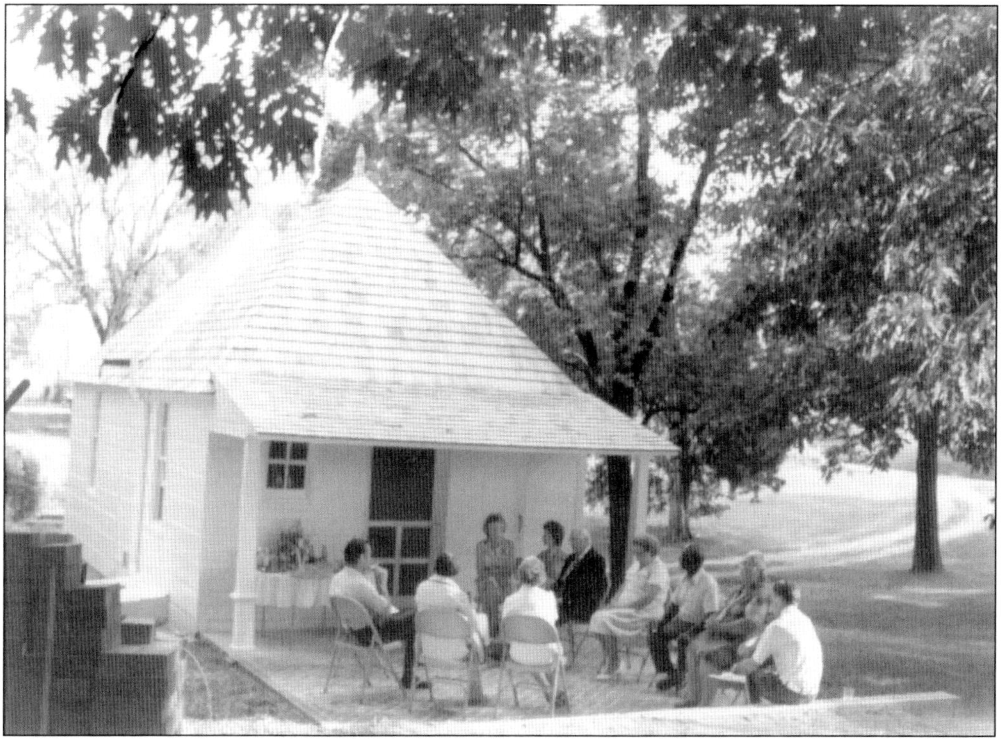

As the museum grew, the gift shop was moved in the mid-1970s to the customs house, a farm building that had been relocated across from the rose arbor. Sotterley staff and volunteers are seen here on the front porch before the grand opening.

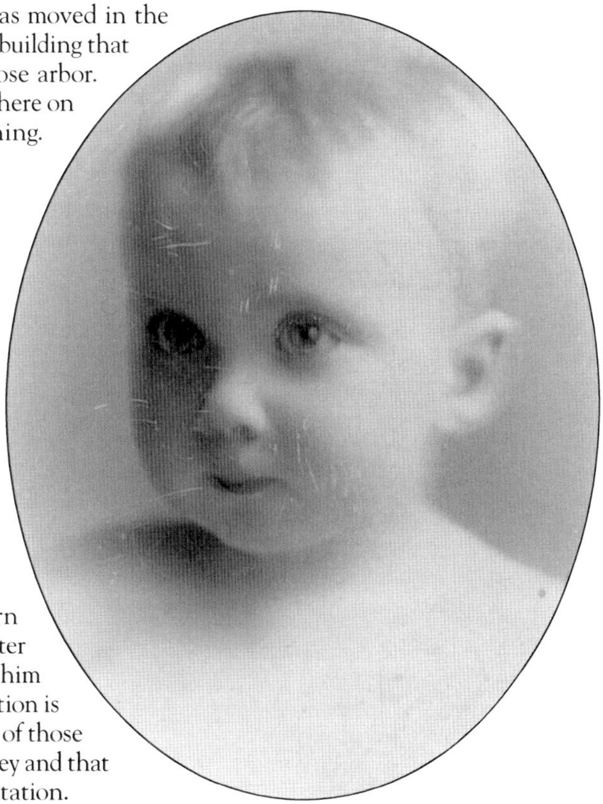

John H.T. Briscoe was the last baby born at the Sotterley plantation house. In later years, Herbert Satterlee would visit with him when he came to Sotterley. The plantation is fortunate to have so many descendants of those that owned, lived, and worked at Sotterley and that can trace their roots to Sotterley Plantation.

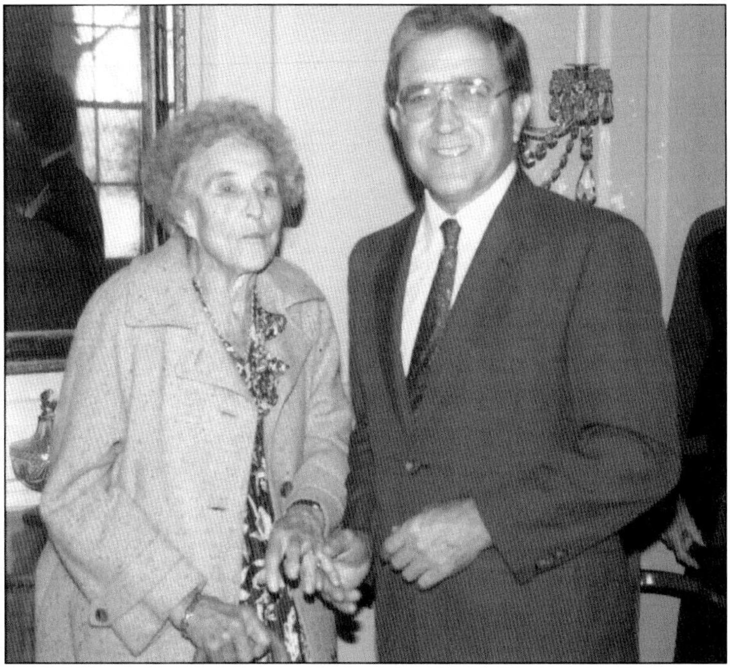

Judge John Hanson Briscoe stands with Mabel Ingalls in the plantation house during a celebration after the county's recognition of Ingalls's contribution to the education of St. Mary's County children in 1990. Judge Briscoe is a descendant of John H.T. Briscoe and has served Sotterley for many years. He is now a trustee emerita.

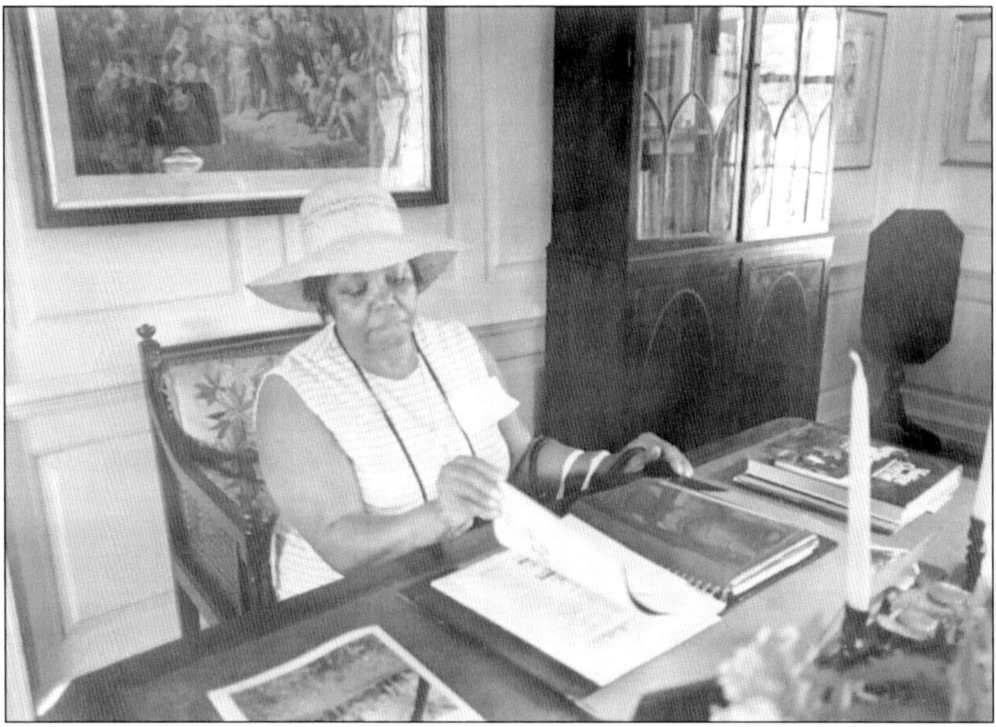

In 1978, Agnes Kane Callum and 103 Cane descendants visited Sotterley Plantation and were greeted by Mabel Satterlee Ingalls. Callum is seen here at Herbert Satterlee's desk in the library, or New Room, looking at records and oral traditions that she presented to Sotterley about her ancestor, Hilry Cane, and his family, who lived as enslaved and then freed people at Sotterley in the 1800s.

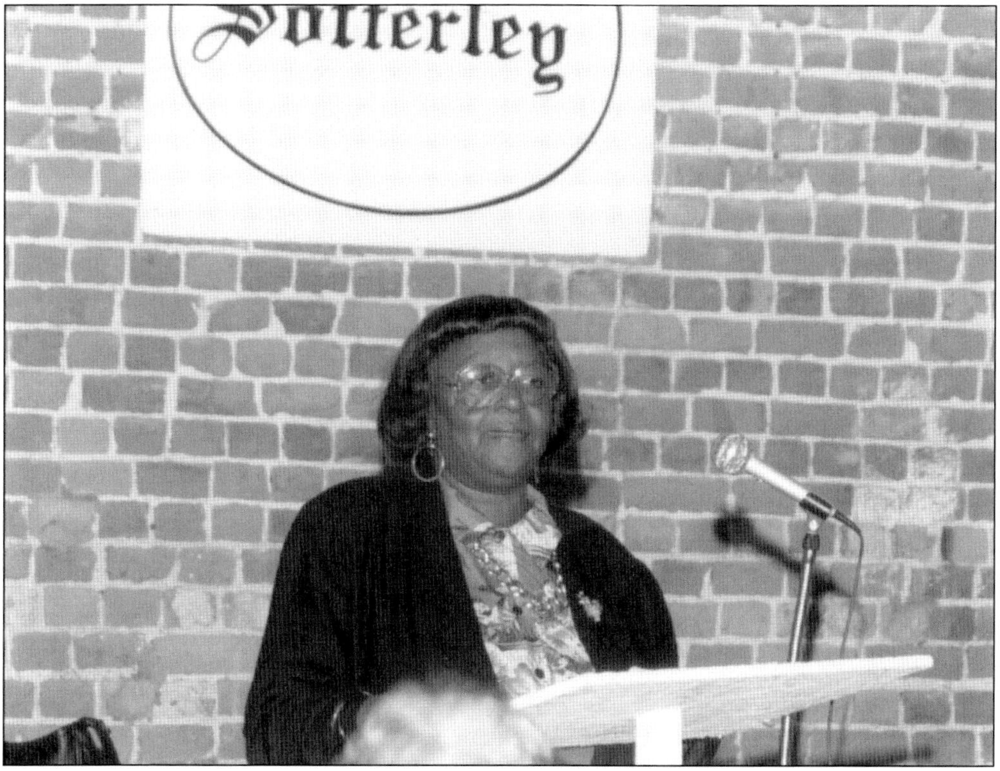

Above, Agnes Kane Callum speaks at a board meeting as a member of Sotterley's board of trustees. Callum is seen below with fellow Sotterley descendant John Hanson Briscoe. The two worked together to promote and raise awareness about Sotterley Plantation in order to save it in the 1990s. This was filmed for the *Today Show* on NBC.

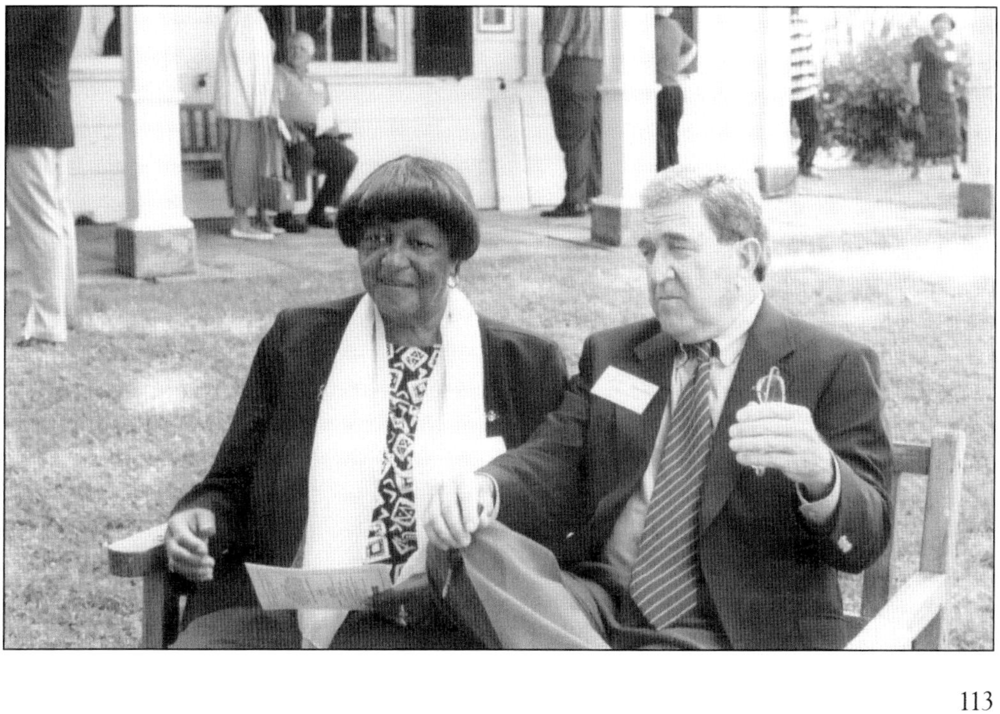

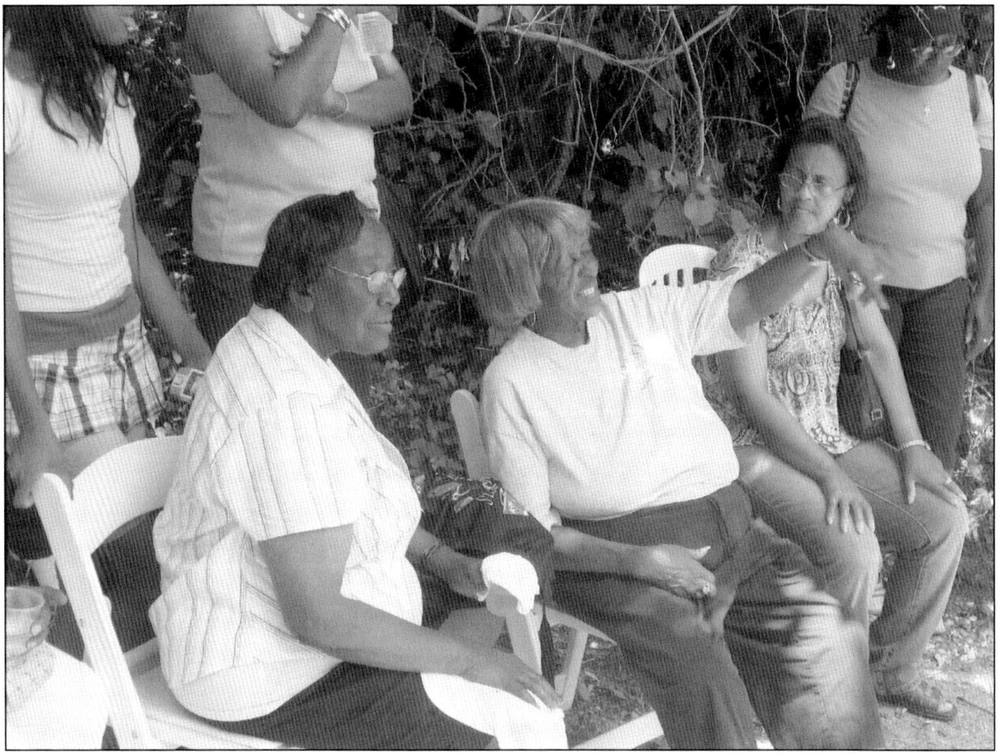

Agnes Kane Callum (above, left) continues to bring people to Sotterley and educate them about her ancestor's history at the plantation. A pilgrimage always includes a visit to Sotterley's only remaining 1830s slave cabin (below). In the 1800s, the Kanes' ancestors lived in this cabin or one like it.

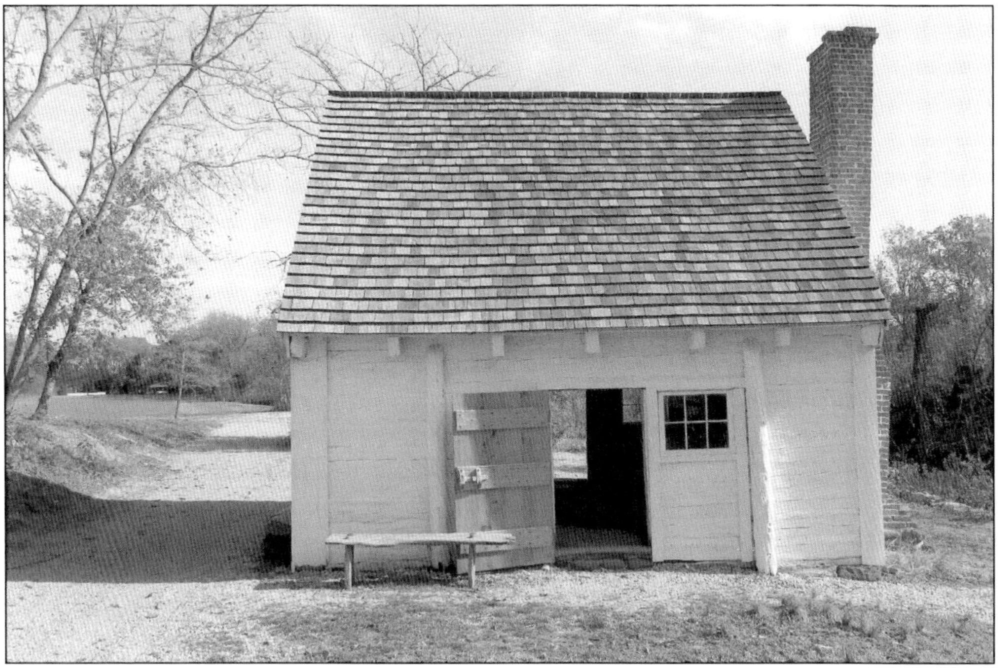

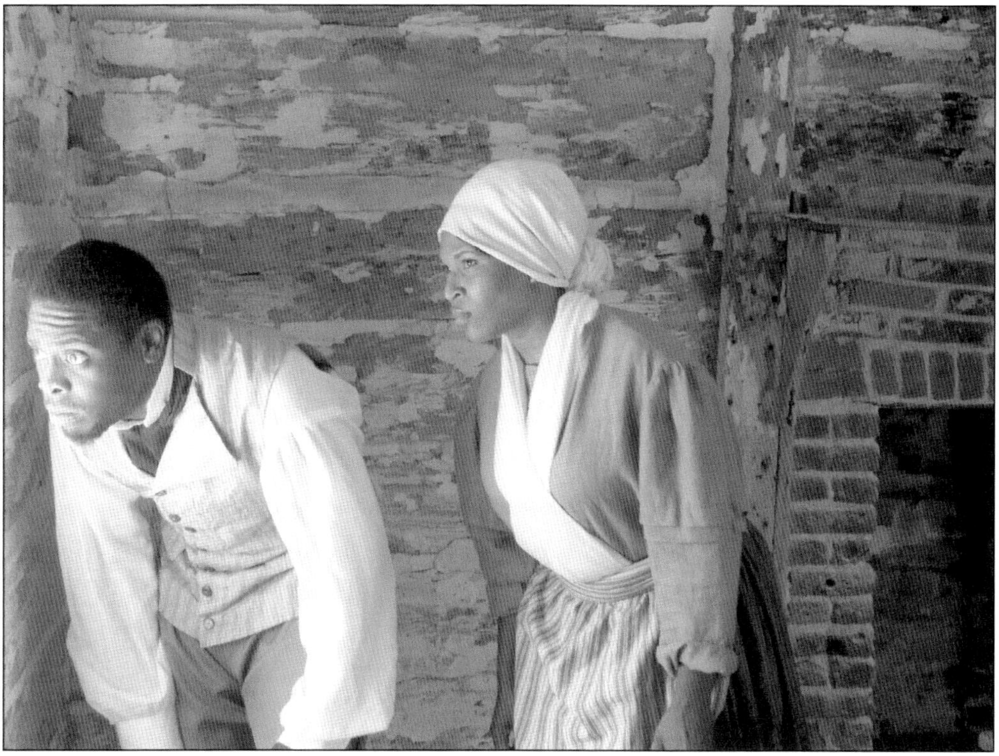

Historic Sotterley continues to bring awareness and education about the history of southern Maryland. To commemorate the bicentennial of the War of 1812, Sotterley produced the living history presentation *The Choice*. Written by Dale Jones, the production incorporated research into the actual events of June 1814, when 49 Sotterley slaves escaped to the British. Local actors Jay Hunter and Shemika Berry (above) brought to life Peregrine Young and Elcie, enslaved people at Sotterley who had to make the difficult choice to leave with the British or to stay. Sotterley's slave cabin is seen below from the plantation house in spring.

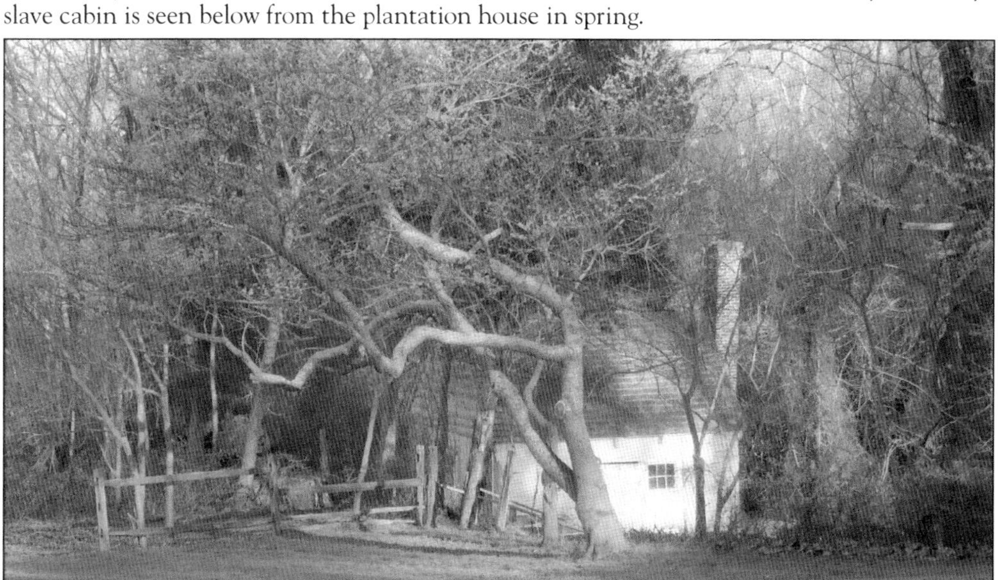

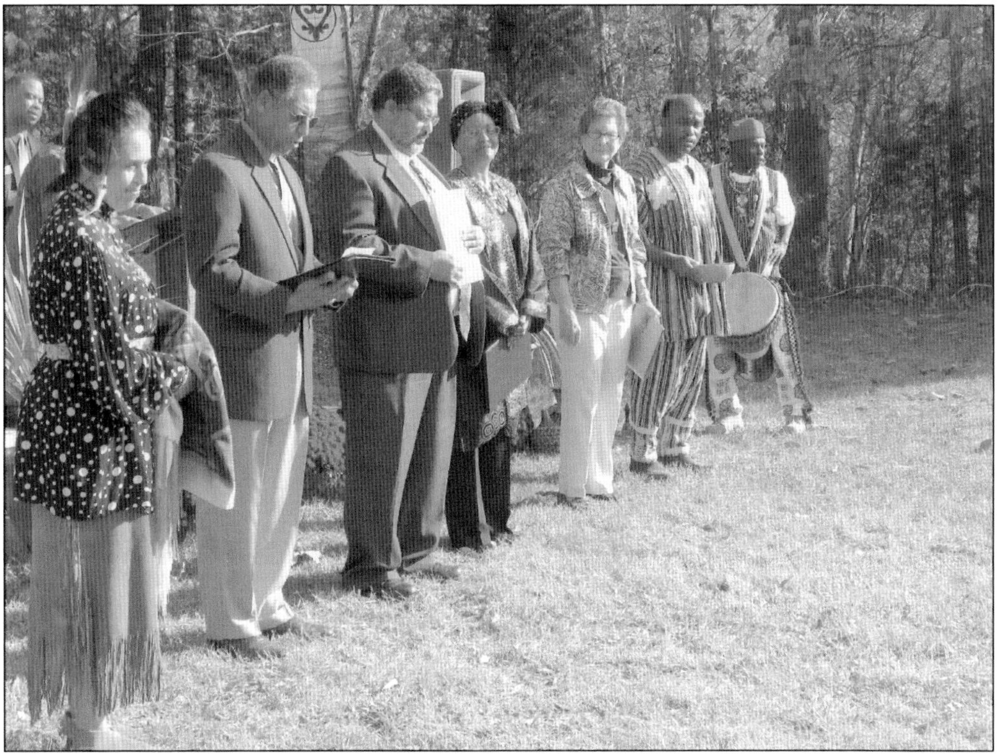

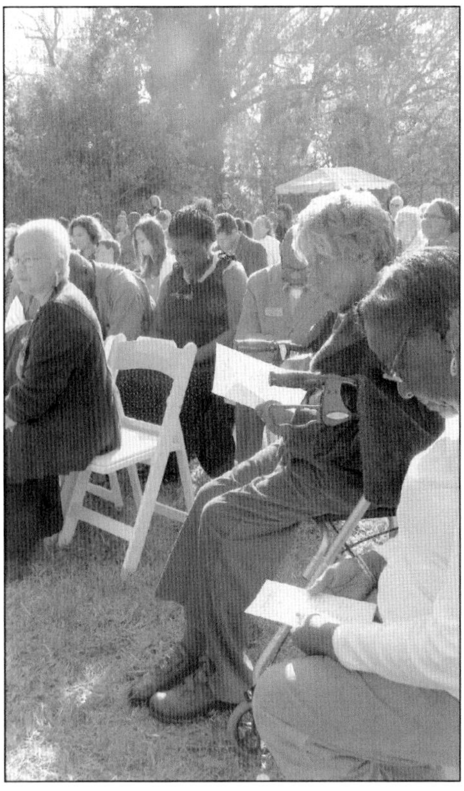

On November 12, 2012, Historic Sotterley Plantation came full circle by becoming part of the Middle Passage Ceremonies and Port Markers Project. As it is only one of three sites in Maryland recognized as a middle passage arrival point, along with Baltimore and Annapolis, a remembrance ceremony was held at Sotterley for all of those who lost their lives being transported here against their will from Africa. Participants represented the different cultures and religious groups whose ancestors were affected by early European settlement and the transatlantic slave trade. Participants included, from left to right, (first row) Natalie Proctor, Piscataway People; Rev. Irvin Beverley, United Methodist Church Bethesda; Rork Brown and Dr. Francine Hawkins, St. Peter Claver Catholic Church, St. Inigoes; Anne Harrison, Patuxent Friends; Kofi A. Ofori, Akan Priest; and Joseph Ngwa, Fontomfrom Drums; (second row, extreme left) Kelsey Bush, commissioner of the Maryland Commission on African American History and Culture. At left, other participants included, from left to right, Ann Chinn, executive director of the Middle Passage Ceremonies and Port Markers Project; Agnes Kane Callum; and Dr. Martina Callum.

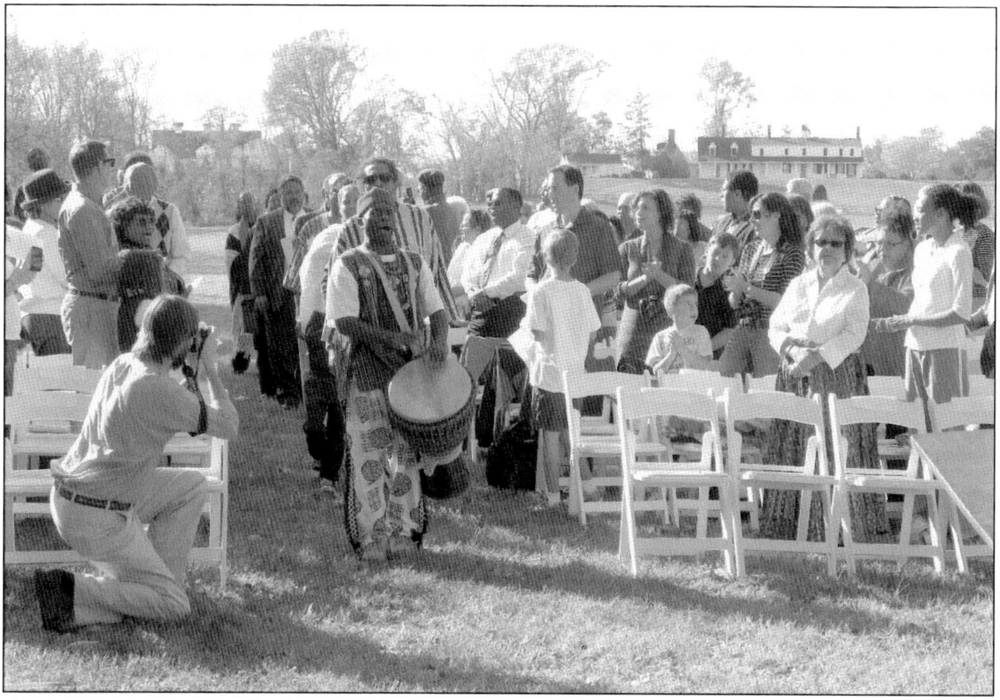

Above, a procession walks through the audience at the Middle Passage Ceremony on November 12, 2012. Sotterley's plantation house and barn are in the background. Below, participants toss 29 carnations into Sotterley Creek to represent all who perished during the middle passage.

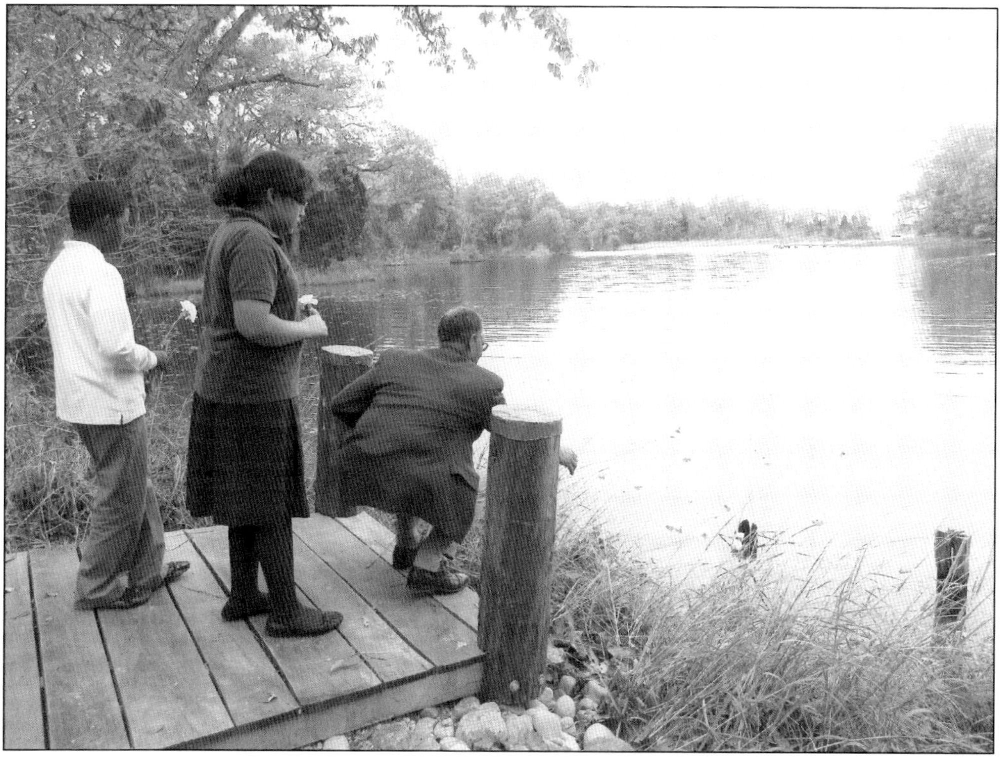

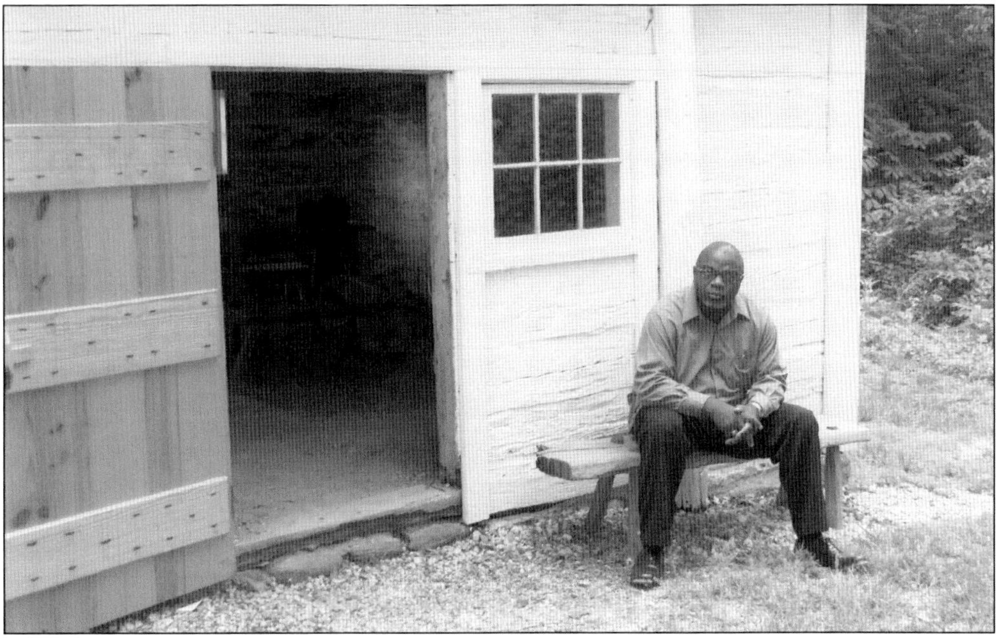

Joseph McGill sits in front of Sotterley's 1830s slave cabin on July 9, 2011, as part of the Slave Dwelling Project. McGill travels around the United States spending the night in slave dwellings, drawing attention and support for these structures and highlighting their importance in American history to help ensure their preservation.

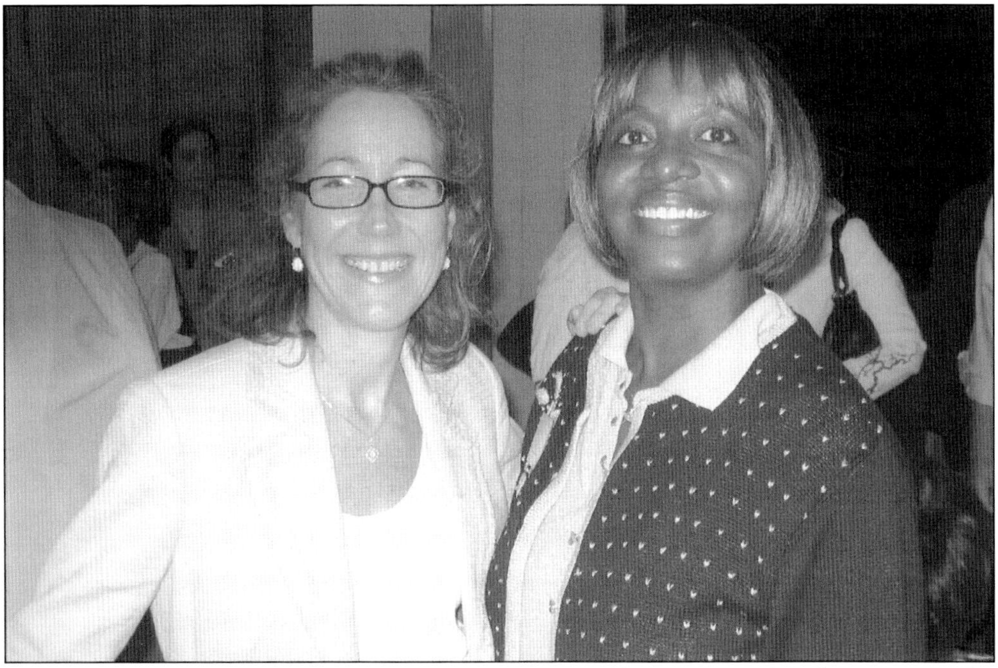

Sotterley descendants Janice Briscoe (left) and Martina Callum pose together during a Sotterley event. Sotterley descendants and trustees, as their parents before them, they both continue to give of their dedication, means, and time to help Sotterley Plantation continue its important mission to educate future generations.

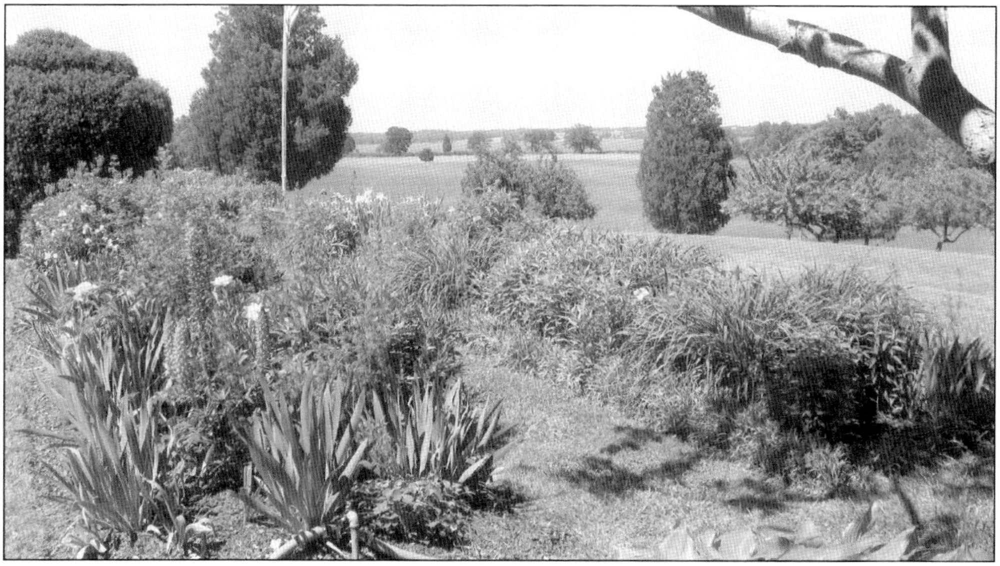

The photograph above shows a breathtaking view of Sotterley's revival gardens looking toward the Patuxent River. The garden is made possible by the tireless work of Sotterley's all-volunteer Garden Guild, which was the brainchild of early museum director Elizabeth Harman to help preserve the gardens. Many members have served in the guild over the years. The photograph below shows members gathering holiday greens for Sotterley's December events. They represent the many dedicated and talented people that share their time and talents so that the public can enjoy this beautiful formal garden. From left to right are Robert Aldridge, Rich Richardson, Mary Roderick, Annie Skaggs, Carol Fugate, Tina Keeler, Liz Delorme, and Gordon Moe.

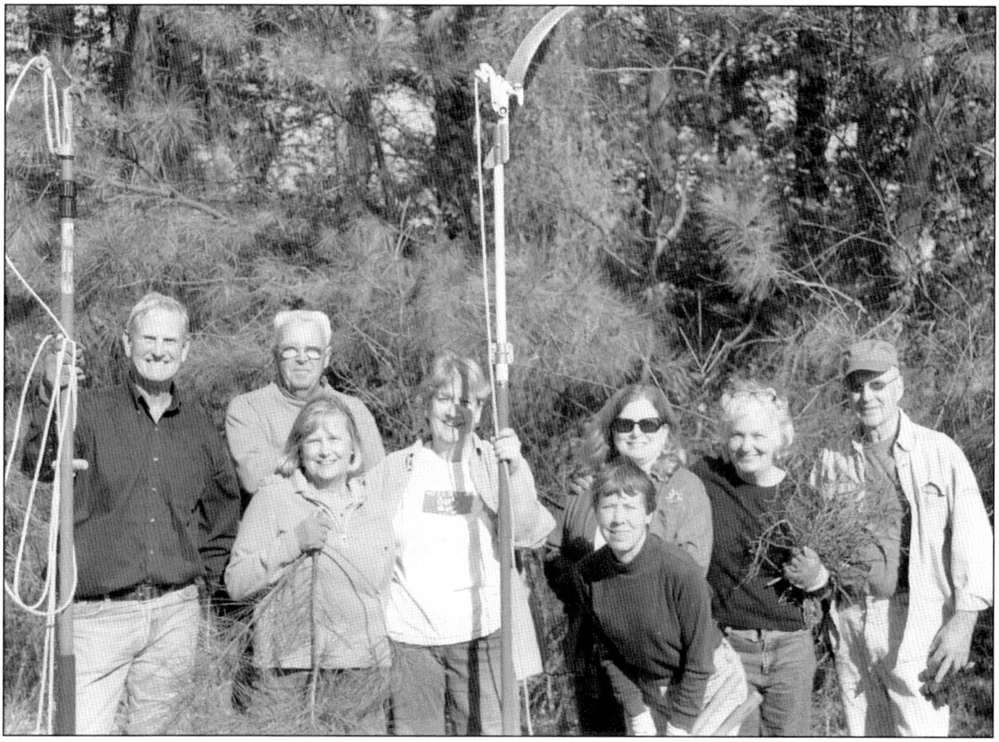

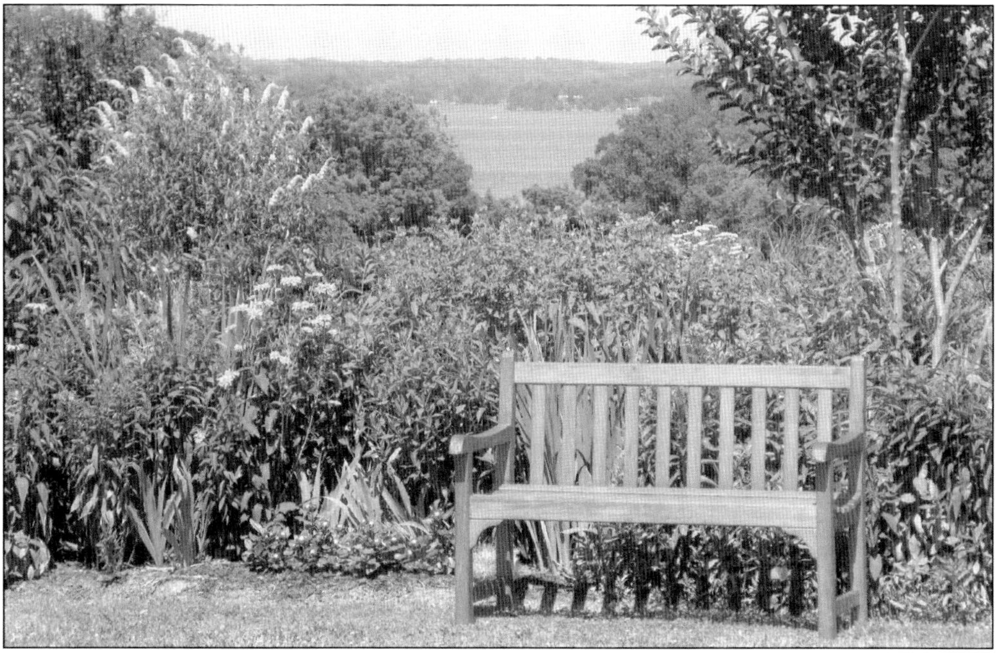

Sotterley's garden in full bloom is as inviting today as it has ever been. Sotterley's location and natural beauty have been drawing people to it for hundreds of years. With a spectacular view of the Patuxent River, visitors can see miles of riverfront and all of the surrounding plant and animal life.

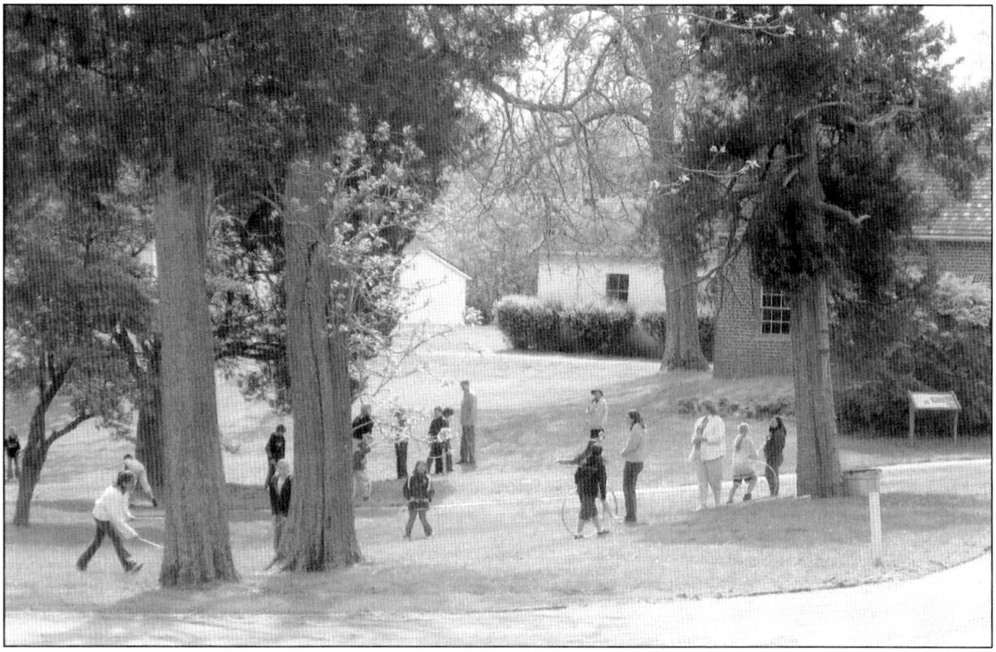

Sotterley Plantation puts all of its resources to good use. This class of schoolchildren is participating in one of Sotterley's education programs on site. The programs provide authentic learning experiences that enhance lessons from the classroom. Thousands of Maryland schoolchildren visit Sotterley each year.

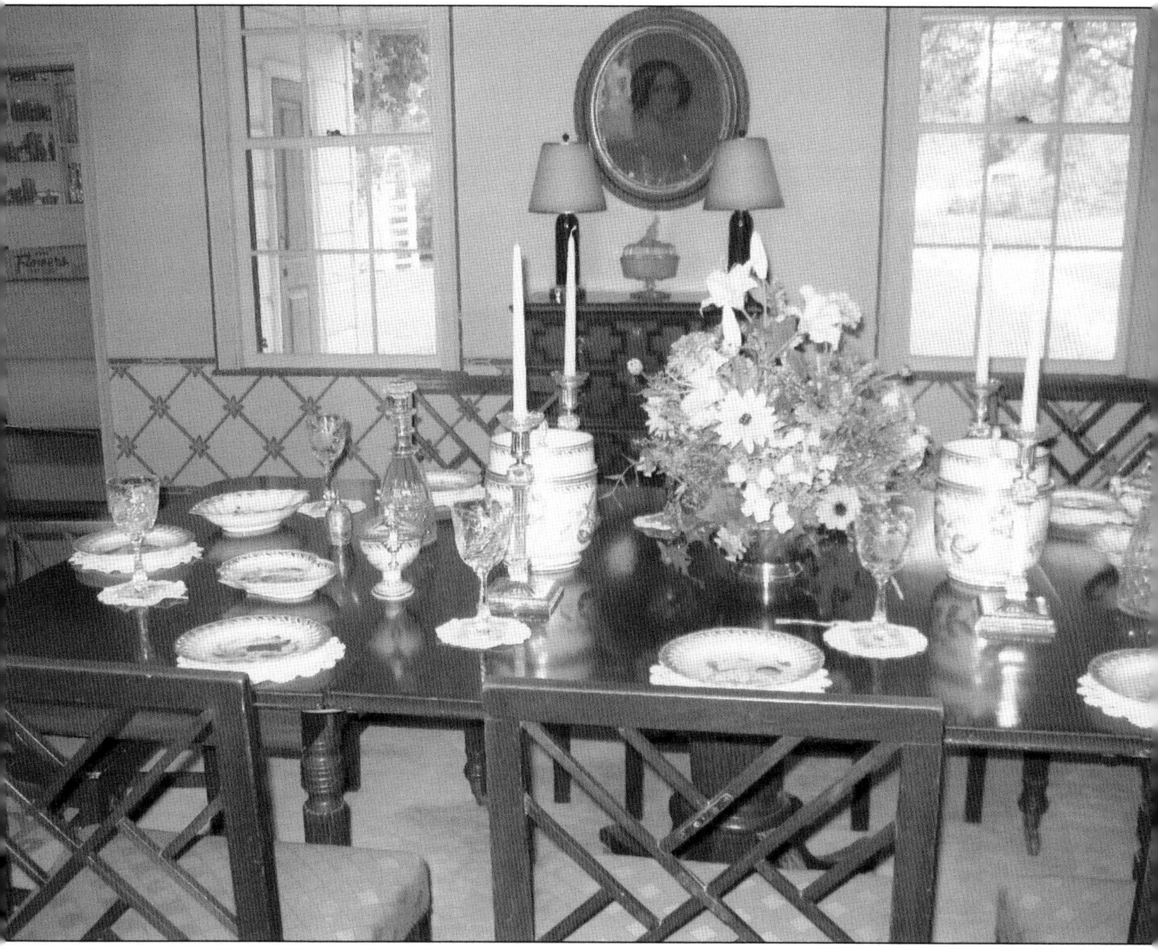

A family home from 1703 to 1993, the plantation house will always be central to the experience of Sotterley. The dining room, an 18th-century room redecorated in the mid-1900s, is always a highlight of any tour. The rose arbor and the north gatehouse can be seen through the dining room's left and right windows, respectively. Herbert Satterlee's mother is depicted in the oval portrait.

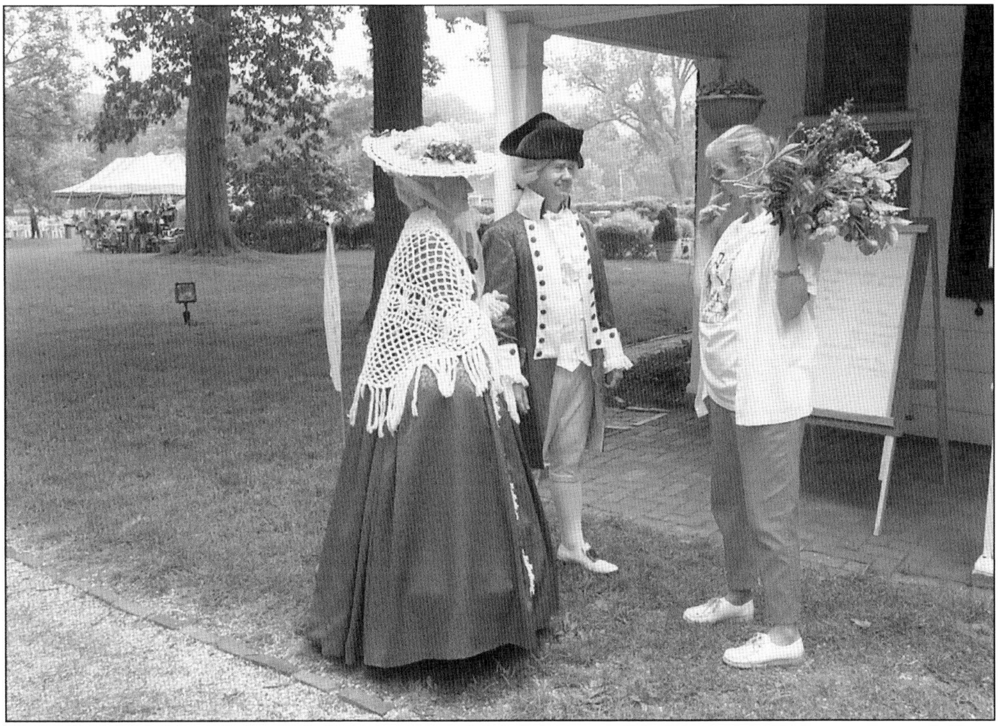

Pat and Frank Greenwell, longtime Sotterley volunteers and supporters, often show up at special events in beautiful period costume as Elizabeth and George Plater. The Greenwells have been wonderful Sotterley ambassadors and can appear in appropriate dress for almost any period in Sotterley's history. Lizette Day (right) also served Sotterley for many years.

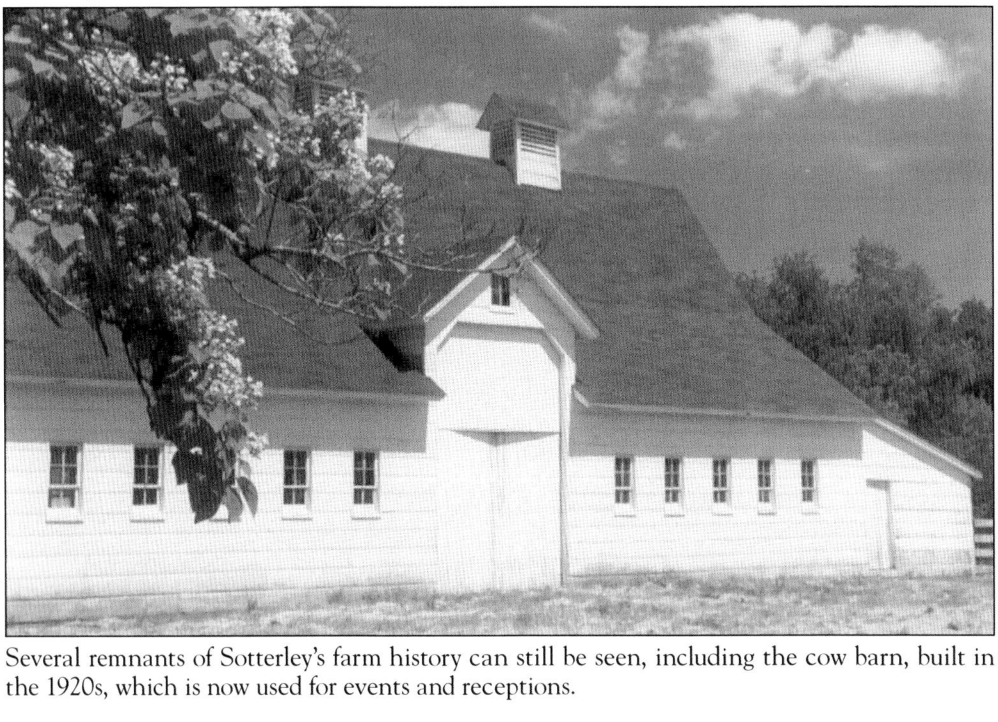

Several remnants of Sotterley's farm history can still be seen, including the cow barn, built in the 1920s, which is now used for events and receptions.

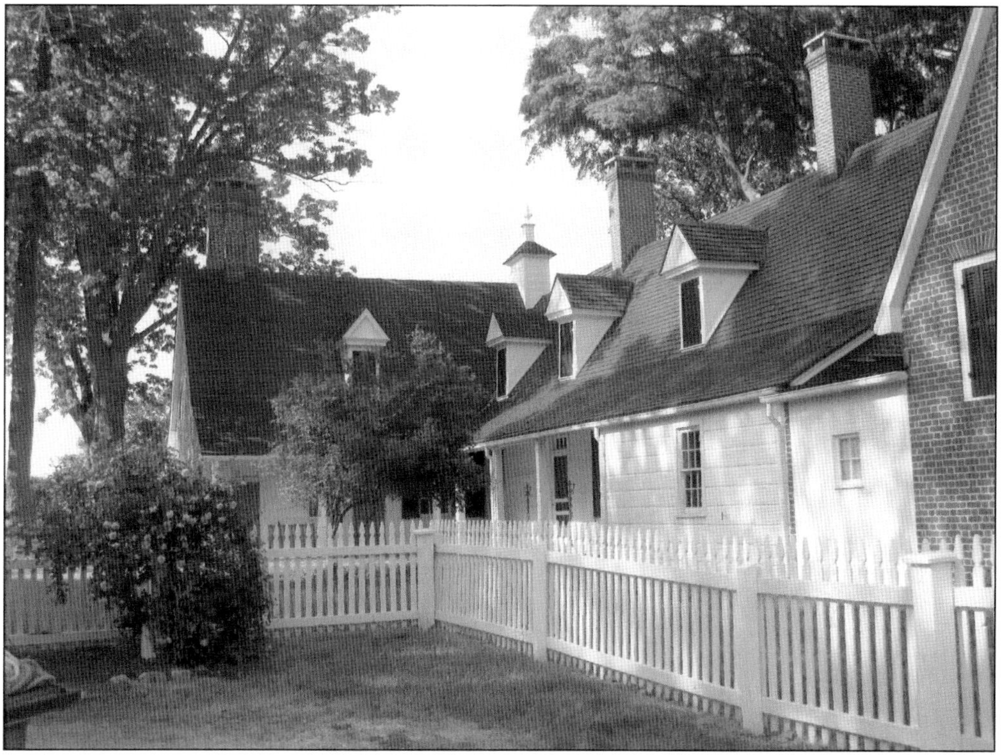

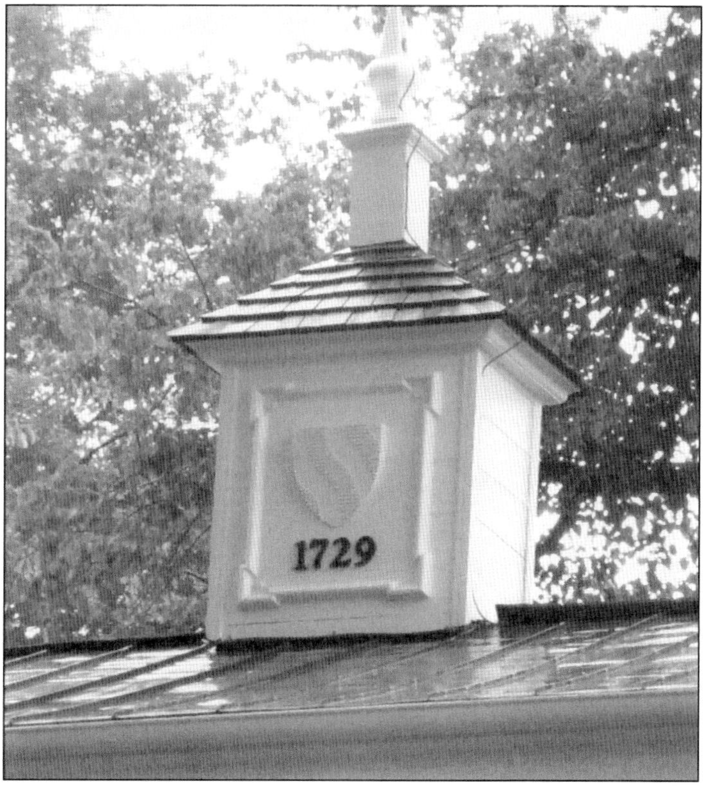

Sotterley's plantation house is still bordered on its road side by the picket fence (above) that Herbert Satterlee installed. The house now features a stained red roof and 300 years of stories to tell. The 18th-century cupola at right, which has been restored over the years, includes a Plater family crest and the year 1729. These features were added to the cupola in the 1970s; Rebecca Bowles married George Plater II in 1729. A bronze plaque commemorating George Plater III was donated by the local chapter of the Daughters of the American Revolution in 1976 and was installed on the north brick wall of the plantation house.

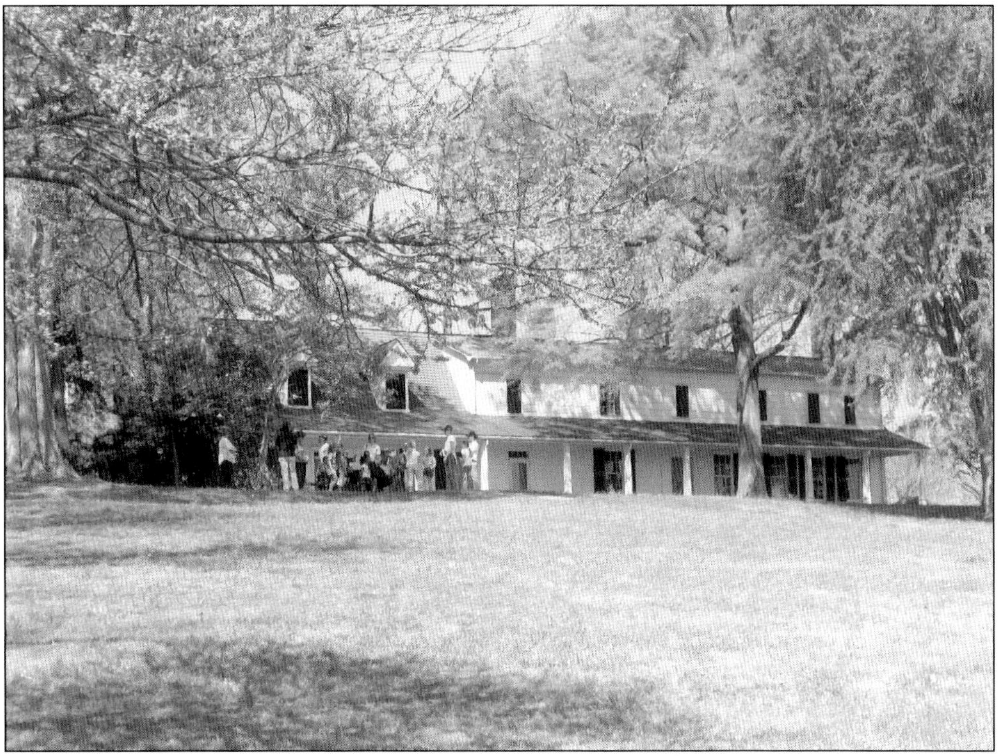

Above, classes of students stand in front of the river side of the plantation house in spring. A postcard-ready photograph of the land side of the plantation house is seen below. Each year, hundreds of people choose to take their wedding vows or attend special events at Sotterley.

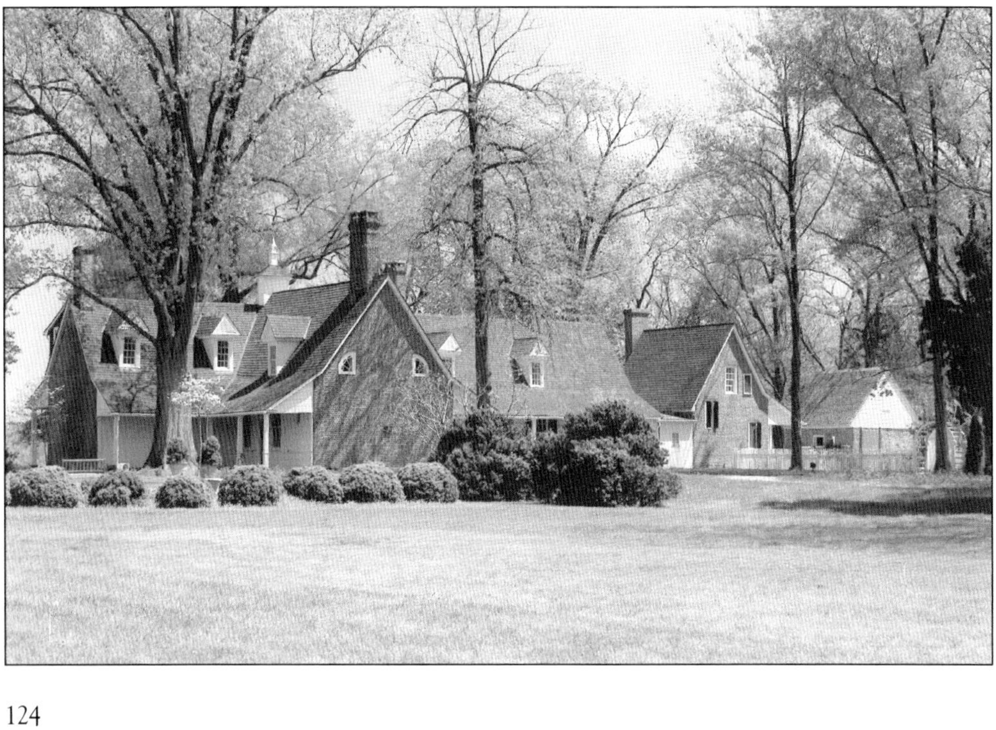

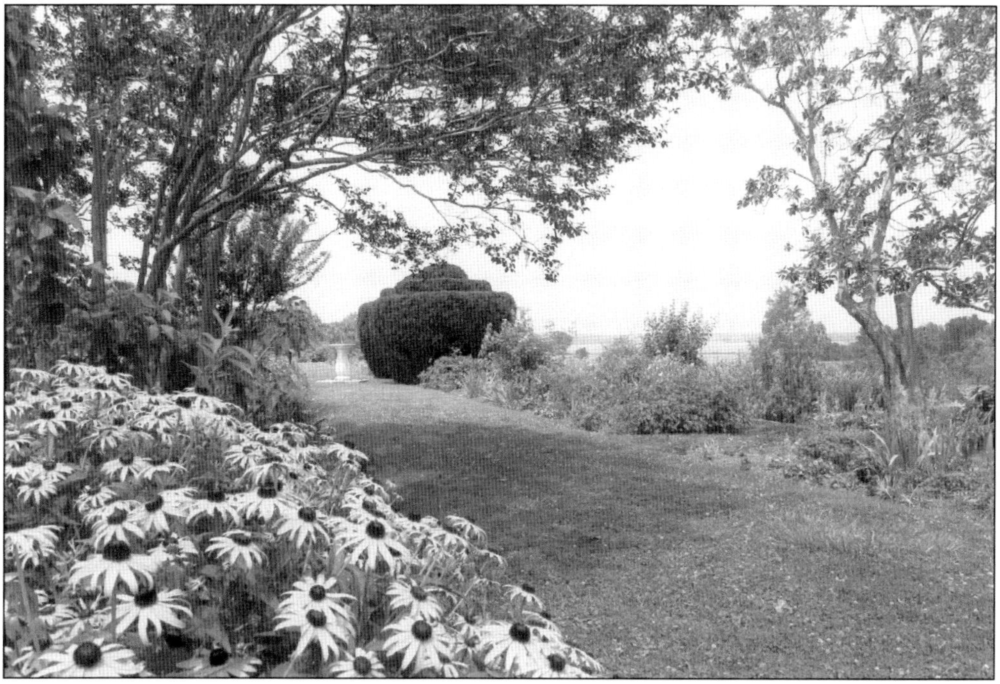

This timeless view of the sundial and garden looking towards the Patuxent River beckons thousands of visitors each year to slow their pace and take in the beauty, history, and culture of Sotterley Plantation. In the left foreground is black-eyed Susan, the state flower of Maryland.

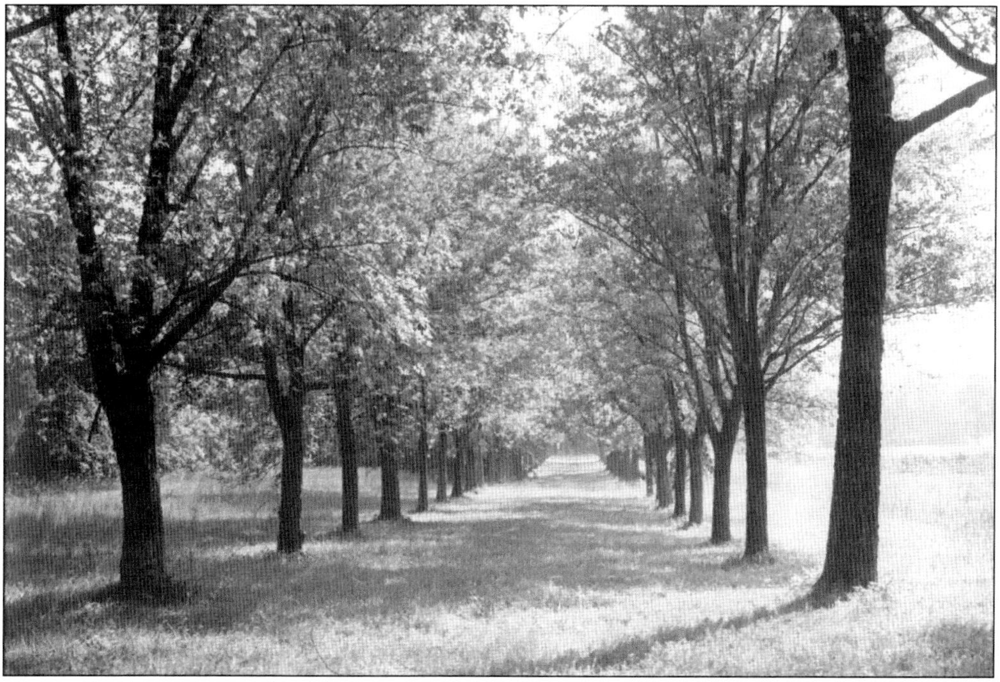

This mid-1900s photograph of the grassy tree allee leading to Sotterley's plantation house harkens to a different time. The allee is now a road traveled by visitors to Sotterley Plantation, leading them to discover the past and learn for the future.

Bibliography

Brown, David. *Sotterley: Her People and Their Worlds*. Baltimore, MD: Chesapeake Book Company, 2010.

Carson, Gary, and Carl R. Lounsburg, eds. *The Chesapeake House: Architectural Investigations by Colonial Williamsburg*. Chapel Hill, NC: The Colonial Williamsburg Foundation by the University of North Carolina Press, 2013.

Ehrenreich, Barbara and Deirdre English. *Witches, Midwives, and Nurses: A History of Women Healers*. New York City: Feminist Press, City University, 2010.

Ellis, Joseph J. *American Creation: Triumphs and Tragedies of the Founding of the Republic*. New York City: Alfred A. Knopf, 2007.

Eshelman, Ralph, E., Scott S. Sheads, and Donald R. Hickey. *The War of 1812 in the Chesapeake: A Reference Guide to Historic Sites in Maryland, Virginia, and the District of Columbia*. Baltimore, MD: Johns Hopkins University Press, 2010.

Galenson, David W. *Traders, Planters, and Slaves: Market Behavior in Early English America*. London: Cambridge University Press, 1986.

Goodheart, Adam. *1861: The Civil War Awakening*. New York City: Alfred A. Knopf, 2011.

Holly, David C. *Tidewater by Steamboat: A Saga of the Chesapeake*. Baltimore, MD: Johns Hopkins University Press, 1991.

Knott, Richard, and Shawn Knott. *Memories of Sotterley*. Hollywood, MD: self-published, 2003.

Mannix, Daniel P., and Malcolm Cowley. *Black Cargoes: The History of the Atlantic Slave Trade 1518–1865*. New York City: Viking Press, 1962.

Oliver, Sandra L. *Food in Colonial and Federal America*. Westport, CT: Greenwood Press, 2005.

Rediker, Marcus. *The Slave Ship: A Human History*. New York City: Penguin Books, 2007.

Tattersfield, Nigel. *The Forgotten Trade*. London: Jonathan Cape, 1991.

Toomey, Daniel Carroll. *The Civil War in Maryland*. Baltimore, MD: Toomey Press, 2009.

Wilson, Richard Guy, Shaun Eyring, and Kenny Marotta, eds. *Re-creating the American Past: Essays on the Colonial Revival*. Charlottesville, VA: University of Virginia Press, 2006.

About Sotterley Plantation

Now in its fourth century, historic Sotterley Plantation offers a wide variety of interactive, research-based programming and exhibits for all ages. Visitors can take advantage of guided, audio, or self-guided experiences that take them back through time. They can explore one of the few original, restored slave cabins in Maryland and tour the plantation house, one of the oldest continuously owned structures of its type in America.

Sotterley's all-volunteer Garden Guild maintains one of the most breathtaking Colonial Revival gardens in the nation overlooking the Patuxent River, which serves as the backdrop for hundreds of weddings and special events each year. Visitors can walk miles of nature trails to view the local species of plant and animal life, relax on a bench recycled and crafted from Sotterley's own trees, or see the film *Sotterley: A Tidewater Legacy*. The museum shop offers books and unique gifts. Sotterley has small group, hands-on educational field trip experiences, workshops, and an acclaimed speaker series. Visitors can also take part in Sotterley's signature events, such as Riverside Winefest, during the first weekend in October; Ghosts of Sotterley; or one of Sotterley's December holiday events.

Historic Sotterley, Inc., is a nonprofit public charity governed by a board of trustees with a mission to research, preserve, and interpret Sotterley's unique cultures and environments and to serve as a public educational and cultural resource. The museum depends on memberships, sponsorships, admissions, rentals, and grants for financial support. Sotterley also depends on its talented, dedicated volunteers and staff.

To support Sotterley Plantation and find out more about dates and hours of operation, scheduling, events, tours, and programs, visit the website, www.sotterley.org, or write to Historic Sotterley, Inc., PO Box 67, 44300 Sotterley Lane, Hollywood, MD, 20636. You can also visit Sotterley Plantation on Facebook and Twitter.